William Mackergo Taylor

Contrary Winds, and Other Sermons

William Mackergo Taylor

Contrary Winds, and Other Sermons

ISBN/EAN: 9783337114596

Printed in Europe, USA, Canada, Australia, Japan

Cover: Foto ©Lupo / pixelio.de

More available books at **www.hansebooks.com**

OTHER SERMONS

BY

WM. M. TAYLOR, D.D., LL.D.

PASTOR OF THE BROADWAY TABERNACLE, NEW YORK CITY

NEW YORK
A. C. ARMSTRONG & SON
714 BROADWAY
1883

COPYRIGHT, 1883, BY
A. C. ARMSTRONG & SON

PRESS OF J. J. LITTLE & CO.,
NOS. 10 TO 20 ASTOR PLACE, NEW YORK.

PREFACE.

THE favorable reception given to the former volume entitled "The Limitations of Life and other Sermons" has moved me, at the urgent and repeated solicitation of my friends the Publishers, to issue a companion to it in the shape of the present work. The discourses here presented to the reader were delivered in the ordinary course of my ministry, and have been chosen simply because of their bearing on topics of great present importance, and because of the testimonies to their helpfulness which I have received from many who heard them. They are printed now as they were preached at first, for the good that they may do, and my prayer is that the Spirit of God may accompany them with his quickening and upbuilding influences.

WM. M. TAYLOR.

BROADWAY TABERNACLE,
   NEW YORK, October, 1883.

CONTENTS.

	PAGE
CONTRARY WINDS	7
CHAFF OR WHEAT?	21
CHRIST BEFORE PILATE—PILATE BEFORE CHRIST	37
CAPTIVITIES AND HOW TO IMPROVE THEM	51
PERSONAL INDEPENDENCE THE RESULT OF DIVINE REDEMPTION	65
THE UNTRODDEN PATH	80
THE PAST IRREVOCABLE	93
THE VISION OF ELIJAH	107
THE PLEASURES OF SIN	121
AFFLICTION AS RELATED TO LIFE	136
OPPORTUNITIES AND THEIR LIMIT	150
THE HARVEST OF RETRIBUTION AND REWARD	169
DEBTORS	186
THE REVELATION AT THE BUSH	200
TRUE GREATNESS	215
THE SEAL OF THE SPIRIT	229
DRIFTING	245
THE INDUCTIVE STUDY OF THE SCRIPTURES	260
AN OPEN DOOR FOR LITTLE STRENGTH	279
THE SORROWFUL "IF"	292
THE HIDDEN SUPPORT OF LIFE	309
THE RECTIFYING INFLUENCE OF THE SANCTUARY	325
THE RESPONSIBILITIES OF LIFE	341
THESE THINGS DONE AND OTHERS NOT LEFT UNDONE	356

CONTRARY WINDS.

MATTHEW xiv. 24.—The wind was contrary.

To get at all the lessons which are suggested by these words to those who care to go beneath the surface of the narratives of Scripture we must have a clear conception of the whole circumstances connected with the spending of this night of toil, by the disciples, on the Lake of Gennesaret. They had just returned from their first preaching tour though Galilee; and as, in the exuberance of their joy, they were telling Jesus " all things both what they had done and what they had taught," the followers of John the Baptist came with the sad tidings that Herod had caused their master to be put to death. This news at once revived in the Lord the remembrance of John's nobleness, and suggested to him the nearness of his own crucifixion. He saw that, with him too, matters were hastening to a crisis; and, therefore, that he might prepare himself for that which was before him, and fortify his disciples against the difficulties and disappointments that were in store for them, he took them with him for a season of rest and retirement to the eastern side of the lake.

But the inconsiderate selfishness of the people gave him no opportunity for relaxation, for as soon as they saw him setting out in the boat they started to walk round the head of the loch in great numbers, and, immediately on his landing, they crowded about him as they had done at Capernaum. Nor did he thrust them from him; but, after having taught them till far into the afternoon, he was so moved with compassion for them that he furnished a feast for them by miracle from the five loaves and two fishes, which were all the provisions available at the moment. The effect of this supernatural work was great. It roused the enthusiasm of the people to the highest pitch, so that they exclaimed "This is of a truth that prophet that should come into the world": and they wished "to take him by force and make him a king." His own disciples, too, seem to have been unwontedly stirred. With their as yet carnal ideas regarding his kingdom, they were all too ready to second and support the proposal of the multitude; and so, for their own sakes, as well as to prevent the crowd from rushing into a reckless enterprise, he sent them away to cross the lake by themselves, and after dismissing the people to their homes, he went up alone into the mountain to soothe and refresh his spirit by fellowship with his Father.

While he was thus engaged, however, his disciples were called to contend with a furious storm, of a kind not uncommon on the sea of Galilee. That lake lies low, being, in fact, six hundred feet beneath the level of the Mediterranean, and the water-courses on its banks have cut out deep ravines which act like funnels to draw down the winds from the mountains, so that the storms are often both sudden and severe. On the present occasion the wind came down with such fury that even strong rowers, like the fishermen apostles, could make little way against it, and after "toiling" for nine hours they had made no more than three miles. Thus it was with them until the fourth watch, when the Lord came to their relief, walking on the waves; and after he entered the boat, the wind ceased, and they speedily reached "the other shore."

Now, with these facts in mind, let us see what help we can derive for our daily lives from this toilsome rowing of the disciples against a contrary wind.

I. Very evidently, the first thing here suggested is that the way of duty is not always easy. In saying that I do not allude to the inner difficulties which we have frequently to overcome before we enter upon the path of obedience, but rather to those hindrances which come upon us from without, while we are honestly trying to go forward in the course which, believing it to be commanded us by God, we have begun. These disciples were not very anxious to get into the boat at first. They had to be "constrained" by the personal effort of their Master himself. Had he not exerted on them such an amount of pressure as to make them feel that they would be going against his will if they should stay, they would much rather have remained with him. But after they had entered the boat, and had begun their rowing, there is no reason to believe that they were slack at their work. The smallness of the progress which they made was owing, not to anything about them, but only to the sudden uprising of a storm of contrary wind.

Here, then, were men doing what had been clearly commanded by the Lord; doing it too because they felt that they could not refuse without wounding his heart; doing it, as there is reason to believe, with all their might; and yet hindered by influences external to themselves, and altogether beyond their control. Now, when we put it so, we see in a moment that the situation of these disciples is not uncommon. I venture to say that there is no one here of any lengthened experience who has not had many days in his life when "the wind was contrary" unto him. We have had a duty laid upon us. It has not been of our own choosing. If we had been left to our own impulses we would much rather have done something else, but in a marvelous manner we have felt ourselves "shut up" to its performance. We have not been able to get past it. We have entered upon it because we felt we must do so. Our loyalty to the Lord has "constrained" us to undertake it; and yet, almost as soon as we begin, "the wind becomes contrary," and we have to contend with the greatest amount of difficulties, so that we are prone to cry "Why is this? Have we mistaken altogether the indications of God's Spirit as to our duty in the case? and if we have not, how comes it that he has hindered us in this fashion?" How often one begins the day with the clear conviction that some important thing must be done by him before the evening! He enters upon it early in the morning, but he has not proceeded far when he is interrupted; and he has scarcely dismissed one intruder before another is announced. Thus it continues all the day, and at its close he sighs, and says, "Ah! me! the wind was contrary." And the next day may be a repetition of the same, so that he is tempted to make a choice between two conflicting obligations, and to neglect one for the sake of meeting another.

And what is sometimes true thus of a single day in our history, may be so, also, of a whole section of life. Take the case, for example, of a youth in his choice of a profession. He is ingenuous, conscientious, prayerful. He does not wish to take any course of which his Saviour would not approve, and at last he feels himself shut in, suppose, to the ministry of the gospel. It is not that he is attracted toward it by any of its outward advantages; but that he is impelled into it by that inner consecration that will not let him stay out of it. He hears the Master's call, not in any mystic voice, but in that irrepressible "I cannot but" which springs up within him. He seems to himself to be drawn on by an irresistible attraction. He could not be happy, he could not say to his conscience that he had obeyed God, if he did not yield. And yet, after he begins to prepare himself for the work to which he thus devotes himself, he is beset with difficulties. Perhaps the parents who have heretofore cheerfully supported him are beggared by some commercial crisis, and can help him no more; or the death of a father may have thrown the weight of a household on his shoulders; or some accident—as men call it—on the railway or in the steamboat may lay him for months, or perhaps longer, on a bed of weakness. And so he too, while following what he believed to be the will of God, is made to feel, to his own dismay and depression, that "the wind is contrary."

What a thrilling illustration of the same thing we have in the case of the Apostle Paul and his visit to Rome! He had long desired to go to that city, not from motives of curiosity, or from any wish to secure worldly fortune, but simply that he might help the Christians there by giving them some spiritual gifts, and might at the very center of the empire touch for Christ some springs of influence which would vibrate to its outermost circumference. Nor is this all. In that desire he had been encouraged by his Lord; and so, feeling it to be clearly his duty, he sets out for Jerusalem, intending to go thence to the imperial city by the directest route. But all the way thither he is met by entreaties not to go, and even by prophecies of coming evil. On his arrival there he is imprisoned in the castle of Antonia. And though, on the second night after his apprehension, the Lord stood by him and assured him that he would still get to Rome, yet he had to go through two years of imprisonment and through peril of shipwreck and long delay at Malta to his destination. That was a dreary duration of contrary wind; and I often wonder what Paul thought as he looked back on the clear assurance which he received from his Master that he should go to Rome, and then glanced at the chain by which he was bound, and the untoward influences by which he was surrounded. Did no misgiving ever arise in his heart as to whether or not he was right in seeking to go to Rome? Or, if he was unwavering in that conviction, was he ever tempted to think that God had no control over the occurrences of human life or the elements of nature? Or, feeling himself unable to unravel these mysteries, did he take refuge in his own words of believing assurance, "We know that all things work together for good to them that love God, who are the called according to his purpose"? I cannot tell. But I can clearly see what a trial came to him thus from hindrances in the very providence of God which kept him from doing that which God himself had laid upon him.

And many of us who have sought the "furtherance of the gospel" among our fellow men, in obedience to the injunction of the Lord, have seemed to be providentially retarded in the same way. We begin, say, in a spirit of simple devotion to Christ, and because he has so brought the matter to our door that we cannot pass it on to another, some effort for the evangelization of the careless in our neighborhood. We are sure we are seeking a good end, but "the wind is contrary." We are met with freezing indifference among those from whom we expected co-operation. One difficulty is suggested after another, and so soon as we surmount one obstacle another makes its appearance. We never seem to get into plain sailing; always there are breakers ahead, or something to be guarded against. If it all depended upon us, we should go on with energy; but alas! our energy evaporates in a large degree in holding those constant negotiations and taking those continual precautions which are needed in order to keep everybody sweet and to prevent friction. Let any one set out in earnest to do anything positive or aggressive for Christ, and all experience declares that before he has gone far he will have to face a contrary wind. These are the conflicts which must have given birth to the following lines of Faber, and the mere repetition of his words may be itself a comfort to us:

> "Oh! it is hard to work for God,
>   To rise and take His part,
> Upon this battle-field of earth,
>   And not sometimes lose heart.
>
> "He hides himself so wondrously,
>   As though there were no God:
> He is least seen when all the powers
>   Of ill are most abroad.
>
> "Or, he deserts us at the hour
>   The fight is all but lost,
> And seems to leave us to ourselves
>   Just when we need Him most.
>
> "Yet, there is less to try our faith
>   In our mysterious creed,
> Than in the godless look of earth,
>   In these our hours of need."

II. Now, what shall we say to sustain ourselves amid an experience like that? This, at least, we may take to ourselves for comfort, namely, that we are not responsible for the wind. That is a matter outside of us and beyond our control, and for all such things we are not to be blamed. Now, that takes the sting out of the trial. It does not diminish the difficulty; it does not make the prosecution of our work less arduous; the "toiling in rowing" will be demanded all the same, but there will be more heart, and better, for its continuance. Nothing breaks the spirit like conscious guilt; but, on the other hand, nothing braces it like conscious integrity. If a difficulty rises before me in God's providence, apart from any agency or culpability of my own, then I am in better mood to meet and overcome it than I should be if I recognized in it some result of my own folly. A feeling of this sort, I think, must have throbbed in Paul's heart when he wrote to the Romans, "If it be possible, *as much as lieth in you*, live peaceably with all men." He had known what it was to have men fired with antagonism to him, but he had known also the riches of the consolation that consists in the consciousness that he had done nothing to deserve it; and so he would have his readers see to it that when they were hindered it should be by a "wind" which they did not raise, and not by a "breeze" which they had themselves created. And the same thought must have been in Peter's mind when he bids his readers be careful that when they suffered it should be for "well doing" and not for "evil doing." The obstacles which we make for ourselves are those which give us the sorest pain; but though that for which I am not responsible may be a great hindrance to me, it can never be a real personal burden. One may grumble about the weather,—though even that would be a sin,—but inconvenient though disagreeable weather is, we do not number that among our sorest afflictions. The contrary wind is in God's providence, and is to be made the best of; nay, so soon as we recognize that it is in God's providence, we will make the best of it.

But another thought, suggested by the history from which my text is taken, comes to our support here, this, namely, that the attention required for bearing up against the contrary wind may take us, for the time being, out of the way of some subtle temptation. Think of the circumstances out of which these disciples had just come. The multitude desired there and then to take measures for the proclamation of Christ as a King; and, with their low and earthly notions of the sort of kingdom which Messiah was to establish, the near prospect of his entrance in this way upon it had a strange fascination for the disciples. They were eager for just such a *dénouement* as the great mass of the people wanted. How eager is evident from the fact that, on the following day, after their Master had refused to be a mere temporal ruler, and had thereby so estranged many from him that they "went back and walked no more with him," he was moved to say to the twelve, as if he saw some signs of wavering even in them, "Will ye also go away?" So we gather that he sent them away across the lake that night, and left them by themselves to contend with adverse winds, just to keep them out of harm's way, and to give them something else meanwhile to think of than the glittering allurements of worldly greatness. And how often have we seen that a contrary wind has done the same thing for ourselves? We have not been conscious of it at the moment; but after the toil has been long past, and we have been able, from the height of some later vantage ground, to look back upon the whole experience, and put everything in it into its proper perspective, we can see that it came just in time to prevent us from being moved by some dear deceitful dream that was at the moment magnetizing us by its influence. We lament the interruptions that have kept us from finishing the work which we had laid out for a day, and feel almost aggravated at the delay; yet somehow, through the experience of these very interruptions, we have been kept from doing that work in a way that would have brought dishonor on ourselves, or given the enemies of the Lord occasion to blaspheme. The mode which at first had a strong charm for us did in the interval lose its attraction, and wiser thoughts prevailed in the end; or the work grew in our idea by the delay, so that it became something grander than, without that, we could have thought of making it.

So, again, when we have been held back by sickness, or other providential restraint from accomplishing that on which, as the servants of God, we were resolutely bent, we have lived to find out that, if that hindrance had not come just then, we should have been in danger of preferring personal ambition to the approbation of the Lord. And, in general, all such adverse providences have operated in keeping us nearer the mercy-seat, and in leading us to depend more implicitly, or, as the hymn has put it, to "lean" more "hardly," on the support of the Lord. Let us not forget, therefore, that the buffeting with an adverse wind has in it a preventive influence, which may help to keep us from something worse. Better far a strong head-wind than a fog; for in the fog an iceberg may be veiled, and collision with that would be destruction. But, here, the fog may be, as in the case of these disciples it was, in the vague and misty notions which we may have of Jesus and his kingdom; and anything that takes our thoughts away from the secret dangers lurking in all such speculations is a blessing, no matter how rough the experience may be.

But still another thought comes to our support here, for there may be much in contending with a contrary wind, like that which we have been describing, to prepare us for higher service in the cause of Christ. Look once more at these disciples. Up till this time they had been in visible companionship with the Lord, from the hour when they had been called to follow him, with but the exception of that preaching circuit from which they had just recently returned. But he was not to be with them thus all through their lives. The day was coming when he would be crucified; and though, after his crucifixion and burial, there was to be a resurrection from the grave, yet that was to be followed by his ascension into glory, after which he would no more be with them in the body. It was needful, therefore, that, before that time arrived, they should have some experience of what it was to be absent from him; and in this night upon the deep they had what I may call a rehearsal in symbol of some of the difficulties with which they would have to contend after he was taken up into heaven. He withdrew to the mountain to give them a foretaste of what should come when he went up to heaven; and I have a firm conviction that much of that persistence of the apostles in the face of persecution which so strongly impresses us as we read the early chapters of the Acts of the Apostles had its root in the remembrance of what they had learned in this night's contending with adverse winds on the Galilean lake. This was one of their first experiments in walking alone, and it helped to steady them afterwards.

Now, it is quite similar with many believers yet. Take the case of a young man studying for the ministry, and compelled, in the course of his curriculum, to do battle with difficulties; and those who have had such a fight to go through will tell you that no college or seminary could ever have given them so valuable a preparation for their life work as that conflict secured to them. Those five years of waiting between the obtaining of his license to preach and the securing of a parish, which seemed at the time even to Thomas Guthrie to indicate that he had mistaken his profession, were, as he himself afterwards declared, among the most useful to him of all his early life; for during a part of these he "walked the hospitals" of Paris, and so fitted himself for work in the dens of the Edinburgh Cowgate; and during the rest, he conducted a bank in his native town, and so familiarized himself with business that he could speak with wisdom and intelligence to men of every occupation, and of all ranks. And the same is seen in many other men. The very necessity of rowing against the wind develops new strength, and brings latent resources into play. It is questionable if John Kitto would ever have been an author had it not been for " the contrary wind" of deafness which blew upon him from the time that he was twelve years old; and so much have difficulties to do with the development of character, and the attainment of a sphere of exalted usefulness in the world, that we may say that the greatest of all misfortunes that can befall a youth is to have nothing but good fortune. It may help to nerve us against despondency, therefore, to know that our present conflicts are the prophecies, if we but fight them bravely through, of future eminence.

But once more here, as we bend to our oars while

the wind is contrary, we may take to ourselves the comfort that the Lord Jesus is closely watching us. — The parallel passage in Mark tells us that "he saw them toiling in rowing." They did not know it, for it was dark. But it is written here for our support in similar circumstances. "He saw them toiling in rowing, for the wind was contrary unto them." If they had known that it would have put new heart into them; for they would have felt sure that no harm would be suffered to come to them beneath his eye, and they would have been convinced that whenever he saw it to be necessary he would come to their relief. But precisely that, this narrative as a whole is designed to teach us. It tells us that though Jesus is unseen, he is still looking down with interest upon us; that he is making intercession for us before the heavenly mercy seat; and that in some way, at the right time, he will come to succor us. So we may leave all care about the issue, and attend, meanwhile, to the rowing. That is our present duty, let us therefore hold to it steadily, bravely, hopefully. Nor let us be disappointed if the fourth watch of the night should come before help appear. Relief will come; so again I say, let us work hopefully. There is all the difference in the world between working with hope and without it; or, using the language of Scripture, between a living hope and the hope that is dying or dead. The sailor on the raft sinks into inactivity so long as there is no vessel in sight; but let a ship appear on the far horizon and immediately he is alert, and seeks by every means in his power to attract the attention of those on board, if haply he may be saved. In the same way, if we lose the hope of Christ's help we shall give up rowing against the wind. But as hope revives within us we shall put forth more strength. Let those in a beleaguered garrison be signaled that relief is near, and though they be on the verge of starvation, they will hold out until it comes; and so let a Christian keep hope, and he will keep persistence, for here, too, comes in that pregnant saying of the Apostle, "we are saved by hope." What a contrary wind that was which blew on Milton during the long years of his blindness! Yet he held on, and held out. Here are his words:

> "Yet I argue not
> Against Heaven's hand or will, nor bate a jot
> Of heart or hope, but still bear up and steer
> Right onward."

And his glorious epic was the magnificent outcome. Thus let us hold on, no matter what we are required to contend against, and let us rest assured that at length Christ will come to us with such strengthening influences that we shall rise to something nobler than without our struggle we could ever have attained. Let us, then, toil on! It is but a little while at the longest. No contrary wind can last forever. By and by Christ will come to us, and then there will be peace. Yes, and after a time we shall reach "the other shore"; and when we touch that we shall be done with difficulties. So, as the father of the well-known Andrew Marvell said, just before he entered the boat in which, as he was crossing the Humber, he went down and was drowned, "Ho! for Heaven!" What though the waves be rough? Ho! for heaven! What though the wind be contrary? Ho! for Heaven! What though the labor be exhausting? Ho! for Heaven!

> And when the shore is won at last,
> Who will count the billows past?

Nov. 28, 1880.

CHAFF OR WHEAT?

JEREMIAH xxiii. 28.—*The prophet that hath a dream, let him tell a dream, and he that hath my word, let him speak my word faithfully. What is the chaff to the wheat? saith the Lord.*

THE prophet Jeremiah lived in evil days. He was, in fact, almost the only witness-bearer for Jehovah in his generation, for the people had sunk into uttermost depravity, and were fast ripening for judgment. At the time when he uttered the words of my text, Jehoiachin, the grandson of Josiah, was upon the throne of Judah, which he filled for only four months; and Nebuchadnezzar was preparing the expedition which, within a few weeks, was to take Jerusalem captive, and to carry to Babylon, as prisoners of war, many thousands of its citizens. In vain the prophet raised his warning voice. To no purpose did he entreat the people to return unto the Lord, and the monarch to make peace with the Babylonian emperor. It was his lot, Cassandra-like, to foretell things which no one would believe; and to have his efforts thwarted by men of whom better things might have been expected. For his most pronounced antagonists were among those who had been educated as prophets, and who called themselves the servants of the Lord. Ever as he gave his message they stood forth to contradict him, and claimed that they and not he truly represented the mind of Jehovah. They despised him, and said, "The Lord hath said ye shall have peace; and they said unto every one that walked after the imagination of his own heart, No evil shall come upon you." But he affirmed concerning them that they "spake a vision of their own heart and not out of the mouth of the Lord"; and, as the test between them, he made his appeal to the results. They were continually exclaiming "I have dreamed; I have dreamed!" "Well then," he cries to the people, "let them tell their dreams, and let me proclaim God's word; then out of the issue ye shall know which of us is his rightful messenger. 'The prophet that hath a dream, let him tell a dream, and he that hath my word, let him speak my word faithfully; what is the chaff to the wheat? saith the Lord.' Put it to the test of experiment, and try it by the results produced in each case, then ye shall know which is the true prophet and which the false."

But primarily applicable as these words are to the utterances of Jeremiah, we may broaden them out so as to include under them the whole word of God; and we may challenge all human dreams which men have set up in antagonism to it with the same confidence; and say "What is the chaff to the wheat?" As the Saviour himself has expressed it, "by their fruits ye shall know them." The Baconian principle is that everything is to be received which stands on the basis of experiment; and, judged by their results, we never need fear for the Sacred Scriptures, for in their own proper department they are "wheat," and everything which men have put in their place and set up against them is "chaff." This is the testimony of human experience as a whole, and in a day when multitudes are seeking to put the Bible once again upon its trial, it may be well to bring this out prominently before your attention.

My theme, then, this morning is the superiority of the

divine word to the merely human dreams by which men have sought to displace it. But, before I enter upon it, let me carefully define what I mean by "human dreams." I do not include under such an appellation the discoveries of science which have made this century illustrious. So far from being "dreams," these are well-accredited facts; and they are a part of God's revelation to men as really as are the writings of prophets and apostles. They have not come to us in the same way, indeed, and no supernatural influence was required either to perceive them or to communicate them. But nature, as some call it, is in my view only the first volume of God's book, and everything which is really found in it contributes to a better understanding of him. Still, just as the Bible was not designed to teach men science, so science is not competent to instruct men in those subjects which are distinctively treated of in the Bible, and when it enters into that department, science is a mere dreamer, even as many who are well acquainted with the Scriptures are no better than dreamers when they speak of scientific topics. I refer now, therefore, not to the discoveries of science, but rather to those views regarding God, and the soul, and the hereafter which multitudes in our times are seeking to put in antagonism to the word of God,—and I say that these "human dreams" when tested by experience are found to be chaff, while the word of God, when similarly tried, is discovered to be wheat. Now let us see whether I can make good my assertion. I shall arrange my statements under one or two particulars.

I. In the first place, then, I remark that the human dream is empty; but the divine word is substantial. Chaff is a mere husk, but wheat is all grain. So the antagonists of the Bible deal in vague speculations, or empty negations; whereas the Scriptures are positive and satisfying. The agnostic says that we cannot know anything save that of which we can take cognizance with our bodily senses; and so he relegates the world of spirit, and even the existence of God, into the category of the unknown and the unknowable. The atheist deals in absolute negation, and affirms that there is nothing but the visible, and the here,— no God, no soul, no future life. And the sceptic alleges that there is utter uncertainty as to whether there is a God, a soul, or a hereafter. Now, this being the case, it is no calumny to say of these systems that they are empty things. They have nothing in them on which a man can lay hold. They are as unsubstantial as a dream; as shadowy as a vision of the night. But the Scriptures, on the other hand, are positive. Their very first utterance— "In the beginning God"—brings God into the front; and there is that within us which is responsive to their assertion of his existence. His I Am awakes an echo in ourselves which is not only the assertion of our own spiritual being, but the recognition of his. Moreover the Scriptures speak to our consciences in such a way as not only to reveal our sinfulness, but also to unfold the way of forgiveness; and, by the resurrection of Jesus Christ from the dead, they bring the future life to light—so that what was before a perhaps, or a mere possibility, becomes an absolute certainty.

But you may say all that is mere assertion. Well, let it be put to the proof. Try the human dream in the hour of bereavement. What has it to say to the mourner weeping over the casket that holds his dead beloved? I challenge infidelity to utter then a word which has in it a single particle of comfort for the stricken one. If he choose to repress the intuitions of his own nature, and shut his eyes to the evidences of intelligent design which exist in the external world, one may affirm that there is no God. But what comfort is there in that at such a time? If he please to turn away from the proofs which so plentifully exist in support of the credibility of the Gospel narratives, another may allege that the whole story of Jesus Christ is a myth, and that his resurrection from the dead is a delusion: but what consolation is there in that under such an experience? If he desires to say something kindly, a third may speak of the "common law," and sadly refer to the universality of death: but what is there in that to dry a tear? and who can wonder at the indignation with which the poet treated it, when, in words which seem to suggest that he had this very text in mind, he cries:

> "One writes, that 'other friends remain.'
> That 'loss is common to the race,'
> And common is the common place
> And vacant chaff, well meant for grain.—
> That loss is common would not make
> My own less bitter—rather more:
> Too common: never morning wore
> To evening but some heart did break."

But now, suppose the friends have been walking together in the faith of Christ, and one has been taken and the other left. Draw near to the survivor, and say, "Let not your heart be troubled; ye believe in God, believe also in me. In my Father's house are many mansions; if it were not so I would have told you. I go to prepare a place for you. We know that if our earthly house of this tabernacle were dissolved, we have a building of God, an house not made with hands, eternal in the heavens." And what is the result? The tears flow on, but the bitterness is taken out of the sorrow. The memory is transmuted into a hope; for the parting is seen to be but for a season, while the reunion is to be forever. The loved one is missed; but even in the sadness caused by the absence there is a bright anticipation of the happy beyond. Now, as I contrast these two ways of dealing with sorrow, am I not warranted to say, "What is the chaff to the wheat?" "No doubt," you reply, "but that does not prove that the Scripture revelation is true." And to that I answer, that there *is* more of proof in it than you think for, since its adaptation to meet the need of the mourner is itself an indorsement of its worth. The specific in medicine has won its recognition when it is seen to be unfailing. In like manner the power of the Gospel to comfort the mourner establishes its claim to be received as the divine specific for his grief, and he will not give it up unless he gets something better in its place; least of all will he part with it for that which is unsubstantial as an airy nothing.

II. But, in the second place, I remark that the human dream is destitute of nourishment for man's spiritual nature, while the divine word is strengthening, and ministers to its growth. Chaff does not feed; but wheat gives nutriment. So mere speculation has in it no educating and ennobling influence. It occupies the mind without strengthening the character. The man who indulges in it makes no progress; but, instead of flowing onward with the current, he is caught in some whirling eddy, round which he is continually revolving. The sceptics of to-day are no farther on than those of the early centuries; and agnosticism was as fully developed in ancient Athens as it is in any of our modern cities. But the Christian believer grows. His character is ever gaining new development. He never reaches his ideal, but still "follows after." The human being lives by faith. He must believe something. He cannot move a single step otherwise; and when he loses all faith he comes to a standstill. That is a general law, and so we need not be surprised to find it hold in reference to spiritual things. Scepticism puts an arrest on progress. It stimulates the critical faculty into excess; and, instead of stirring a man up to the formation and development of his own character, it makes him a mere anatomist of the characters of others. I think, if you examine, you will find that the great majority of mere critics have become so through their lack or loss of personal religious faith. What a contrast, in this regard, there is between the lives of the two Frenchmen, Vinet and St. Beuve! They were companions in youth, and, indeed, friends through life. But St. Beuve lost his religious faith, and became a literary critic, one of the very best of critics, indeed, yet only a critic, delighting the readers of his "Causeries du Lundi" with his expositions of the systems of other men and his estimates of their worth; but Vinet, who retained his faith to the last, became a producer himself, added something great to the thought and work of his time, and earned the right to be called the "Chalmers of Switzerland."

Now that is a typical instance. But if you wish to find my statement confirmed by an American experiment, take the case of those who went into the Brook Farm enterprise, and you will find that the growth of them all had been checked by speculation ending to a greater or lesser extent in unbelief. They all had the critical faculty sharpened; but they were all, even then, at their full growth, and they never got farther. They had little or nothing of the constructive about them; and the most they have done, either in literature or in society, has been in the way of criticism. Their work has been serviceable to those who are already believers, and who know how to take advantage of it for their constructive purposes; but they did little in that way themselves. To the same class belongs that eminent English philosopher who has lately been visiting our shores, and who, after having been entertained by the evolutionists of our country, set sail yesterday for his home.* You read, I doubt not, with interest, his exceedingly thoughtful remarks about Americans in the interview with which he honored a privileged reporter. Among other wholesome truths he said, regarding fitness for free institutions, "It is essentially a question of character, and only in a secondary degree a question of knowledge." And again, in regard to indifference among the people to public abuses, he reiterated the opinion, "Not lack of information, but lack of certain moral sentiments, is the root of the evil." This emphasis of character is most admirable; and in that, as you well know from my frequent references to it, I thoroughly agree with him. His diagnosis is excellent; but what does he propose as the remedy? How are we to get this character and these moral sentiments? Alas! in answer to such questions he is very largely silent. He has a small sneer at "the little which religious teachers have been doing these two thousand years," and a vague inference from biological truths to the effect " that the eventual mixture of the allied varieties of

---

* The reference is to Mr. Herbert Spencer.

the Aryan race will produce here a more powerful type of man than has hitherto existed"; and that is all! So moral sentiments are to be the growth of a mixture of races, and the only hope for us of the present generation is that we are in the way of evolving for the far-off future a very high ultimate form of national life. Said I not truly that in all these men the critical was the predominant quality, and that they had little or nothing of the constructive in them? Evolution! as well may a man endeavor to lift himself by his own garments as seek to elevate himself through such means. Nothing can be evolved that has not first been involved; and though it may "split the ears of the groundlings" to talk of the little that religious teachers have done, there is nothing that can make character or elevate the race like the gospel of the Lord Jesus Christ. What made the Pilgrim Fathers, and gave its character to New England? Was it not the faith of the gospel of the Lord Jesus? It is true, indeed, as our own poet has said, that

"God had sifted three kingdoms to find the wheat for his planting,
Then had sifted the wheat, as the living seed of a nation."

But they were "the believers" who remained. Their faith made them the "fittest" to survive. And to mention no more, what made Scotland, and put its people in the van of Europe? Was it not the same faith in the same gospel? The truth is, that all that has been secured in character during the last eighteen centuries, in the way of deepening, broadening and elevating it, has been secured in connection with the efforts of religious teachers. The progress of the past has been owing more to the word of God than to all else combined; and so, even in the face of Mr.

Spencer's allegations, I dare to ask, "What is the chaff to the wheat?"

III. But this leads me to remark, in the third place, that the "human dream" has no aggressiveness in it to arrest or overcome the evils that are in the world, but the divine word is regenerating and reforming. "Is not my word like as a fire? saith the Lord, and like a hammer that breaketh the rock in pieces?" A venerable old man, who has been during the greater part of a long life before the public, and who has been highly respected by all his associates, is now lying seriously ill.* He has been known mostly as a politician; but within the last six years he has given very serious attention to religious matters, and in a long conversation which I had with him some months ago he delighted me with the insight which he gave me into his spiritual experience. His eye was dimmed, for he was nearly blind; but his mind was clear and bright as ever, and I will not soon forget the radiance which illumined his countenance when I thanked him for a letter on this very subject which he sent two years ago to the *New York Herald*, and which is now printed as a tract by the American Tract Society. I speak of Mr. Thurlow Weed; and I am glad here to direct attention to his words, since no one can accuse him of professional prejudice, and every one must accept him as a competent and unbiased witness. Let me quote the following sentences, illustrative of the regenerating influence of the truth: "Our city furnishes many examples of the beneficence of religion. Forty years ago a locality too well known as the 'Five Points,'

---

* Mr. Weed died a few days after this sermon was delivered.

with a population of several thousands, was the home of the vilest of the vile, and the resort of others equally debased. Men, women, and children, of all nationalities and colors, herded together, differing only in the degrees of crime and the depths of profligacy habitually practised. Their days were passed in either idleness or depredations. Their nights were spent in dance-house debaucheries. All healthy or wholesome influences were excluded. Children grew up to become either street beggars or inmates of the almshouse, and their parents filled penitentiaries and prisons. These orgies continued year after year, defiant and aggressive, until that pandemonium was invaded by Christian men and women whose patience would not tire, whose courage was indomitable, and whose devotion has been rewarded by a moral and religious reformation so complete that no part of our city is now more quiet and orderly than the once dreaded 'Five Points.' Thousands of children, then growing up either vagabonds or culprits, are now attending schools, in which they are stimulated by precept and example to live industrious and virtuous lives. Instead, therefore, of going forth idle, ignorant, and vicious children to prey upon society, the destitute and orphan children of the 'Five Points,' prepared for usefulness by moral and religious training, find happy homes in our rapidly-developing Western States and Territories.

"Again,* eight years ago, Water Street and its surroundings northward from Peck slip had a notoriety almost as unenviable as that of the 'Five Points.' That region was rife with drunkenness, burglaries, pugilism, and their kindred vices. Jerry McAuley

---

* Now ten.

was conspicuous in all that was wicked and demoralizing. He had the reputation of being a terror to the precinct, a reputation which, by his own confession, was deserved. But this disturber of the public peace was converted, and then he resolved to devote the remainder of his life to the service of his Master, and, with a faithful, affectionate wife as a helper, he has given himself to labor for the salvation of others. For a long time the hisses and howlings of his former associates seriously disturbed his meetings, but courage, perseverance and patience finally prevailed, and his work now progresses without interruption. The general character of the neighborhood has been improved; its social and moral tone and atmosphere have been purified. Sailor boarding-houses have been reformed. Sailors now carry their Bibles with them to sea. Moody and Sankey hymns are sung in forecastles. Hundreds of half-naked and hungry wives and children, by the conversion of drunken husbands and fathers, now rejoice in comfortable and happy homes. The Mission church is crowded every week day and evening, and three times on Sunday, with intelligent Christian men and women, who, rescued from garrets and gutters, are now reputable citizens, enjoying the fruits of their industry, and relating with grateful hearts the miseries of their past, the joys of their present, and the hopes of their future. By all who 'went to scoff, but remained to pray,' Jerry McAuley and his exemplary wife are regarded with affection, and will be remembered with gratitude."*

---

* Mr. McAuley has since removed to the Cremorne Mission in West Thirty-second Street, where he carries on a work equally remarkable with that above described; while Mr. O'Brien has succeeded him in Water Street, with, if possible, still more marked success than his predecessor had.

These are some of the recent fruits of the gospel in reformatory and regenerating work, of which we are ourselves eye-witnesses. But now, where shall we look for anything like similar results from those who are the votaries of the human "dreams" of agnosticism, scepticism or infidelity? What has any one of these done to improve the characters of individual men, or elevate society, or bless the world? And had not Mr. Weed a right to conclude his letter with this challenge: "And now I invite the advocate of infidelity, or any of his followers, to inform the public how and to what extent they have profited by his missionary labors in this city; what salutary reforms he has inaugurated, or even suggested; or in what manner and to what extent he has contributed to the general welfare or happiness of his fellow-citizens"?

There is an annual record of Christian work in this city, issued by Mr. Lewis Jackson, of the City Mission, which may illustrate the same thing. It is an extensive document, and represents many agencies, and much expenditure of effort and of means. It shows, too, that large results have been secured; but where is the report of similar doings among the "dreamers of dreams"? What hospitals have they reared? what missions have they inaugurated? what sinners have they reclaimed? You read, as I did, with deepest interest, those recent articles in the *New York Times* about our city churches. Many things in them were glaringly inaccurate, but some were calculated to awaken very serious thoughts in our minds; yet one was to me matter of devoutest gratitude, and that was the fact that by these churches two millions and a half of dollars are given annually for enterprises of benevolence, which have for their object not merely the physical, but also, and especially, the moral and spiritual welfare of men. All these agencies are in full operation, and all of them are attended, through the blessing of God's Spirit, with a larger or smaller measure of success. What is agnosticism, or scepticism, or infidelity attempting in the same direction? and what success would any of them meet, if it should make the effort? I ask these questions without any fear for the answer, and here again I dare renew my challenge: "What is the chaff to the wheat? saith the Lord." Let the advocates of infidelity either *do* more than we have accomplished, or let them forever hold their peace.

IV. But I have time only to name my fourth remark, which is, that the human dream is short-lived, but the divine word is enduring. Chaff is easily blown away, but the wheat remains. And so the "little systems" of human speculation "have their day and cease to be"; but "the word of the Lord endureth forever." Each new antagonist, as he has arisen, has boasted that he would destroy the influence of the gospel; but, somehow, he passes away, and it continues. Like some impregnable fortress, in the hollows around which you may pick up specimens of the various missiles which from age to age have been hurled against it, whilst its walls remain unbroken, the word of God has withstood for centuries the attacks of many successive armies of antagonists. The assailants have gone—the Book abides; and as of old it was written, so we may write again—"They are dead who sought the young child's life." The arguments of the first antagonists of the gospel are now read only in the pages of the apologists who replied to them. And in more recent times, how many adversaries have advanced to assail it, with haughty boasting that it would speedily be defeated, but with the same result? Voltaire said that it took twelve men to establish the gospel, but he would show that one man could overthrow it. Yet the gospel is here studied by millions, and how few now read Voltaire? A certain German rationalist alleged that the gospel was not worth twenty-five years' purchase; but half a century has gone since he wrote, and the gospel is more vigorous than ever, while he is forgotten. Again and again, in the estimation of its adversaries, it ought to have been demolished; but it *will* not die, for there is deep truth in Beza's motto for the French Protestant Church, which surmounts the device of an anvil surrounded by blacksmiths, at whose feet are many broken hammers, and which I once heard Frederick Monod translate thus:

"Hammer away, ye hostile bands :
Your hammers break, God's anvil stands."

Now, what does your boasted doctrine of the survival of the fittest say to this? Come! do not flinch, but carry it through. Is not the inference from your own principle irresistible—that by its survival the gospel has proved its fittestness?—and may I not, therefore, repeat my challenge: "What is the chaff to the wheat?"

But what is the inference from all this? Can we express it better than in the words of the text: "He that hath my word, let him speak my word faithfully"? Let us first of all seek to possess it for ourselves, and then let us present it faithfully to our fellowmen. If we would see its power, we must preach it as we have received it from the Lord. It was to this same Jeremiah that Jehovah said: "Preach the preaching that I bid thee; diminish not a word"; and the most successful evangelist the world ever saw was he who could say with truth, "I have not shunned to declare unto you all the counsel of God." So let us imitate his example, and set forth before men the whole truth as we find it in this book. Let us expose the dreadful nature and evil consequences of sin; let us publish the good news of salvation righteously wrought out by God, in love, for all who choose to accept of it; let us show that such salvation is to be had alone through faith in the Lord Jesus Christ; let us exalt the life-giving agency of the Holy Spirit, by whom alone men are quickened into newness of life—and let us enforce all these statements by the solemn sanctions of eternal judgment. Then we may expect to see God's arm made bare again, as in former days, in the conversion of multitudes; and even if in that expectation we should for a time, like Jeremiah, be disappointed, we shall have at least the consolation that we have delivered our own souls and have sown seed which shall yet germinate in the hearts and lives of men. And now may God help us to lay these things to heart, that his name may be glorified. Amen.

November 12, 1882.

CHRIST BEFORE PILATE—PILATE BEFORE CHRIST.

MATTHEW xxvii. 22.—Pilate saith unto them, What shall I do, then, with Jesus, which is called Christ?

DURING my late visit to my native land I had the great enjoyment of seeing, and somewhat carefully studying, Munkacsy's famous picture of "Christ Before Pilate." Rarely, if ever, have I been so much moved by a work of art; and I propose this morning to give to you, as nearly as I can recall it, the sermon which it preached to me as I sat and silently contemplated the figures, which, even as I looked at them, seemed to grow before me into life.

But, first, I must try to describe to you the picture itself. The canvas is large, and the figures, all of which are on the line of sight, are of life size. The scene is in the pavement or open court before the governor's palace, which was called in the Hebrew tongue Gabbatha, and in which, after all his efforts to wriggle out of the responsibility of dealing with the case, Pilate ultimately gave up Jesus to be crucified. At one end of the court, on a raised bench, and dressed in a white toga, Pilate sits. On either side of him are Jews, each of whom has a marked and special individuality. The two on his left are gazing with intense eagerness at Christ. They are evidently puzzled, and know not well what to make of the mysterious prisoner. On his right, standing on one of the seats, and with his back against the wall, is a Scribe, whose countenance is expressive of uttermost contempt, and just in front of this haughty fellow are some Pharisees, one of whom is on his feet, and passionately urging that Jesus should be put to death, presumably on the ground that, if Pilate should let him go, he would make it evident that he was not Cæsar's friend. Before them again is a usurer, sleek, fat and self-satisfied, clearly taking great comfort to himself in the assurance that, however the matter may be settled, his well-filled money-bags will be undisturbed. Beyond him stands the Christ in a robe of seamless white, and with his wrists firmly bound; while behind, kept in place by a Roman soldier, standing with his back to the spectator, and making a barricade with his spear, which he holds horizontally, is a motley group of on-lookers, not unlike that which we may still see any day in one of our criminal courts. Of these, one more furious than the rest is wildly gesticulating, and crying, as we may judge from his whole attitude, "Crucify him! crucify him!" and another, a little to the Saviour's left, but in the second row behind him, is leaning forward with mockery in his leering look, and making almost as if he would spit upon the saintly one. There is but one really compassionate face in the crowd, and that is the face of a woman who, with an infant in her arms, most fitly represents those gentle daughters of Jerusalem who followed Jesus to Calvary with tears. Then, over the heads of the on-lookers, and out of the upper part of the doorway into the court, we get a glimpse of the quiet light of the morning as it sleeps upon the walls and turrets of the adjacent buildings. All these figures are so distinctly seen that you feel you could recognize them again if you met them anywhere; and a strange sense of reality comes upon you as you look at them, so that you forget that they are only painted, and imagine that you are gazing on living and breathing men.

But, as you sit awhile and look on, you gradually lose all consciousness of the presence of the mere on-lookers and find your interest concentrated on these two white-robed ones, as if they were the only figures before you. The pose of the Christ is admirable. It is repose blended with dignity; self-possession rising into majesty. There is no agitation or confusion; no fear or misgiving; but, instead, the calm nobleness of him who has just been saying "Thou couldst have no power at all against me, except it were given thee from above; therefore he that delivered me unto thee hath the greater sin." The face alone disappoints. Perhaps that may be owing to the lofty ideal we have of the Divine Man, so that no picture of our Lord would entirely please. But though the painter has wisely abandoned the halo, and all similar conventionalisms of art, and has delineated a real man, for all which he is to be highly commended, yet the eyes which look so steadily at Pilate as if they were looking him through, seem to me to be cold, keen, and condemnatory, rather than compassionate and sad. It is a conception of the Lord of the same sort as that of Doré, in his well-known picture of the leaving of the Praetorium, and the eyes have not in them that deep well of tenderness out of which came the tears which he shed over Jerusalem, and which we expect to see in them when he is looking at the hopeless struggle of a soul which will not accept his aid. It is said that the artist, dissatisfied with his first attempt, has painted the Christ face twice; but this, also, is a partial failure, and here, so at least it seemed to me as I looked upon it, is the one defect in his noble work. But if there is this defect, it is one which it shares with every other effort that human art has made to delineate the Lord. The Pilate, however, is well-nigh faultless. Here is a great, strong man, the representative of the mightiest empire the world has ever seen, with a head indicating intellectual force, and a face, especially in its lower part, suggestive of sensual indulgence. There is ordinarily no want of firmness in him, as we may see from the general set of his features; but now there is in his countenance a marvelous mixture of humiliation and irresolution. He cannot lift his eyes to meet the gaze of Christ; and while one of his hands is nervously clutching at his robe he is looking sadly into the other, whose fingers, even as we look at them, almost seem to twitch with perplexed irresolution. He is clearly pondering for himself the question which a few moments before he had addressed to the multitude, "What shall I do with Jesus which is called Christ?" He is annoyed that the case has been brought to him at all, and as he feels himself drifting on, against his own better judgment, toward yielding to the clamor of the multitude, he falls mightily in his own conceit, and begins to despise himself. He would, at that moment, give, oh, how much! to be rid of the responsibility of dealing with the Christ, but he cannot evade it; and so he sits there, drifting on to what he knows is a wrong decision, the very incarnation of the feeling which his own national poet described when he said, "I see and approve the better course; I follow the worse." Thus, as we look at these two, we begin to discover that it was not Christ that was before Pilate so much as Pilate that was before Christ. His was the testing experience. His was the trial; his too, alas! was the degradation; and at that coming day when the places shall be reversed, when Christ shall be on the judgment seat, and Pilate at the bar, there will still be that deep self-condemnation which the painter here has fixed upon his countenance. It is a marvelous picture, in many respects the most remarkable I ever looked upon, and, even from this imperfect description of it, you will easily understand how as I sat intent before it it stirred my soul to the very depths.

But now, with this portrayal of the scene before us let us see if we can account, first, for the hesitation of Pilate to give up the Lord, and then for his final yielding to the clamor of the people. Why all this reluctance on his part to send Jesus to the cross? He was not usually so scrupulous. A human life more or less gave him generally very little concern. He had all a Roman's indifference for the comfort of those who stood in any respect in his way; and had no compunction, as we know, in mingling the blood of certain turbulent Jews with the very sacrifices which at the moment they were offering. Had Christ been a Roman citizen, indeed, he would most likely have been very watchful over his safety, for in regard to all such the imperial law was peculiarly strict, but the life of a mere Jew was a very small thing in his estimation. Wherefore then, this unwonted squeamishness of conscience? It was the result of a combination of particulars, each of which had a special force of its own, and the aggregate of which so wrought upon his mind that he was brought thereby to a stand.

There was, in the first place, the peculiar character of the prisoner. A very slight examination had been sufficient to convince him that Christ was innocent of the charge which had been brought against him. But in the course of that examination much more than the innocence of Christ had come to view. He had manifested a dignified patience altogether unlike anything that Pilate had ever seen; and his answers to certain questions had been so strangely suggestive of something higher and nobler than even the most exalted earthly philosophy that he could not look upon him as a common prisoner. He was no mere fanatic; neither was he after the pattern of any existing school, whether Jewish, Greek, or Roman. There was about him an "other-worldliness" which brought those near him into close proximity, for the time, with the unseen; and an elevation which lifted him above the tumult that was howling for his destruction. Probably Pilate could not have described it to himself, but there was something which he felt unusual and exceptional in this man, marking him out from every other he ever had before him, and constraining him to take a special interest in his case. Add to this that his wife had sent to him that singular message—"Have thou nothing to do with that just man, for I have suffered many things this day in a dream because of him,"—a message which, in those days of mingled scepticism and superstition—for the two always go hand in hand—must have produced a deep impression on his mind. Moreover, there seemed some fatality about the case. He had tried to roll it over upon Herod, but that wily monarch sent the prisoner back upon his hands. He had attempted to release him, as the passover prisoner for the year, but neither was there any outlet for him in that, for the people had preferred Barabbas. And so the responsibility had come again to his own door, and could not be passed on to another. Still again, he saw that the Jews were acting most hypocritically in the matter. It was a new thing for them to be zealous for the honor of Cæsar, and he could easily see through the mask they wore, into the envy and malice which were the motives for their conduct. The deeper he went into the case he discovered only the more reason for resisting their importunity, and, however he looked at it, his plain duty was to set the prisoner free.

Why then, again we ask, was his perplexity? The answer is suggested by the taunt of the Jews, "If thou let this man go thou art not Cæsar's friend; whosoever maketh himself a king speaketh against Cæsar." He foresaw that if he resisted the will of the rulers he would make them his enemies, and so provoke them to complain of him to the emperor, who would then institute an inquiry into his administration of his office—and that he was not prepared to face. He had done things as a governor which would not bear the light, and so at the crisis of his life he was fettered by deeds of the past from doing that which he felt to be the duty of the present. You may, perhaps, remember that expression of the prophet, which thus reads in the margin: "Their doings will not suffer them to turn unto their God";[*] and that other, which affirms, concerning Israel: "Their own doings have beset them about."[†] Now, these descriptions most accurately define the cause of Pilate's perplexity here. His conduct in the past had been such that he had not the courage to take any course which might lead to an investigation of that. If he could deliver Christ without provoking that, then he would most cheerfully do so; but if by delivering Christ he would provoke that, then Christ must be given up to the cross. Hence his perplexity at the first, and

---

[*] Hosea v. 4.   [†] Ibid, vii. 2.

hence, also, his yielding in the end. His past misdeeds had put him virtually into the power of those who were now so eager for the condemnation of the Christ. On three several occasions his arbitrariness had been such as all but to instigate a rebellion among the people, and his cruelty and contempt for justice, when he had a personal end to gain, were sure, upon appeal to the emperor, to be severely punished; so to save himself from banishment and disgrace, if not even death, he delivered over Jesus to the will of the Jews. He wished to do right in this case more than ever he had wished before; there was something about it which in his view made it more important that he should do right now than ever before; but through all his past official life he had, by his enormities and oppressions, been unconsciously weaving round himself a net, in the meshes of which he is now inextricably caught. His guilty conscience made him a coward at the very time when most of all he wanted to be brave. He had come to his "narrow place," where he could turn neither to the right hand nor to the left, but must face the naked alternative "yes" or "no"; and he fell because in his former life, when he was thinking of no such ordeal, he had sold himself by his evil deeds into the power of the enemy.

Now, what a lesson there is in all this for us! Men think that they may live for the time being as they please, and that at a convenient season they can repent and turn to God. But the present is conditioning the future, and making it either possible or the reverse for us to do right in the future. He who neglects the laws of health every day, and lives in intemperance and excess of all kinds, is only making it absolutely certain that when fever lays him low he will die, for he has eaten out the strength of his constitution by his follies. And, in the same way, he who sets all morality at defiance in his ordinary conduct only makes it inevitable that when his convenient season does come, when his time of privilege and testing does arrive, he will fail to rise to the occasion, and be swept away into perdition. The tenor of our ordinary life determines how we shall pass through exceptional and crucial occasions, therefore let us bring that up to the highest level by doing everything as unto God, and then we shall be ready for any emergency.

Nor let me forget to add here, that in spite of all his efforts to keep back investigation, Pilate's day of reckoning with the emperor did come. The Jews complained of him after all, in spite of his yielding to them now; and as the result he was banished, and afterwards, so tradition says, he committed suicide. Thus the ordeal and the disgrace came, notwithstanding all he did to avert them, and he had not under them the solace which he might have enjoyed if only he had stood firm on this great and memorable occasion. Therefore let us all, and especially the young, take to ourselves, as the first lesson from this deeply interesting history, that we should be careful not to hamper ourselves for the discharge of duty in the future by the guilt of the present. By our conduct now we are either coiling cords around us which shall hold us fast at the very time when we most desire to be free, or we are forming and fostering a strength of character which, through God, will triumph over every temptation. If "to be weak is to be miserable," it is no less true that to be guilty is to be weak. Preserve yourselves, therefore, from this danger, and seek above all other things to keep your consciences clean; then when you need all your strength for a crisis, you will not sit, like Pilate here, in nervous perplexity, bemoaning your helplessness even while you yield to the adversary; but you will shake the temptation from you with as much ease as the eagle shakes the dewdrop from his wing. Keep yourselves pure: so shall your youth be full of happiness, and you shall go forth out of it with no encumbering past to clog the wheels of your endeavor. How happy he whose youth time thus leaves him with a smile and sends him forth upon the duties of manhood with a benediction! But he, how miserable! whose early years heap bitter maledictions on his head, and push him forward into active life with a conscience already laden with guilt, and a soul as weak before temptation as a reed is before the wind. ——

But while there is thus in this history a lesson for all time, I think Munkacsy, by the appearance of his wondrous picture now, has made it evident that there is also something in it specially adapted to these modern days. It is with artists in the choice of their subjects as it is with ministers in the selection of their themes. Both alike, consciously and unconsciously, and most frequently perhaps, unconsciously, are affected by the spirit of their age. The atmosphere—literary, moral, political, and religious—which is round about them, and which they are daily breathing, does, insensibly to themselves, so influence them that their thoughts are turned by it into a channel different from that in which those of a former generation flowed. Hence, whether the painter would admit it or not, I see in this picture, at this juncture, at once a mirror of the times and a lesson for them. The question of Pilate, "What shall I do, then, with Jesus which is called the Christ?" is pre-eminently the question of the present age. No doubt we may say with truth that it has been the question of all the Christian centuries, and each one of them has faced it and solved it after its own fashion. It has tested the centuries even as it tested Pilate, and those in which Christ was rejected have been the darkest in the world's history; while those in which he has been hailed as the Incarnate God have been the brightest which the earth has ever seen, because irradiated with truth, and justice, and benevolence and purity. But though we are always prone to exaggerate that in the midst of which we are ourselves, it seems to me that in no one age since that of the primitive church has this testing question been so prominent as in our own. All the controversies of our times, social, philosophical, and theological, lead up to and find their ultimate hinge in the answer to this inquiry, "Who is this Jesus Christ?" If he be a mere man, then there is for us nothing but uncertainty on any subject, outside of the domain of the exact sciences; and we must all become agnostics, holding this one negative article of belief, that nothing can be known about anything save that of which we can take cognizance with the bodily senses. But if he be Incarnate God, then he brings with him from heaven the final word on all subjects concerning which he has spoken; and though in his person he is the mystery of mysteries, yet, once received, he becomes forthwith the solution of all mysteries, and faith in him is at once the satisfaction of the intellect and the repose of the heart. It is perfectly natural, therefore, that all the controversies of the day should turn on him. The Lives of Christ which have been written during the last thirty or forty years would make in themselves a very respectable library; and the cry even of the sceptic is, "I could get on very well with unbelief, if I only knew what to make of Christ." Yes, that is just the difficulty. Christ is here in the Scriptures a character portrayed in literature; he was in the world for thirty-three years, and lived a life exceptional in every respect, but most of all in the moral and spiritual departments, so that of him alone perfection can be predicated; he has been ever since a most potent factor in history, for through his influence all that is pure, and noble, and exalted, and lovely and of good report, has come into our civilization. Now, these things have to be accounted for. If he was only a man, how shall we explain them? and if he was more than a man shall we not take his own testimony as to his dignity and mission? If we are to be unbelievers, we must account for Christ on natural principles; but if we cannot do that, then we must receive him as he claims to be received. There is no alternative. Those in the age who have the spirit and disposition of Pilate will anew reject him; but those who are sincere and earnest in their inquiries will come ultimately out into the light, for "if any man be willing to do his will, he shall know of the doctrine whether it be of God."

And what is true of the age, as a whole, is true also of every individual to whom the gospel is proclaimed. For each of us, my hearers, this is the question of questions, "What shall I do with Jesus which is called Christ?" Shall I reject him and live precisely as if I had never heard his name? or shall I accept him as the Lord from heaven in human nature, trust in him as my Saviour, and obey him as my king! I must do the one or the other; and yet how many are seeking, like Pilate, to evade the question? They try to escape the responsibility of dealing with it as a direct alternative of yes or no. But as one has well said, "necessity is laid upon us. The adversaries of Christ press upon us to give our verdict against him. We are troubled and perplexed, for we have long heard about him, and have had each of us his own convictions. We would still remain neutral. We try—and try in vain—to escape from the spirit, the conversation, the literature, the question of the times. Again and again we wash our hands. But neither our silence nor our actions are of any avail; and so we are found sitting, conscious of the presence and the claims of our Saviour, and, like Pilate, not daring to look at him, as we puzzle over the answer which we must give to the question that is being forced upon us—Who is this Jesus Christ?" Perhaps this description accurately portrays some one here this morning. If so, let me give him one parting word. It is this: You cannot evade the decision, BUT BE SURE THAT YOU LOOK AT THE CHRIST BEFORE YOU GIVE HIM UP. Nothing is so remarkable in the picture to which I have so often this day referred as the evident persistency with which Pilate keeps his eyes from Christ; and few things are so saddening as to meet with men who profess to have, and really have, difficulties about Christ, but who have never read the gospels or the New Testament with any attention. Let me urge you, therefore, to study these gospels and epistles before you give your voice against the Lord, and I am very sure that if you ponder them thoroughly you will soon accept him. Give over trying to solve all the difficulties and so-called discrepancies in the Scriptures which form the stock-in-trade of the infidel lecturer—all these are but as dust which he raises that he may blind your eyes to the really important question, "Who is Christ?" Settle that, and if you do, all other difficulties will vanish. Turn your face to the light, and the shadow will fall behind you. LOOK AT THE CHRIST BEFORE YOU GIVE HIM UP. And remember, if you do reject Christ, you have still to account *for* him. It is unreasonable for you, if you believe only in the natural and material, to leave such a phenomenon as Christ unexplained. Yes, and I must add, if you reject him you must yet account *to* him. Go, then, and ponder this text; yea, may it continue sounding in your inmost heart until you have determined to receive and rest upon him as your only Saviour, and say to him, like Thomas, "My Lord and my God."

OCTOBER 15, 1882.

CAPTIVITIES AND HOW TO IMPROVE THEM.

JEREMIAH xxix. 10-14.—For thus saith the Lord, That after seventy years be accomplished at Babylon I will visit you, and perform my good word toward you, in causing you to return to this place. For I know the thoughts that I think toward you, saith the Lord, thoughts of peace, and not of evil, to give you an expected end. Then shall ye call upon me, and ye shall go and pray unto me, and I will hearken unto you. And ye shall seek me and find *me*, when ye shall search for me with all your heart. And I will be found of you, saith the Lord: and I will turn away your captivity, and I will gather you from all the nations, and from all the places whither I have driven you, saith the Lord; and I will bring you again into the place whence I caused you to be carried away captive.

WHEN God sends his people on a pilgrimage, he gives them a staff to support them by the way. So, after ten thousand captives had been taken by Nebuchadnezzar from Jerusalem to Babylon, he caused his servant Jeremiah to write them the letter which is contained in this chapter, and in which he cheers them with the prospect of ultimate deliverance. They had been very unmindful of his covenant, and most disrespectful to his prophet, yet he had not forgotten them, and through the instrumentality of the messenger whom they had formerly despised he sends them the strongest consolation. Now, in all this we discover certain similarities to our own experience, and I am sure that you will not accuse me of any unwarrantable accommodation of the passage which I have just read, if I seek to bring out of it some great truths which hold in all circumstances, and which are profitable both for warning and for comfort.

I. To begin with, then, we may describe every real affliction which comes upon the Christian as a captivity. We have now, indeed, no such deportations as those made by Eastern warriors when they carried the populations of conquered countries away from their homes to foreign lands. They designed thereby to break up the sentiment of nationality among the captives themselves, and to remove from the newly acquired provinces all incitement to insurrection; while, at the same time, they strengthened the centers of their empires by the addition of skilled artisans, scholars and agriculturists. Those who were thus removed from their native homes were for the most part generously treated. They were regarded as colonists rather than as slaves; nevertheless, they were taken whither they did not desire to go, and they were prevented from going to the land after which their hearts were longing. It is not wrong, therefore, to speak of them as captives. They were led through experiences into which they would never have gone of their own accord, and they were held back from the pleasures and occupations to which they would willingly have returned. That was the essence of their captivity. But is it not also the essence of every sort of affliction? To be in a condition which we never should have voluntarily preferred, or to be held back, by the power of something which we cannot control, from that which we eagerly desire to do,—is not that the very thing in an experience which makes it a trial? Take bodily illness, for example, and when you get at the root of the discomfort of it, you find it in the union of these two things: you are where you do not want to be, and where you would never have thought of putting yourself, and you are held there, whether you will or not, by the irresistible might of your own weakness. No external force has been exerted upon you; no sentinel keeps visible guard at your chamber door to prevent your exit, yet you are a prisoner as really as if you were encelled in the Tombs. You do not relish the situation. There is nothing in it, in itself considered, to attract you to it. You would not have been in it if you could have helped it; and now that you are in it you cannot go about your ordinary duties. Your business has to do without you. The appointments you have made have to go unkept. The transactions you expected to complete have to be let alone. You are a captive.

But the same thing comes out in every sort of affliction. You are, let me suppose, in business perplexities. Well, that is not of your own choosing. If you could have accomplished it, you would have been in quite different circumstances. But, in spite of you, things have gone crooked. Men whom you had implicitly trusted, and whom you would have had no more thought of doubting than you have thought now of doubting your mother's love to you, have proved deceitful. Or, perhaps, the partner whom in days gone by you had been the means of enriching has turned against you, and is seeking to worry you into the sacrifice of that which you know is really yours. And so you are at a standstill. You have been carried from the Jerusalem of comfort to the Babylon of perplexity, by no effort of yours, nay, perhaps, against the utmost resistance on your part, and now you can do nothing. Your resources are locked up, if they be not lost, and when your sympathies are moved for some suffering fellow-man, or for some deserving cause, or for some Christian enterprise, you feel that you cannot give as you did formerly, or it may be that you cannot give at all,—that is, you are a captive.

So sometimes, also, our providential duties are a kind of affliction to us. We had no choice in determining whether we would assume them. They came to us, unbidden, at least, if not undesired, and they have chained us to themselves, so that when we are asked to take part in some effort for the benefit of others we are compelled to say "No." We would a great deal rather have said "Yes": it is a trial to us to refuse; but we are hemmed in by prior and pressing obligations, and we cannot do otherwise. Which of us knows not an experience like that? The chain that binds us may be one that has come to us clearly in the way of Providence. Yet for the moment we would that we were free. Our very most sacred responsibilities—God help us! what weak creatures we are!—are sometimes felt by us as fetters which hold us back from enterprises of great pith and moment. Thus this old captivity, which marked an era in the history of God's ancient people, and which forms the theme of so many plaintive psalms, repeats itself, in some degree, in the life of every believer, and our modern trials furnish us with a key wherewith we may unlock for ourselves the prophetic casket in which such treasures of consolation are laid up.

II. For now I proceed to remark that every captivity of which the Christian is the victim will have an end. Jeremiah here declares that after a set time of seventy years the enforced absence of the people from their own land would cease. And the student of ancient history knows that this all came to pass. At the date at which the prophet wrote, indeed, there was, to human view, but little likelihood that such a change would come. Nebuchadnezzar was in his glory. The Babylonian empire was at the zenith of its splendor, and it did not seem probable that it would be speedily overthrown. Yet, in a wonderful way, Cyrus, who had been called the servant and the shepherd of the Lord by Isaiah, obtained possession of the dominions of Belshazzar, and the very first year of his Babylonian reign was signalized by the issue of that famous decree which gave the Jews permission to return to their own country, and encouraged them to rebuild the temple of their God. Now, in a similar way, we may be sure that sooner or later our providential captivities will come to an end. "Time and the hour run through the roughest day." "Be the day weary, or be the day long, at last it ringeth to even-song." It is but a little while, at the longest, and we shall be where " sorrow and sighing shall forever flee away." This state of limitation, this conflict between our aspirations and our abilities, is not to last forever. We may hope that it will come to an end even here upon the earth, but we may be sure that it will not continue beyond the grave. And there is much even in that thought to give us comfort. "The things concerning us have an end." Not forever shall we be in bondage to the weakness of the body, hampered by its liability to disease, and hindered by its proneness to fatigue. Not always shall we be at the mercy of the unscrupulous and dishonest. Not continually shall we be held down by the encumbrances that overweight us here on earth. For in the fatherland above we shall work without weariness, and serve God without imperfection. So in the prospect of that home we may well be reconciled for a season to the discomforts of our present exile.

But, while there is much in this view of the case to sustain us, we must not lose sight of the moral end which God has in view in sending us into our captivity. Mark these words of the Lord, "I know the thoughts that I think toward you, thoughts of peace and not of evil, to give you an expected end." He sees the result from the beginning, even as at the first the eye of the artist beholds the finished statue in the rough block of marble that has just come to him from the quarry; and all the afflictions which he sends are but like the hammer-strokes of the sculptor, each of which removes some imperfection or brings some new loveliness to view. Observe how it was with the Israelites in the case before us. During all the years of their history, from the very exodus on to the captivity, their besetment was idolatry. Ever and anon they were falling into the worship of some of their neighbors' gods; sometimes they followed Baal, and sometimes, as in the days of Ahaz, altars were erected on the very roof of the Temple, apparently for the worship of the heavenly bodies. But from the time of their removal to Babylon all that disappeared. Their captivity gave the death-blow to their idolatry, and thenceforth they worshiped only God. Moreover, their absence from Jerusalem, and the cessation of their Temple ritual, threw them back on God himself, and from this date prayer assumed an importance among them that it had not before possessed. Cut off from access to the house of God, they sought God himself the more earnestly, and found, in very deed, that he was not confined to temples made with hands. Now, also, the written word began to be studied by them, and synagogues for its weekly public reading were instituted among them. Thus they increased in spirituality of character; they learned to walk more by faith and less by sight; and the forms of their religion, instead of being ends in themselves, became to them only the means of ministering to their fellowship with Jehovah.

Now, is it not precisely in these ways yet that God, through affliction, works out the sanctification of our souls? Ah! how many of our idolatries he has rebuked and rectified by our captivities! We had been worshiping our reputation, and lo! an illness came which laid us aside, and our names were by and by forgotten, as new men came to the front; and then, learning the folly of our false ambition, we turned from the idolatry of self to the homage of Jehovah. Or, we had made an idol of our business. We had great ideas of what we should make of it, and we thought of leaving it as a legacy to our children, and perpetuating our name in connection with it; but now it is in ruins, and as we see the perishableness of earthly things, we turn to Him who is unchanging and eternal. Or, we had made a god of our dwelling, and by some reverse of fortune it is swept away from us, just that we might learn the meaning of that old song of Moses, "Lord, thou hast been our dwelling-place in all generations."

How many portions of his word, also, have been explained to us by our trials! There is no commentator of the Scriptures half so valuable as a captivity. It unfolds new beauties where all had appeared to be beautiful before; and where formerly there was what we thought a wilderness, it has revealed to us a fruitful field. The old psalms have quavered for us with a new pathos as we sat by our "Babel's stream," and have sounded for us with a new joy as we found our captivity turned as the streams in the South. The man who has seen much affliction will not readily part with his copy of the word of God. Another book may seem to others to be identical with his own; but it is not the same to him, for over his old and tear-stained Bible he has written, in characters which are visible to no eyes but his own, the record of his experiences, and ever and anon he comes on Bethel pillars or Elim palms, which are to him the memorials of some critical chapter in his history. How many of us, too, might say with truth that we had never really prayed until God sent us into captivity! Our worship had been outward, formal, cold; a thing of duty, not of sincerity; an affair, shall I say, of luxury rather than of need? But now we have found out what the mercy-seat means, and know that prayer is the surest and the sweetest solace in the hour of perplexity. This is God's "end and expectation" in our captivity; and when that is realized is there one among us who would affirm that the result is not worth the price? By such experiences it is that Christians are made; and if we would be great in holiness, we must lay our account with the discipline through which alone that greatness can be given. Nor must we imagine that God is changed toward us while thus he is dealing with us. In all and through all he is working for our good, that at the last he may present us to himself without spot or wrinkle or any such thing; and whensoever we are apt to suspect him he falls back upon his own conscious love to us and says, "I know the thoughts that I think toward you, thoughts of peace, and not of evil, to give you an expected end."

III. But now we must not forget to add, in the third place, that if we would have such results from our captivity, there are certain important things which we must cultivate. What these are will appear if we look narrowly at the verses which form my text, and at those by which they are immediately preceded:

I mention first among them a willing acceptance of God's discipline, and patient submission to it. It would seem that before the date of Jeremiah's letter there were among the captives certain persons claiming to be prophets or diviners who were seeking to incite them to revolt against their conqueror, and promising that thereby they would have a speedy return to Jerusalem; but Jeremiah endeavored to impress upon them that the shortest way to their deliverance lay through a contented accommodation of themselves to their new circumstances, and a patient endurance of their trials. So he says to them, Make the best of your position—"Build ye houses and dwell in them; and plant gardens and eat the fruit of them"; and, so far from hatching schemes of rebellion, "Seek the peace of the city whither I have caused you to be carried away captives and pray unto the Lord for it; for in the peace thereof shall ye have peace."

Now, in the same way, if we are to receive benefit from our captivity we must accept the situation and turn it to the best possible account. Fretting over that from which we have been removed, or which has been taken away from us, will not make things better, but it will prevent us from improving those which remain. The bond is only tightened by our stretching it to the uttermost. The impatient horse which will not quietly endure his halter only strangles himself in his stall. The high-mettled animal that is restive in the yoke only galls his shoulders; and every one will understand the difference between the restless starling of which Sterne has written, breaking its wings against the bars of its cage, and crying, "I can't get out," "I can't get out," and the docile canary that sits upon its perch and sings as if he would outrival the lark soaring to heaven's gate, and so moves his mistress to open the door of his prison-house and give him the full range of the room. He who is constantly looking back and bewailing that which he has lost, does only thereby unfit himself for improving in any way the discipline to which God has subjected him; whereas the man who brings his mind down to his lower lot, and deliberately examines how he can serve God best in that, is already on the way to happiness and to restoration. This is a most important consideration, and it may, perhaps, help to explain why similar trials have had such different results in different persons. One has been bemoaning that it was not with him as in months past; while the other has been discovering that some talents have been left him still, and has been laying these out for his Lord. One has been saying, "If I had only the resources which I once possessed I could have done something, but, alas! they have gone"; the other has been soliloquizing thus: "I can at least do this, and if I put it into the hand of Christ, little as it is, he can make it great"; and so we account for the misery and uselessness of the one, and the happiness and usefulness of the other. Nor will it do to say that this difference is only a thing of temperament. It is a thing of faith. The one recognizes the hand of God as a loving father in his affliction; the other sees nothing but his own calamity, and that only increases his affliction in the end.

Thus, paradoxical as it may appear, acquiescence in adversity is the best way out of it; for he who accepts the situation and begins on the lower level to do his best has already stepped on the first round in the ladder up which he is to ascend to a renewal of prosperity. This is true, as every one will admit, in temporal things, but it is no less true in spiritual matters, for not until we have forgiven God for the wrong which we imagine he has done us, or rather not until we have come to see that there was no wrong in his discipline, can we receive the full measure of the blessing which he desires to bestow upon us.

But the second thing to be cultivated by us, if we would secure the full benefit of the trial, is unswerving confidence in God. If we doubt him we at once become the prey to despondency, impatience, and rebellion. We are ready then to take counsel of false prophets and diviners, and to open our hearts to every kind of evil. But so long as we hold fast our faith in him, everything that comes upon us will in the end only minister to our spiritual growth. "He that believeth shall not make haste;" and the man who has the fullest persuasion that the providence of God is universal, including everything in his lot, while at the same time it is directed to a special end, namely, the greatest good of those who truly love him, will "hold still," no matter what may come upon him. Thus this unfaltering trust in God is intimately connected with the willing acceptance of our captivity, to which I have just alluded, and so it comes to be closely allied also with that progress in holiness which it is the great design of our afflictions to promote. And why should we not trust God? He has given us his word, and that ought to be enough; but, as if in accommodation to our weakness, he has confirmed that promise by his oath, and has at the same time opened up a way, through the cross of his own Son, by which he may righteously keep his pledge. So we have no ground for suspecting him; and if we do distrust him, we can have no better reassurance of his faithfulness than that which this verse affords: "I know the thoughts that I think toward you, thoughts of peace and not of evil, to give you an expected end." Brethren, ponder well these words. They are unique even in the sacred Scriptures, and they have a comforting influence such as few other passages possess. Years ago they came to my own heart with peculiar power, and the Bible now would scarcely be the same book to me if I could not find them in it, and fall back upon the assurance they give. They are almost like a soliloquy of Jehovah, in which he comforts himself, under the suspicious and accusations of his wavering people, by the consciousness of his own loving purposes. As if he had said, "You may think of me as you please; you may utter hard things against me, and accuse me of having a controversy with you; but no matter. I know all that is false, I know the thoughts that I think toward you, and whatever you may allege to the contrary, they are thoughts of peace and not of evil, to give you an expected end." Now, may it not be with some of us that we have failed to receive the full benefit of trial just because we have been misjudging God? Confidence in your physician is itself more than half the cure, and trust in God is absolutely essential if we would gain benefit from his discipline. Yet because a change in men's conduct toward us is usually the indication of a difference in their disposition toward us, we think that God has ceased to care for us when he puts us into trial or sends us into captivity. But it is not so. To-day the medical man gives his patient liberty to take anything he chooses; to-morrow he cuts off all indulgence, and uses severe and painful remedies; but does he care the less for him because he thus changes his treatment, or has his purpose regarding him undergone an alteration? Not at all. In both cases he is equally earnest to have his health restored. And it is quite similar with God in his dealings with his people. He is not an amiably indulgent father, giving his children whatever they ask just because they desire it; but he is a wise and judicious educator, who gives or denies according as he sees it will promote the training of his pupils for the higher life of heaven. So let us trust him, and beneath every other sentiment of our souls let there be that of humble submission to his will, not because it is inevitable, but because it is for our good.

The last thing needed by us if we would derive the full benefit from our captivity is fervent prayer. Hear these words, "Then shall ye call upon me, and ye shall go and pray unto me, and I will hearken unto you, and ye shall seek me and find me, when ye shall search for me with all your heart." Now, as I have already said, this was all fulfilled in the case of the captive Jews. They did seek God with all their hearts, and they did enjoy the blessing promised them by the mouth of Ezekiel, in that chapter of his book that is such a wonderful anticipation of the Gospel. It is noteworthy, also, that out of the songs in the Psalter which are not the production of David, a large proportion belongs to the age of the captivity. The people thus did turn to God, and he *was* found of them because they sought him with the greatest earnestness. So let us make our captivities, whatever they may be, the occasions of new prayers. Let us take them to God, not in a formal and superficial manner, but really and sincerely, emptying our hearts before him, and pleading his promises even as Daniel took Jeremiah's prophecy which we have to-day been considering: and who can tell but he will give us not only the relief we seek, but also such revelations of his grace and goodness as shall correspond to the vision of the seventy heptades with which the Babylonian prime minister was blessed? No calamity can be to us an unmixed evil if we carry it in direct and fervent prayer to God, for even as one in taking shelter from the rain beneath a tree may find on its branches fruit which he looked not for, so we, in fleeing for refuge beneath the shadow of God's wing, will always find more in God than we had seen or known before. It is thus through our afflictions that God gives us fresh revelations of himself; and the Jabbok ford, which we crossed to seek his help, leads to the Peniel, where, as the result of our wrestling, we "see God face to face," and our lives are preserved.

I cannot but feel that these truths are designed for some one here to-day. I came from the country with quite another sermon for this morning's service. But after I reached my home this discourse came to me, and would write itself, whether I would or not. So I know it is meant for some one, though I know not who he is. I draw the bow at a venture, but as I do so the hands of the Master, unseen, are over mine, and the arrow, which to-day is one of deliverance and not of destruction, will surely find its mark. Take it to thyself, O captive, and he will give thee "songs for sighing," and turn for thee "the shadow of death into the morning."

June 9, 1878

PERSONAL INDEPENDENCE THE RESULT OF DIVINE REDEMPTION.

1 Cor. vii. 23.—Ye are bought with a price; be not ye the servants of men.

The first Gentile converts to Christianity had to confront many perplexing problems arising out of their relationship to those who remained heathens, and their daily contact, in one way or another, with the institutions of paganism and the enactments of imperialism. It is not wonderful, therefore, that in their difficulty as to what they should do in certain matters, the members of the church of Corinth had applied for advice to the Apostle Paul; and the counsels which he gave to them were, as indeed might have been expected, pre-eminently wise. One of the things concerning which they had specially desired his guidance was marriage, and the chapter from which my text is taken is almost exclusively devoted to that subject. It is remarkable at once for the broad principles which it lays down, and for the recognition which it gives to the modifying influence of exceptional circumstances. Indeed, so largely does this last element enter into the discussion of the subject, that, unless we take into account what Paul has elsewhere written on the dignity and importance of the married relationship, we might be apt, from the perusal of this chapter alone, to take away an entirely erroneous impression respecting his views. But we have to remember that much that he has here advanced was for a then "present necessity," and with that thought in mind it is not difficult to distinguish between the great abiding principles which he lays down for all time, and the hints which he has given to guide his correspondents through a temporary difficulty. He affirms that, in their circumstances, at the time, celibacy would be the prudent course for the Corinthian believers; yet he declares that he was not authorized to issue to them any command to that effect. Each must judge for himself, and act accordingly; and they might all have the comfort of the thought that, whether they married or not, there was no sin in taking either alternative. Only, if they did marry, he would remind them that, by the law of God, the tie between husband and wife was for life, and was not to be broken, save for the one great reason which the Lord Jesus specified. He affirms also that if for any other cause husband and wife should separate, it was the duty of both to remain single, and make no other connection. How different all that is from the divorce laws in some of our States, and how much these laws are doing to poison family happiness, and degrade public morality, I will not now pause to point out. I will only say that while such laws remain unrepealed the States in which they exist have too much glass in the walls of their own houses to make it safe for them to throw stones at the Mormons.

Another question which emerged from the circumstances in which some of the Corinthians found themselves was this: What was to be done in cases where the wife had become a Christian, while the husband continued to be an idolater? or where the husband was converted, while the wife remained a pagan?

And to that Paul's reply was that even in such instances the indissolubleness of the marriage tie remained, and that the believing partner was to continue in the relationship. If the unbelieving wife did not object to dwell with a believing husband, he was not to put her away, and if the unbelieving husband did not refuse to dwell with a believing wife, she was not to think of leaving him. If a separation came, it was not to be the act of the believer. But if the unbelieving party to the contract broke it, of his own motive, by wilful desertion, for no other reason than the Christianity of the other, then the clear statement is made, "a brother or a sister is not in bondage in such cases." And the ground on which this advice is given by Paul is the same as that suggested by Peter in dealing with the same question. The apostle of the circumcision thus writes: "Likewise, ye wives, be in subjection to your own husbands; that if any obey not the word, they also may, without a word, be won by the conversation of the wives"; and in a similar strain Paul says here, "What knowest thou, O wife, whether thou shalt save thy husband? or how knowest thou, O man, whether thou shalt save thy wife?"

The apostle, you observe, says nothing whatever here about, and gives no encouragement to, the deliberate choice by a believer of an unbelieving partner; but when, both having been unbelievers, the husband or the wife should be converted while the other remains as before, his unequivocal advice is that the believer should continue the relationship, and make the best of its opportunities for Christ; and in reference to all similar questions of what may be termed casuistry in a good sense his great law is, "Let every man abide in the same calling wherein he is called." His first duty is to sanctify that, and through the performance of that duty God will open to him a higher opportunity. This law he applies, first, ecclesiastically, to the questions between Jew and Gentile, and affirms that it is not necessary for the Jew to abjure his Jewish customs when he becomes a Christian any more than it is for the Gentile to become a Jew in order to be a thorough follower of Christ. Then, advancing to ground that was still more delicate, he shows its bearing, socially, in regard to slavery, saying, "Art thou called, being a slave, care not for it? but if thou mayest be made free, use it rather." Do not, as if he had said, by any violent or dishonorable means seek to regain your freedom; but let your solace in your bondage be, that the Christian is the Lord's freeman. Still, do not despise liberty, for in itself that is better than slavery. If, therefore, you can peacefully and Christianly secure your freedom, thankfully embrace it, and let your spiritual ballast be in the reflection that the believing freeman is the slave of Christ.

Thus the apostle clearly indicates that Christianity is a regenerating force for the individual, and only through that a reformer of society. It was not to create a sudden revolution that should overturn everything as with the shock of a devastating earthquake; but it was to bring on a gradual change, working like the leaven in the meal on individual particle after particle, until the whole mass should be leavened. "God hath called us to peace" was the apostle's watchword in all such matters; and any one who knows the social condition of the Roman Empire when he wrote this letter, and thinks on the influence of his words on that, and on the countries into which, in after times, the gospel has been introduced, will be forward to admit that they were not only admirably judicious, but eminently far-seeing.

All this I have said, not only that I may lay bare to you the intellectual and spiritual strata in which the words of my text lie; but also that I may bring up before you principles of social and civil economics which are far too frequently lost sight of in these days. We are so impetuous in our eagerness to gain certain ends that we take what seems to us the shortest way, though that may lie through strife and misery. But "he that believeth shall not make 'such' haste." He will abide in his calling and serve God there, waiting for results. These may not come at once, but they will come, and when they do they will prove by their wholesomeness and their permanence that they were worth waiting for.

Now, it is in connection with the commanded preference of freedom to slavery, when that can be secured, that Paul says, "Ye are bought with a price; be not ye the servants of men"; as if he would have put it thus: use freedom rather than slavery, for Christ has bought you, and it is well to keep yourselves for his divine ownership. But the words thus appropriate to Paul's primary purpose have a much wider range than that here given to them, and the longer one thinks on them the more significant they become. They suggest the truth that spiritual redemption is the root of personal independence; and to the elucidation of that—opposed as it is to many modern notions about Christianity—I shall devote the remainder of my discourse.

First, let us look at the assertion "Ye are bought with a price." This is one of the ways in which, in Scripture, the great effect of Christ's death in the room of sinners is described. That which, in modern theological phraseology, we have called the atonement, is spoken of in the word of God in four different, yet not inconsistent, aspects. It is called a sacrifice, as when Christ is said to have borne our sins;* and is designated by the Baptist as "the Lamb of God that taketh away the sins of the world."† It is styled a redemption, as when Paul says, "In Christ we have redemption, through his blood, even the forgiveness of sins,"‡ and when the Lord himself affirms that "the Son of man came to give his life a ransom for many."§ It is characterized, as a declaration of God's righteousness in the forgiveness of sins, that "He might be just and yet the Justifier of him that believeth"; ‖ and the same phasis of it is presented to us when the apostle alleges that ¶ "it pleased the Father, having made peace by the blood of his cross, by him to reconcile all things unto himself," for the making of peace by the blood of the cross was something prior to and in order to the effecting of the reconciliation, and must, therefore, be equivalent to the declaration of righteousness whereby he is just and yet the Justifier of the believer. And finally, it is all traced up to the love of God, "Who gave his only begotten Son that whosoever believeth on him might not perish but have everlasting life."** Thus the death of Christ did not purchase God's love for sinners, but manifested that love, and opened for it a righteous channel through which it might flow to guilty men.

---

* 1 Peter ii. 24.
† John i. 29.
‡ Eph. i. 7 ; Col. i. 14.
§ Matthew xx. 28.
‖ Rom. iii. 26
¶ Col. i. 20.
** John iii. 16.

Now, the mere fact that this vast subject is presented to us in so many different ways is a proof that no one mode of speech can fully describe its character; and the great source of the discussions which have been held regarding it is that each of the disputants has adopted one of these statements concerning it, as if that contained the whole truth about it and involved in it the negation of all the rest. But the true inductive spirit is that which accepts all the four, and maintains that the atonement is the great whole which holds them all in harmony. Christ's death was the manifestation of God's love, in the provision of an all-sufficient sacrifice for human sin, whereby his righteousness is declared in the forgiveness and salvation of believing men—usually called their redemption. In this way of putting the matter, the redemption will describe the result in the case of believers of their acceptance of Christ as their sacrifice; and that is borne out by the use of the word in many passages of Scripture. For in one place we have "waiting for the adoption, to wit, the redemption of the body;" and again, believers are said to be "sealed until the day of redemption"; while more than once we have "redemption" identified with "the forgiveness of sins." The Redeemer is Jesus Christ, the price is his precious blood, and the redemption is the result of his payment of that price in his absolute ownership of those whom he has thus purchased. This ownership involves on his part the bestowment of pardon and salvation upon them, and on theirs the giving up of everything which is inconsistent with his service according to Peter's words, "Ye know that ye were not redeemed with corruptible things as silver and gold, from your vain conversation received by tradition from your fathers; but with the precious blood of Christ;"* and that exhortation of Paul, "Ye are bought with a price, therefore glorify God in your bodies and your spirits which are God's."† The language, of course, is figurative, and if, in the case of an ordinary analogy, it is not possible, as Macaulay says, to make it go on all fours and run it out into every little detail, we may be sure that any such attempt is hopeless here. It was in seeking to do that, as is well known, that the theologians of the Middle Ages—and even some of the post-Reformation era—fell into the atrocious absurdity of affirming that the redemption price of Christ's blood was paid to Satan, because sinners are held captive by him at his will. So we must be warned by their example, and walk warily. The following things, however, seem to me to be clear, namely: that the price is the blood of Christ; and that the effect of the payment of that price is that believers belong body, soul, and spirit to Christ as his purchased property or possession; while the act of payment appears to me to be equivalent to that "making peace by the blood" which Paul has spoken of as a declaration or manifestation of righteousness made by God in the setting of Christ forth as a propitiation for the forgiveness of sins through faith in his blood. But in the words of my text, the apostle, without caring to press the analogy so far as to specify to whom or why the price was paid, gives prominence to the result in the case of believers—"Ye are bought"; or, as he has elsewhere put it, "Ye are not your own"—you belong, by right of his purchase, to Christ; your intellects are his to be instructed by him; your consciences are his to be regulated by him; your lives are his to be ruled by him, ab-

---

* 1 Peter i. 18. † 1 Cor. vi. 20.

solutely and entirely you are his. Now at first sight that reads like a consignment of us to the most abject slavery; for no human oppression can thoroughly enchain the spirit. But here it must be remembered that what on the Lord's side is a purchase, is on the believer's side a voluntary consecration, and that the Master is not a man but the God-man, with whom oppression is impossible. Thus it comes about that this divine ownership of us by Jesus is the charter of our deliverance from our fellow-men, and the paradox that the service of Christ is perfect freedom is made good. "Ye are bought with a price; be not ye the servants of men."

Now in looking at this inference from the fact of our redemption by Christ, we must beware, on the very threshold, lest we fall into mistake. Paul does not mean to say that all manner of service of men is inconsistent with our ownership by Christ. We have only to read his exhortations to servants in his various epistles to be convinced of that. What he desires to allege is that Christ's property in us emancipates us from abject slavery to men in every form which is inconsistent with that property. No man can deprive us of that which already belongs to Christ; and it is through the assertion of that principle by Christians that all the victories of religious freedom have been won in the world.

Take, for example, the slavery of the intellect, as that was attempted to be fastened upon men by authority in matters of faith. You know the degradation to which popery reduced the people in this department; and you know, too, how the yoke was broken when Luther and his compeers in other lands exalted the gospel, and told their hearers that it was their blessed privilege, as Christ's blood-bought ones, to take their belief from him. For the right of private judgment, as they expounded it, was not the liberty of every man to think as he pleased, but the inalienable privilege of the believer to take the truth from the lips of his Lord. And you can see, at once, how this same principle delivers us to-day from the yoke of party and the dictation of men. If I am a redeemed man, I belong to Christ, and have no master but him. I refuse, then, to be told by any man what I must believe. I refuse to allow any man to come between Christ and me to interpret his words. I have to do directly and immediately with Christ alone. What he says to me I will accept simply because he says it; but I will have no interference from others, since that is a dishonor to him. This is as different from rationalism, on the one hand, as it is from Romanism, and every other ism which arrogates to itself intolerance and authority, on the other. Rationalism repudiates Christ, and takes only what pleases itself; Romanism enthrones a human infallibility which lays down the law as to the interpretation of Christ; but the consciousness that I am bought with a price enthrones Christ over my intellect, and I take my faith implicitly and immediately from him. He has purchased me wholly for himself, and by that purchase he has emancipated me from the interference of men, for now I follow him. There may be doubt in a man's mind as to whether he will accept Christ's redemption or not; and after he has accepted redemption, there may be doubt in his mind as to the meaning of some of Christ's sayings; but when he has accepted Christ as his Saviour, and has come to a clear understanding of what Christ has affirmed, the redeemed man receives that; and claims, rightfully too, that in receiving it, he shall not be troubled with human intervention. That does not mean that if by following this rule he is led to the adoption of views inconsistent with the terms on which he holds his position, say as a minister in a church, he has still a right to hold that position. As an honest man, in such a case he will give up his position, counting the loss as nothing for the sake of Christ, and, in doing that, he will secure the respect of every one; whereas by taking the opposite course he will forfeit the confidence of all who love righteousness; and if he draw down upon himself remonstrance, or discipline, or disfellowship, he has no more right to call out that he is persecuted than one who breaks a contract has to complain of injustice when he is arraigned before a court of law. Thus the personal independence in matters of faith which is secured for us by our redemption is different from rationalism, which repudiates all authority in religion, and from latitudinarianism, which acts as if it were quite a proper thing for one who has received a position on a certain condition, to retain that position even when the condition annexed to it has been broken. And yet this liberty, thus regulated by allegiance to Christ, is a very real thing, for it keeps the man in his own proper orbit, throwing off human intolerance on the one side, and accepting divine direction on the other. If he yielded to the one, there would be slavery; if he abjured the other, there would be license; but the course he takes is one of freedom, and the result secured by taking it differs as much from latitudinarianism as the Reformation from Popery differed from the first French Revolution.

But leaving now the department of the intellect, I think it is easy to see how the principle on which I am now insisting leads directly and immediately to liberty of conscience. If I am bought with a price, then my conscience is Christ's. He alone is its Lord, and I am bound to hold it sacredly for him. That is the holy of holies of my nature, wherein none but the Divine High Priest may enter; and when he sprinkles his blood of atonement there, he marks it as inalienably his own. What I solemnly in the light of his word and by the illumination of his Spirit feel to be my duty, that I must do because I am his, and no power is to be allowed to coerce me into the violation of these sacred convictions. This was the principle which the English Puritans maintained; and this too, only more as it respects the church, perhaps, than individuals, was the ground on which the Scottish Covenanters planted themselves. It cost them a great deal to hold it; but their loyalty to Christ gave them their courage, and in the end they won their victory. Men sneer nowadays indeed, when in these old histories they come across the phrase "the headship of Christ," and, pronouncing it with sniveling ridicule, they style it the very essence of cant. But that phrase was for the men who used it the crystallization of the principle that is beneath Paul's words "ye are bought with a price," and when they unfurled their banner it bore upon it the strange unworldly device "for Christ, his Crown, and Covenant." Their struggle, therefore, was not like that of Tell in Switzerland, or of Wallace in Scotland, or of Washington and his comrades in America, for merely natural or national rights, glorious as all these conflicts were. Their struggle was not for any claim of their own, but for Christ's redemptive right of ownership over their consciences. They resisted unto blood because they wished to preserve the sacred kingdom of their souls from being polluted and profaned by other lordship or royalty than that of Jesus; and by their effort to secure that they attained also to civil freedom. The outcome of that conflict is seen to-day, not only in the difference between the Great Britain of the present and that of two hundred years ago; but also here in America, for the Declaration of Independence and the Constitution of this Republic, with its recent amendments, are only the expansion and development of the work which these blood-bought men began. Sneer now, if you dare, at "the headship of Christ"! or ask me now, will you, if I am not talking in paradoxes when I speak of Christ's absolute ownership of his redeemed ones as the root of personal independence and well regulated freedom?

But, not to mention other illustrations of this principle, you may see finally how it operates in emancipating us from slavery to worldly fashion, or to the public opinion of men. For if we belong to Christ, and if we are only sure that he would have us pursue a certain course of conduct, what does it matter to us what others think or say regarding us? There is, I know, such a thing as a love of singularity for its own sake, or a contempt of fashion, even in things indifferent, simply because it is fashion, or a defiance of public opinion only to insult it. But Christianity gives no countenance to any of these things. Paul in all things non-essential became all things to all men that he might by all means save some: and we may be very sure that no principles advocated by him would ever condemn such conduct in others. But when fashion would usurp the place of Christ, or when we are moved more by the consideration of the good will of our fellows than we are by regard to the Master's word,—then we are disloyal to him and are robbing him of that which he has purchased by his blood. Now, it is from that unmanly deference to customs and opinions, when conscience says that it is right to ignore them, that the sense of Christ's ownership sets us free; and every man who says "no" to those influences which Christ has commanded him to resist is as really fighting for liberty as were the "minute-men" in the days of the Revolution; and is as true a hero as those who bled at Marathon or Leuctra. Aye, and if he fight on he may yet work out emancipation for multitudes besides himself. See how much has been accomplished in this way by our Christian Temperance men. They have not only earned their own freedom—so that now there is nothing unfashionable in their course—but they have made their position such that no one needs be ashamed to take it, thereby, as I believe, diminishing temptation in many homes. Nor should we forget others who have wrought out like emancipation for their fellows. I never meet a Friend with his peculiar dress and his methodical speech without having some admiration for the stand he has taken. It may be that now that which was in the outset a protest against formalism has itself become a form. It may be that what was a real voice in the case of George Fox and his first disciples has too largely now become merely an echo. It may be that there is as much pride to-day in wearing that quaint attire as there was in the fashion of the period against which it was a protest. But still there is a right noble history beneath the broad-brim. The position of its wearer was taken originally out of regard to Christ's redemptive right over his people; and the outcome of it is seen in the fact that in every struggle for liberty, humanity, education, and the personal protection of the weak, you will find a Quaker in the foreground. So his personal independence was rooted in spiritual redemption, and bore its fruit in the larger liberty of the nation. Ah! if we were to remember always that we belong to Christ, from how many dangers we should be set free, and how many temptations we should then overcome with ease! Take, then, this truth with you, ye men of business, into your daily conduct, and when others taunt you with being under restraint because, as belonging to Christ, you cannot do what they would ask, tell them that you are really battling for a larger liberty, and that the stand you make is, in that aspect of it, even more truly for their advantage than would be your yielding to their desires. And you, ye young men whose cry is for liberty; whose aspiration is for manhood; and whose watch-word is independence, learn here how you can find all three safely, surely and permanently through the acceptance of the redemption of Christ. The most absolute devotion to Christ is the most complete declaration of individual independence; even as the defiant rejection of Christ on the score of liberty issues in the most degrading form of slavery. These things may seem to be contradictory, but they are true, and they have been often demonstrated to be so in the history alike of individuals and of the race. Make your choice between them, and do not let yourselves be beguiled by first appearances, for here, too, the prize is in the leaden casket, and the highest liberty is to be found in that which is the lowliest service. Therefore choose to be ransomed by Christ that you may be delivered from servitude to men.

January 9, 1881

THE UNTRODDEN PATH.

Joshua iii. 4.—Ye have not passed this way heretofore.

AFTER their weary wilderness journey of forty years, the tribes of Israel had come to the Jordan, the crossing of which was now the only difficulty that lay between them and the promised land. Strangely conflicting must have been their emotions during their three days' encampment by the river side. As they looked back upon the past thankfulness would predominate, though the absence of their old men, and notably that of Moses and Aaron, would tinge their gratitude with sadness; as they gazed upon the far landscape, and thought of the time when the fertile fields of Canaan would be all their own, hope would whisper to them of the blessings which were yet in store for them; but when at length their eyes rested on the rapid river raging in autumnal flood, as if defying them to pass over its waters, everything else would be forgotten in the immediate peril that was before them, and the one great absorbing question with them all would be, "What shall we do in these proud swelling waves? how shall we ford that broad, deep, rapid, roaring river?"

To meet that state of heart among them, Joshua issued minute directions to the host. He told them that the priests bearing the ark of the covenant would go before them, and he commanded that they were to follow at the distance of a thousand yards, assuring them that, as they did so, the Lord himself would make a passage for them. But to ensure their careful attention to his instructions he added, "Ye have not passed this way heretofore." As if he had put it thus: "This is a new experience for you; there has been and there can be no opportunity of rehearsing for it; it is the first thing of its kind that has come in your history, therefore be sure that you keep a clear, open space between you and the ark, so that each of you may see it, and may be cheered and encouraged by the consciousness of the presence of Him whose glory hovers ever symbolically over it." They had become perfectly familiar with the order of march in the wilderness, so that each tribe could now almost mechanically take its place; and elevated as the pillar of cloud and fire was, they could all see that with ease, whether they were near to it or far away from it; but, in this instance, the ark was to be the means of their deliverance, and, borne as that was upon men's shoulders, if they followed close upon it only those in the few foremost ranks would be able to get a glimpse of it. Hence that it might be fully in the view of all, an open space of two thousand cubits was to be reserved between it and the crossing host. Had they been well acquainted with the matter, had it been the second or third time in their experience that they had crossed a river thus, there would have been less need to give such particular admonition, but as they were to be in circumstances entirely new to them, as they were to pass over an untrodden path, peculiar care was requisite. The event justified the assurance of Joshua, for, when the feet of the priests touched the water, the river stood still, and when the people reached the other shore they raised a memorial with stones taken from the bed of the Jordan to attest to future generations the goodness of their covenant God.

4*

Now from this memorable incident in Israel's history we may deduce a general principle which will be very helpful to ourselves. The crossing of the Jordan may stand for any new experience of peculiar uncertainty through which a man is required to pass; the ark of the covenant, with its mystic symbol of God's presence hovering over the blood-stained mercy-seat, may be taken as representing God's presence with his people, as reconciled to them through Jesus Christ; and the direction to keep the ark in view while crossing the river, may for modern life, be formulated into the maxim that in all new and untried circumstances our true safeguard is to let nothing come between us and the perception of the truth that God is in Christ reconciling the world to himself, and guiding his people to safety and immortal blessedness. Frequently, in the course of a man's life, he is brought to a standstill before some new difficulty of which till then he has had no experience. Things which he has to do or suffer every day become familiar to him, and he acquires a facility in reference to them; but when he has some duty to discharge of a delicate and important character, and like to nothing that he has ever had before, or when he has a trial to bear which is different from every other which he has been called to endure in the past, there comes a time of thoughtful pause, like those three days spent by the Israelites on the bank of the Jordan, during which he asks himself how he is to discharge the duty or to endure the cross. Now at such an emergency here is the answer that is given by this ancient story: Put the ark of God in the river before you, and keep it fully in your sight, then though it be overflowing all its banks, you shall go over dry shod. This is the thought which to-day I mean, by God's help, to vivify and illustrate.

With the Redeemer as our atoning sacrifice and our priestly intercessor clearly before our faith-eye, we are safe not only in pursuing the beaten track of daily life, but also in entering upon and passing over new and untried pathways. Let us take a few instances.

There is the young person leaving the parental home and beginning independent life. The lad has known all the experiences of school, and has, perhaps, also made trial of business duties, while yet his evenings and mornings have been spent in the loved society of the family circle; but now he is to go forth a stranger to an unknown city, mayhap even to cross the ocean to a foreign land. The faces he is to look upon he has never before seen; the duties he is to discharge he has never before performed; the dangers he is to encounter he has not heretofore met; the temptations he is to be exposed to he has never yet confronted; everything is to be new. Hence, whatever else there may be in his heart, there is beneath, unspoken and almost unspeakable, a nervous anxiety as to what is before him, and as to how he shall get through it. High hope will brighten the future for him with its visions of honor and success. There will be a natural and laudable self-gratulation at the assumption by him of the responsibilities of manhood, and he may be able so to repress his feelings in bidding father and mother farewell that a superficial observer may think that he is setting out in highest spirits; but in the depths of his soul there will be, and the more thoughtful he is the more there will be, a solicitude about the future, and he will be ever considering how he will fill his new position with honor to himself, satisfaction to all concerned, and glory to God. Now to all, in such circumstances, there comes the principle which I have deduced from this interesting portion of Scripture narrative. Keep the ark clearly before you, young man, and you have nothing to fear. Let your heart ever turn to the Lord Jesus, let your soul ever feel the constraining influence of his love; let your eye ever rest upon his holy example; let your faith ever fix itself upon his atoning death, and that will make darkness light before you, and crooked things straight, and rough places smooth. The mariner who can use his quadrant can always tell where he is if he can but get a glimpse of the sun at noon-day; and you may always know your way if you keep unclouded before your faith eye the Sun of Righteousness. What the pocket compass is to the traveler over the trackless moor, that the sight of the ark is to the Christian. Let nothing, therefore, intervene between you and that. Do not allow gain, or pleasure, or honor, or fashion, or applause to come between you and your covenant God. Wherever you are, look to him, and go not where you cannot get a clear and uninterrupted view of him, for with him in sight it will be safe for you to go where foot of man has never trodden, but without him you will be sure to stumble, even though your path should lie along the broadest and the smoothest and the most frequented highway.

But that I may not seem to imply that only young men have anxiety in beginning what I have called independent life, we may farther apply this principle to the young woman, on the day when she leaves her father's house to be the center of the home circle of another. What hopes have gravitated toward that day! what preparations have been made for it! what congratulations have been uttered regarding it! Yet now that it has dawned there is, at her heart, a fluttering of strange anxiety. She knows the life that is passed, but what life shall that be which lies all undiscovered and unexplored before her? That is the question which will press itself in upon her thoughts, and which gives to her countenance the absent expression that seems so peculiar. All is mirth and gayety around her. Her parents will not let her see any of the shadow that rests upon their spirits at parting with her. Every one is loading her with presents and following her with good wishes. Her husband's face is beaming with unalloyed delight, and she tries to reciprocate his joy. But, in spite of herself, she feels a palpitating solicitude about the future. It is not that she has any, the slightest, element of distrust in him with whom she has linked her lot, but rather that she distrusts herself, and is questioning whether she is equal to the new duties that devolve upon her. So on the very verge of the river she seems to stand with " reluctant feet," as if she hardly dared to cross. But here there comes the principle of which I have been speaking. Let her put the ark in the river and keep that in sight, and all will be well. Let her resolutely look to Jesus as her Saviour and sovereign, and the duties of her new life will become easy. No matter what cares or crosses may come, with Christ in sight nothing can come wrong; and if she will only keep earthly things from hiding him and his salvation from her view, she will find that she carries everywhere with her a quiet happiness in her heart, and that, like Spenser's Una,

> —" her angel face,
> As the great eye of heaven, shines bright,
> And makes a sunshine in a shady place."

The most perplexing things will become easy when we see Jesus in them; but if we let him be hidden from us by any influence whatever, then the merest trifle may become a fretting source of never-ceasing misery.

But, passing from the consideration of the entrance on a new sphere of life, the principle on which I am now insisting is admirably appropriate to the case of those who find themselves face to face with a difficult duty such as has never before confronted them. In general every man's life, after he has fairly set out upon its labors, has what we might call an "even tenor." There is an ordinary routine of work to be done. Every day is very much like every other; and after a time his anxiety almost disappears, because he feels himself able to meet the general demands which are made upon him. But now and then this tranquillity is interrupted. Something comes that he has not forecast. There is a danger before him the like of which he has never faced. There is a work to be done of which he has had no experience. He is distrustful of himself in the matter. He knows not whether he shall be equal to the exigency. He is, as the psalm expresses it, "at his wits' end." He is like the medical man before a new and unheard-of disease, or like the young seaman, when for the first time the dreaded hurricane comes howling down upon him. He knows not what to do. Now here again our practical maxim becomes valuable. Send the ark before you and keep it in sight. Remember Jesus and his atoning death. Think of the mercy-seat, and of him who sitteth thereon as "the hearer of prayer." Let the truths about Christ and his sacrifice and intercession fill your soul. Open your hearts for the reception of the Holy Spirit, and then you will be guided as safely through your difficulty as were the tribes through the swollen river. Men of business! here is a most useful directory for you. Amid the cares and harassments of your daily engagements, you are too apt to think that religion and the work of Jesus have nothing to do with such concerns; and so, even in times of hitherto unexperienced difficulty, I fear that it is only rarely that you think of looking to him. Too often, indeed, it is not until, in the attempt to cross the river without his help, you are borne away by the flood, that you dream of calling upon him; whereas, if you had only thought of him in time, he would have given you strength to breast it, or he would have parted it before you and led you over it dry-shod. Not for spiritual difficulties alone, not for religious duties merely, as men too commonly use these words, does our maxim hold. To the Christian every difficulty is a spiritual difficulty, and every duty is a religious duty, and so in every emergency he is warranted to look to Christ; nay, he is guilty of a sin not more against God than against himself, if he does not. The ark is as much in its proper place in the counting-house as in the family or in the church; and if in your business perplexities you had more recourse to Jesus directly and immediately, without letting any intervening human element come in to hide him from your thoughts, you would more frequently have deliverances to tell of, and would find yourselves singing "new ebenezers" to his praise. Depend upon it, you will not soon lose yourselves if you keep him in view. Some years ago a party of travelers were passing over one of the Swiss mountains. After they had gone a considerable way it began to snow heavily, and the oldest of the guides gravely shook his head, and said, "If the wind rises we are lost." Scarcely had he spoken when a gale arose, the snow was whirled into multitudinous drifts, and all waymarks were obliterated. Cautiously they moved on, not knowing where they were, and almost giving themselves up for lost. At length one of the guides, who had gone a short way before them to search out the path, was heard shouting, "The cross! The cross! We are all right." And what had the cross to do with it? It was one of those religious memorials which we so frequently meet in Roman Catholic countries, and this one, set up at first by some private individual for a personal reason, had become at length a well-known and easily recognized landmark for the traveler. Hence the moment the guide saw it he knew where he was, and what direction to take. But what was true of that symbol in their case is true in all instances of the thing which it signifies; for we may always know where we are when, with our faith eye, we can see Christ crucified. That reveals every peril, and pierces through every disguise of evil. That bars the way to every dishonor, and barricades the entrance to every pathway of iniquity. Keep that, therefore, in uninterrupted view and you will never lose your way. Get hold of the principles which underlie the work of the Lord Jesus as the Redeemer of men; receive into your hearts the Holy Spirit whom he has promised, then difficulties will become easy, and your way will be opened up before you as you move forward; for as the rod of Moses divided the sea, and the mantle of Elijah parted the waters of Jordan, even so faith in the crucified Redeemer will find or make a way in every emergency.

But, taking another line of remark, the maxim to which I have referred may be applied to those who are called upon for the first time to bear some heavy trial. Sorrow, in some form or other, *must* come upon us in the world. But the commonness of it does not make its experience a whit less bitter to those who are required to drink its cup. No matter how many others have suffered before us, our first acquaintance with grief is ever keen and poignant. It may be occasioned by different causes, and each one thinks he could better have borne it if it had taken him in some other form. In some it may be produced, as it was occasionally in David's experience, by the treachery of friends; in others, by the ingratitude and ungodliness of a disobedient son; in others, by the painful and peculiar illness of those dearest to them; in others, by personal affliction; in others, by the visit of the angel of death to their home. But, however it comes, the first experience of sorrow is a thing that cuts the soul to the quick, and leaves upon the heart an ineffaceable record. Like the highest tide upon the shore, it sweeps up with it the remains of the lower, and leaves its mark longest upon the strand. I dare say there are few here who do not know from their own histories how true these words are. Thus, to take one illustration from those I have just mentioned, how terrible the earliest acquaintance with bereavement! It is a solemn time when first Death knocks at our door for admission, and will not be gainsaid, and whoever be his victim, whether a venerable parent, or a beloved partner, or a darling child, the anguish of the moment is intense. I shall never forget, while memory lasts, the strangeness of the experience through which I passed when first the reaper "whose name is Death" came into my home, and "with his sickle keen" cut down, at one thrust, two of my children. The stroke blinded me for the moment, and I was like one utterly forlorn; but when at length I opened my eyes, I saw the ark in the river, and that instantly steadied me. I knew *then* where I was. I remembered then that he who had done it was my covenant God, to whom I had given my little ones in baptism, and since he had chosen so to accept my gift, I asked myself why I should be dismayed? From my own experience, therefore, I can attest the efficacy of this consolation, and commend it to all who are in trouble, more especially to those who have been bereaved. Let the truth symbolized by that ark be but accepted in simple faith, and even in the moment of utter desolation there will come the calmness of resignation, and the confidence which only the hope of reunion with our loved ones can impart. This alone can avail us at such a time. The sympathy of friends is soothing and sweet, the kindly offices rendered by self-forgetting neighbors are valuable, and the memory of them is laid up in the holiest recesses of our hearts; but these alone would not take the sting out of the sorrow, or the bitterness out of the cup. Only the revelation made by Jesus, in and through his life, death, and resurrection, as the substitute of men, can lift the heart out of its sadness and link the recollections of the happy past with the hopes of the golden and glorious future. No matter what else we look to, we shall still find ourselves in the swelling of the river; but the moment we see Jesus our feet stand on dry ground. He assures us that our loved ones live still, only in a higher and more blessed condition, and he awakens thus within us a desire to depart and to be with him and them.

This leads me naturally to remark, in the last place, that the maxim which I have been illustrating may be applied to our own death. That is an experience which must be always unknown to us until we die. However many we may have seen depart, the path to ourselves must be strange and untraversed. Nothing can acquaint us with it save the treading of it for ourselves. But Jesus, by his own death and resurrection, has put the ark before us, and looking at that we shall find the river dry. Brother! sister! you *must* die! That experience you must pass through, not as the Israelites crossed the Jordan in the midst of a crowded company, but alone. O, see to it that you can keep Christ in view, for he alone can then sustain you. Through death he has himself delivered them who, through fear of death, have been all their lifetime subject to bondage. These, too, are his precious words: "When thou passest through the waters I will be with thee, and through the rivers, they shall not overflow thee. When thou passest through the fire thou shall not be burned, neither shall the flame kindle upon thee." "I will never leave thee nor forsake thee." By the free gift of pardon he has taken the sting out of death, and by his resurrection from the dead he has robbed the grave of its victory. What, then, have we to fear? When we can see him we can calmly sing:

> "The hour may be nigh when our bosoms, faint heaving,
> Shall breathe their last sigh in the peace of believing.
> And Thou, from our pillow all darkness dispelling,
> Wilt calm the rude billow of Jordan's proud swelling.
> Hallelujah to the Lamb who has brought us a pardon,
> We will praise him again when we've passed over Jordan."

But there may be some here who have never yet made Jesus their saviour by simple trust in him; and to them I must address one parting word. You have had many difficulties to confront in the past. You know how you failed before them. When your business went from beneath you, and you had no prop to lean upon, how dreary were you then without the Lord! When your child died, and all the world seemed to you draped in sadness, how utterly prostrate were you then in the consciousness that you had no hold on Christ! When you were laid aside with serious sickness, and you thought that you should die, how was your heart filled with dread at the prospect of meeting God! Oh, let the experience of the past warn you for the future! If you failed under the lesser trials, how will you endure the greater? "If thou hast run with the footmen and they have wearied thee, how shalt thou contend with horses? and if in the land of peace wherein thou trustedst they wearied thee, what wilt thou do in the swellings of Jordan?" "None but Christ; none but Christ," said Lambert at the stake; and there is none else can be a real helper unto you, either in life or death. Put the ark before you, then, and keep it full in view. That only, but that always, will make the channel dry.

December 30, 1877.

THE PAST IRREVOCABLE.

DEUT. xvii. 16. *Ye shall henceforth return no more that way.*

THESE words in their primary application are a prohibition. They occur in that section of Deuteronomy which has been supposed by certain modern critics to prove that the book, as a whole, is not the work of Moses, but belongs to a much later period in Jewish history. Forecasting the future, and contemplating the contingency that after their settlement in Canaan the tribes would desire a king, like other nations, the great lawgiver, guided by the Spirit of God, lays down the principles which, in such a case, they were to follow, and specifies certain things which their king should particularly guard against. But if we admit the possibility of the supernatural in the shape of prophecy at all, there is absolutely nothing in all this inconsistent with the common belief that Moses himself gave these directions; and if we deny the possibility of the supernatural altogether, the question goes farther back than the matter of the authorship of Deuteronomy, and becomes one involving the existence and personality of God himself. That, however, is not a matter of criticism, but of philosophy; and just as on a trial for high treason the prosecutor does not feel himself bound to enter on a long argument to prove the legitimacy of the government, so when objections of the kind which I have indicated are raised against the authenticity of certain portions of the Scriptures, the defender is not required to establish anew the possibility of the supernatural. If reasons of another sort are given, these must be weighed and answered; but if, on the simple ground that all prophecy must have been written after the event, it is proposed to deny the earlier date of the book which contains a prediction of it, then we may safely dismiss the plea as inadmissible, at least at that stage; and so refuse to be diverted from our purpose by the attempt to debate any such question. This volume, as a whole, professes to be a revelation from God. If there be no God, or if it be impossible for him to make known his will to men through a book sealed by miracles and prophecies, then there is an end of the matter. But if there be a God, and if the possibility of his working miracles and giving through his servants predictions of future events be conceded, then there is no relevancy whatever in the objection to the Mosaic authorship of this book, on the ground that here we have a reference to a state of things which did not exist until centuries after Moses lived. This consideration, then, removes the question from the region of criticism altogether, and makes it not so much one of Moses or not Moses, as of God or no God.

But while the matter of the kingdom did not come up until long after Moses' day, there is in this injunction against the multiplication of horses, with its appended explanation, something which to my mind clearly indicates that the prohibition belongs to a date immediately subsequent to the journeyings of the people through the wilderness. So far as the history makes manifest, there was not, in the days of Samuel, any tendency among the people to go down again into Egypt. Amid all their struggles with surrounding tribes under the Judges, we never read of any desire among the Israelites to call in the aid of those who had formerly been their oppressors. But it was otherwise immediately after the exodus; for then the burden of their exclamations in any time of trial always was regret that they had left Egypt; and even in the very year before they entered Canaan, within twelve months of the time at which Moses spoke these words, when they were suffering from thirst, they cried, "Wherefore have ye made us to come up out of Egypt to bring us into this evil place?" So in the words here used concerning the king: "He shall not multiply horses unto himself, nor cause the people to return to Egypt, to the end that he should multiply horses," there is that which is clearly Mosaic, as resting on his knowledge of the repeated hankerings of the people after the material comforts of their house of bondage. Here was a reason admirably appropriate in the mouth of one who had heard the murmurings of the tribes at being deprived of the good things of Egypt, but scarcely such as would have been given by a person writing at the beginning of the Jewish monarchy. The prediction relates to things a long way before; but the argument by which the injunction accompanying it is enforced rests upon experiences which, to Moses, were still things of yesterday.

I have referred to these matters only because of the prominence into which recent controversies have brought this section of the book of Deuteronomy; and because I think that sufficient attention has not been given to the point which I have just brought out.

But now, leaving this discussion, which is perhaps more appropriate for the lecture-room than for the pulpit, let me, before proceeding to outline the train of thought which the words of my text have suggested to me, put distinctly before you the great lesson which this prohibition enforces. It tells us that they who have left Egypt must never return thither. The Christian convert must keep clear of his old bondage-house. He must have nothing more to do with sin. Having named the name of Christ, he is to depart from all iniquity. From and after the "henceforth" of his conversion he must not serve sin, but must live unto him who died for him, and rose again. The time past of his life must suffice to have wrought the will of the flesh. There must be no steps backward; no casting of "longing, lingering looks behind"; no hankering after former indulgences. He has enlisted under the banner of the Lord Jesus, and must be loyal to the great captain of his salvation. His heart is not to be divided between Christ and the world, but having left Egypt he must "henceforth return no more that way." Nay, so thorough must the renunciation be that he must keep away from everything that has a tendency to allure him back, even although, in itself considered, it may not be a sinful thing. There is in itself no harm in the use of horses. They are noble animals. They were, moreover, designed by the great Creator to be subservient to the comfort and convenience of men. Yet because, in those early days, horses could be had in perfection only in Egypt, and because the going thither for them might awaken the old longing in them for those worldly comforts which had formerly beguiled them into, or reconciled them to, their slavery, the law is laid down for the King of the Hebrews, and through him for the people themselves,— "Ye shall not multiply horses."

Now, similarly, the Christian is to keep away from

everything that has a tendency to draw him back to the slavery of the world which he has renounced. No matter if it should be a thing which is in itself as harmless as the use of a horse, yet if it bring him into associations and alliances which endanger his holiness, or weaken the force of his protest against sin, he is to keep away from it. He is to look at things not in the abstract, but in connection with their tendencies and surroundings; and so as respects fashions, amusements, beverages and employments, he is to give up those which would bring him into dangerous fellowship with the ungodly and the depraved. To make sure of his not entering Sodom he must not even "pitch his tent toward" it. To guard against his going back to Egypt he must not "multiply horses." To prevent his returning to sin he must not go in the way that leads to it. Here is a principle far-reaching and important, and I am thankful that it has come up now, when, as it seems to me, with returning prosperity in the country we are in danger of being sucked back into the world's ways. Take it, I beseech you, and act upon it, that you may keep yourselves pure and undefiled.

Thus far I have been dealing with the text in its primary and proper application; but when, in connection with the service of this morning, it first suggested itself to my mind, its words shaped themselves to me as a simple statement rather than as a positive prohibition; and, in that sense, they seemed to me to be peculiarly appropriate to the closing year. We have come very near the end of another cycle of recorded time. Before another Sabbath dawns we shall have entered upon a new year, with all its unknown duties, responsibilities and trials; and as we stand to-day looking back upon the past, there comes out of it a voice which says, "Ye shall henceforth return no more this way." This I know is an accommodation of the words, rather than an interpretation of them, and yet it is, in my judgment, important enough to have our serious and solemn attention. The past is lived. We cannot go back over it again. We cannot unwind it to a certain point, and there start afresh to face the same difficulties and meet the same responsibilities as those which we have had to encounter. Not even the power of Omnipotence can put us where we were twelve months ago, or roll back the year that we may live it over again. The wheels of Time's chariot have ratchets to them, and they move only forward. The incidents, opportunities, and events of the past are irrecoverably gone, and "we shall henceforth return no more that way."

Now, I can conceive that to some of us there may be relief and even comfort in this assurance. The experiences through which we have come may have been such that we cannot wish for their renewal. The path over which we have passed may have been so rough, and steep, and dangerous that we cannot contemplate traversing it again without a shudder. When I was in Chamonix, last summer, a friend who had crossed the glacier and come down by the "Mauvais Pas," on which the iron railing put for the safety of travelers had parted from its fastenings in his grasp, assured me that he would not go through that experience again for all that earth could give. And there may be not a few among us who feel just in the same way concerning some chapters in our last year's life. We are, perhaps, thankful to be through them, but we do not wish to repeat them. We feel regarding them as one does who has come safely out of a terrible railway accident, or who sets his foot on land after a dangerous and tempestuous voyage. We are glad that we have escaped, but, even although we should escape another time, we do not desire to be again in the same peril. Take any one of those terrible catastrophes, so many of which occurred last year in this neighborhood, and ask those who came out of them unscathed whether, with the assurance of similar preservation, they would relish a repetition of their experience, and they will answer, with a solemn intenseness, "No! not for worlds!" One hears, as he replies, the rumble of the falling hippodrome; another sees again the flames of the burning ship, and the passengers leaping in wild haste and confusion into the waters; and yet another seems to feel anew the waves choking his cry for help. These memories give almost a passionate vehemence to their gratitude as they cry: "Thank God that is all over!" For them, therefore, there is comfort in the thought that "they shall henceforth return no more that way."

Some, too, may have had such a time of labor and anxiety that they are glad to think that it is now behind them and not to be renewed. If they had known of it before they entered on it they would have shrunk from it, and now that they have had actual trial of it they say that they could not do it over again. They are grateful to God that they did not break down under the strain, but they have had enough of it, and henceforth, whatever comes, they must carry a lighter load. There are not a few, also, whose past months have been so filled with afflictions that they do not hanker after a repetition of them. They have hardly ever been out of the sick room; or they have been compelled to look day by day on the gradual decay of dear ones whom they have had ultimately to follow to the grave; or the pressure of worldly anxiety has been so heavy upon them that the rolling back of the year and the renewal of its trials would be to them a thing to be deprecated rather than to be desired. And some there are who have had such a fierce fight with temptation, and have come out of it, victorious indeed, yet with such exhaustion that they cannot but rejoice in the thought that now it is all behind them in "the irrevocable past." They are glad for the result, but they would not willingly go back into the agony of the conflict, any more than we in this land would like to pass again through those terrible years when North and South met each other in hostile array on so many bloody fields. So this text, taken as an assurance that we cannot re-live our lives, or go again through the experiences of the past, has in it an element of comfort. It is a relief to know that some things are over and done with. It is an unspeakable satisfaction to think that whatever new trials may be in store for us, those in the past have been borne, and are not to be borne again.

But there is another side to the subject, and that is full of solemnity, not unattended with sorrow. For in the past there are many things which now we wish had been otherwise. Our afterthought has shown us much to which our forethought was blind; but we cannot alter anything now. All is done; and nothing behind us can be undone. The past is always seen more correctly after it has become the past than it was when it was present; and so, as we take a review of the year now nearing its close, we perceive more clearly where we have failed, or in what we have been to blame, than we did at the time when we were in the thick of the things themselves. We mark positive sins now where we saw perhaps only shrewdnesses or matters of prudence at the moment. We can tell now where we missed opportunities of doing good in the service of God and our generation which we scarcely observed as we came up to them. And we have to mourn over the fact that many of our most sacredly formed resolutions have been sadly broken. If we could only put these things right now! If we could only take back with us the experience which we have since acquired, and begin again, say, at the commencement of last year, how different would its record be made by us! But that cannot be. We shall "return no more that way"! What is done is done. Lost opportunities cannot be recalled, and no cement of human device can mend a broken vow. Ah! what a sad reflection have we here. No matter how tenderly you may now feel, young man, you cannot go back and undo the follies of these months, nor can you arrest their consequences! You cannot recall the profane word; you cannot wipe out the impure act; you cannot undo the sins you have committed. The past remains fixed, unalterable; not to be washed out by tears, nor to be amended by repentance.

What then? What is to be done with it? I answer, that if we cannot cancel it, we can confess the evil that is in it, and seek through Jesus Christ forgiveness for that. If we please, we can obtain, through the great atonement, acceptance with God notwithstanding our sins. We never can get rid of the fact that they have been committed; but we may be cleansed of the guilt of committing them. We may be received by God precisely as if we had never sinned; and so the sting of our guilt may be extracted, and the past may cease to be a clog upon our spiritual progress. By faith in Jesus we may be enabled in a very true sense to forget even our sins; and, taking the good out of our experience, we may make the future so full of the service of our generation that God may seem almost to "restore to us the years that the locust has eaten." The reformed drunkard can never go back and undo his own intemperance. It will forever be a fact that he sinned in that particular way. But in Christ he may obtain forgiveness and regeneration, and when, like a Gough, or a Bunting, he gives his life to the reclaiming of those who are now in the degradation out of which he has been raised, he has, in a sense, brought good out of his evil, and has made even his sinful past subservient to his present usefulness. The thief can never make it true that he never stole; but he may obtain forgiveness from the Lord, and may by the Holy Ghost be renewed after the image of Christ; and when, like a Jerry McAuley, he gives his days and his nights to labor for the conversion of the criminal population of the city, he too is showing that even out of the darkest chapters of a man's history may be drawn that which may make him specially useful to some classes of his fellow men. Now what is so conspicuously true in instances like those which I have named may become true also in the case of all the evils that are behind us. We cannot undo them, yet we can prevent them from undoing us. We cannot cancel them, but we can have them forgiven, and we can, by God's grace, secure the wisdom which will enable us to utilize our experience in connection with them for our own good, and for the benefit of others. When we are converted from them we may be able by the blessing of God to strengthen our brethren all the better from our having fallen before them. This is, of course, no excuse for any one's committing sin; neither does it in any way undo the sin; but it casts it behind us and keeps it from fettering us in our future progress; yea, it makes it even a minister to our usefulness. So, even if we cannot go back to repair the past, we may gather wisdom from it to make the future more blessed.

And then, turning the thought which the words of my text express, we may make it full of admonition to ourselves for the future. We are about to enter upon a path in which there will be no possibility of retracing our steps; let us be very careful, therefore, where we plant our feet. We have only once to live; therefore let us live to purpose. The day that dawned this morning will never dawn again. The opportunities which it brought with it will never come again; and if we fail to fill it with the service it requires of us there will be no possibility of returning into it to repair the mischief. The year on which we are about to enter will come only once; if, therefore, we trifle away any of its hours, or abuse any of its days, or miss any of its opportunities, the evil is irreparable. So let us seize every moment as it comes, and use it as we shall wish we had done when we look back upon it from eternity. Remember, the year does not come to you all at once, in twelve months at a time, nor even in twelve distinct installments of a month each; no, nor yet in three hundred and sixty-five separate portions of a day apiece: but in individual moments. Do not, therefore, lose the moments in thinking that you will secure the year; but consider that the year is to be redeemed by the consecration of each moment to the Lord Jesus. Fill every day with his service. Meet every duty that confronts you as a duty to be performed for him. Face every trial that comes to you as a trial to be endured for him. Bear every affliction that falls upon you as an affliction to be suffered for his sake. Think not that by and by you will turn to him, and that will secure life as a whole for him; but let every moment be his, and that will be giving him the life. I referred a little while ago to the fall of the hippodrome wall, and in this connection I am sure many of you will recall the remarkable words which were found in the note-book of one of the victims of that accident to this effect: " I expect to pass through this life but once; if, therefore, there be any kindness I can show, or any good thing I can do, to my fellow human beings, let me do it *now*. Let me not defer or neglect it, for I shall not pass this way again." Some of you, too, will remember the lines of Horatius Bonar in which the same thought is expressed:

> " Not many lives, but only one, have we,
> One, only one;
> How sacred should that one life ever be,
> That narrow span.
> Day after day filled up with blessed toil,
> Hour after hour, still bringing in new spoil."

But there is no enforcement of this truth to be compared with that which comes from the example of our Lord himself. These are his words: "I must work the work of him that sent me while it is day: the night cometh when no man can work"; and so constantly did he act out that resolution that when the time of the crucifixion arrived he could say not only, "Father, the hour is come," but also, "I have glorified thee on the earth, I have finished the work which thou gavest me to do." For every hour he had his appropriate work, and so the life and the work were finished together. And when you ask how that was accomplished you may find the open secret in his saying to his followers, "My meat is to do the will of him that sent me, and to finish his work." On that he lived, and therefore for that he lived. His first recorded words were these: "Wist ye not that I must be about my Father's business?" and to that he kept himself until the last. More than food, more than rest, yea, better than life itself to him, was the doing of that will; and when we fully imbibe his spirit our lives will come to be, like his, rounded into finished completeness and filled with blessing and beneficence to our fellow men. Remember that for everything God gives you to do there is a day when it can be done, and a night when the doing of it is no longer possible: so seize the opportunity and do everything in its own day. It is told of Dr. Samuel Johnson that he had engraven on the dial-plate of his watch these two Greek words, νύξ ερχεται, "the night cometh," in order that every time he looked upon it he might be stimulated to greater activity by the anticipation of death. But, though that use of the phrase is very suggestive, its reference may be greatly widened. For every duty there is a day when it can be performed, but if that day be trifled past and the duty left undone, there comes a night which says, "Ye shall henceforth return no more that way." God give us grace to lay this more earnestly to heart, and then when death comes we shall not be haunted by the ghosts of neglected opportunities or embittered by the pangs of unavailing regrets. This is the true Christian philosophy of life, and I would exhort you to adopt it, and begin to act upon it to-day. Remember that you cannot go back a single step to make the past different in the least degree; therefore let each step as you take it be in "the right way": a step of which Christ will approve; a step which will bring you nearer to him ; a step which will take you into higher experiences, and furnish for you a nobler vantage ground for usefulness ; and, as you look forward to the commencement of another year, let your aspirations shape themselves into this simple supplication :

> "O Saviour, Christ, I pray thou wilt be near
> To consecrate this newly opening year ;
> O may thy love, omnipotent and free,
> Bind every fiber of my heart to thee,
> And every power and every wish complete
> Be laid in full surrender at thy feet."

December 26, 1880.

THE VISION OF ELIJAH.

1 Kings, xix. 12.   And after the fire a still small voice.

"Elijah was a man subject to like passions as we are," and at no time are we more convinced of that than when we find him here at Horeb. Not long before, he had been on the top of Carmel, where he had gained a decisive victory over the priests of Baal; but now he has fled from the post of duty, and the cruel threat of a vindictive woman has frightened him almost into despair. We might well wonder at this, and speak of it as a moral incongruity, if not also as a psychological impossibility, if we did not ourselves know from experience something of those alternations of ebb and flow in faith and feeling which seem to be inseparable from the excitement of public life in the service of the Lord. After such a day as that on Carmel, followed as it was by his earnest wrestling with God for the coming of the rain, and his long race before the chariot of Ahab to the gates of Jezreel, a reaction was sure to come, and, as the hollow corresponds to the hill, so in one who was by nature so intense as Elijah the depression was sure to be terrible when it did come. Yet, let us not do him injustice by imagining that he was most deeply distressed about his own individual interests. It is true that once and again he refers to his belief that he alone was left in Israel to be jealous for the Lord God of hosts, and that they sought his life. But he valued his life only in so far as he could use it in securing the triumph of Jehovah's cause, and it was because that seemed to him to be lost that he was so dreadfully cast down. His heart was set on the regeneration of Israel. He had, as he believed, inaugurated a great reform, and he supposed that God would carry it to immediate success. But instead of that he found Jezebel as determined, as unscrupulous, and as cruel in her antagonism as ever, and thinking that the conflict would have to be fought over again, he became dispirited, and fled. He expected that from the moment of his Carmel victory everything would go right, and that the whole people would enthusiastically declare themselves, not by an emotional cheer, but by a lifelong determination for Jehovah; but when he found that this was far from being the case, he gave up the struggle, and went into the wilderness. Strange as it may seem in one whose great and repeated message was "The Lord God of Israel liveth," he forgot to take Jehovah himself into the account, and for the moment he acted as if the indifference of the people and the bitter opposition of Jezebel were mightier than Omnipotence. Possibly, too, he had been trusting too much in mere power, and so, when he found that it had not changed the heart of the nation, he fell into despondency.

Now, such being his state of mind, we cannot but admire and adore the wisdom of the course which the Lord took with him. When he lay beneath the juniper-tree the angel did not upbraid him, but ministered to his wants in the kindest manner, and let him rest awhile; then, after preparing for him a second repast, he led him to Horeb, where the very associations of the place with the greatest events in the history of Moses might preach to him of the majesty and yet the mercy of the Most High. Then, when before him, as erst before Moses, the Lord passed by, his glory was once again seen to be especially in his goodness, for he was not in the wind, or the earthquake, or the fire, but in "the still small voice," to teach his servant that, however useful these might be in calling attention and in silencing objection, it was not by such "*coups d'état*" as that on Carmel that the work of regenerating Israel was to be accomplished, but by the quiet influence of love. There had been much about him of the austere and the denunciatory. He had said much to terrify and alarm; but the greatest glory of God was not secured by these things. The earthquake, the whirlwind, and the fire were but the out-riders of the divine majesty, but that majesty itself is "gentleness," for it is by that he makes men "great." The one lesson, therefore, good for all the ages, of this Horeb symbolism is that "the kingdom of God cometh not with observation," and that the salvation of the world is to be wrought out by him of whom it could be said, "He shall not cry, nor lift up, nor cause his voice to be heard in the streets. A bruised reed he shall not break, and the smoking flax he shall not quench." Not John the Baptist, with his stern denunciation and his austere asceticism, but Jesus, with his love, and tenderness, and self-sacrifice, is the regenerator of humanity; and though John must always, in some form or other, go before Jesus, yet to expect that he alone shall succeed in reforming the world is as absurd as it would be to anticipate that the plowshare and the harrow will of themselves cause the ground to produce a harvest without the genial heat of the sun, and the kindly rain of the clouds. Now there are three respects in which this one lesson may be helpful to us in these days:

I. In the first place, it reminds us that in the order

of God's government the quietest influence is often the most powerful. God's greatest works are carried on in silence. All noiselessly the planets move in their orbits; "there is no speech, nor language; their voice is not heard" as they sweep on through their appointed paths in space. No sound attends the crystallization of the dewdrops on the myriad blades of grass in the summer evenings; and while the crops are growing in the fields, so profound sometimes is the stillness that all nature seems asleep. What greater revolution can there be than that which recurs at every morning's dawn when night quits her "ebon throne," and resigns her empire to the king of day? Yet how quietly it is accomplished! There is first a streak of light along the edge of the eastern horizon, so faint that you wonder whether it has not shot out from that brilliant star; then a few stray gleams of glory, as if the northern aurora had flitted to another quarter of the heavens; then a flush of ruddy beauty before which the stars begin to pale, and as we watch how one by one these faithful sentinels put out their lamps, the sun himself appears, and becomes the undisputed monarch of the heavens. But it is all so silent that the sleeper is not awakened on his couch, and the pale, sick one who has been longing for the morning knows not it is there until through the shadowed casement it looks in upon him with its benignant smile. In like manner the kingdom of God cometh not with observation. There is no crying of lo! here, or lo! there! Its simple presence is its own announcement and its mightiest power.

Now this is a truth which, as it seems to me, we are in these days very apt to forget. We have fallen upon a generation of fuss, and bustle, and trumpet-blowing, and advertising. It would almost seem as if many of us believed that we were to take the world by storm. We get up excitements in mass-meetings, and pass resolutions, and listen to eloquent orators, and make thundering plaudits, as if these alone were to win the day. We think, alas! too often, like Elijah, that the victory has been gained when we are but entering upon the struggle. We have more faith in the whirlwind and the earthquake than in the still small voice; and we mistake a momentary out-flashing of enthusiasm for the celebration of a final triumph. The sensational is everywhere in the ascendant. We see it in the extravagance of dress that seeks to call attention to itself; we see it in the domain of literature, in the highly colored and hotly seasoned romances that circulate by thousands among the people; we see it in the department of business, in the feverish speculations carried on by individuals who are ambitious to bottle up the trade of a whole continent for their own particular benefit; we see it in the wide field of national affairs, where a "vigorous foreign policy" is pursued, and nations are embroiled only that a Beaconsfield may wear a garter, and one nearer home may have his name kept prominent; we see it in the church, where a high ritual has been adopted, as if that would save men's souls; and that I may carry through my enumeration with absolute impartiality, we see it in the very pulpit, where men too frequently discourse on every topic but the gospel, and sometimes discourse on that under ridiculous announcements which are meant to draw the multitudes, as if that were equivalent to the regeneration of their hearts. Surely, therefore, there is something in this vision for our sensation-loving life. The Lord is not in these noisy and demonstrative manifestations. These of themselves will not avail, either for abiding success or real happiness, or extended usefulness. The earthquake may shake the ground, the whirlwind may rend the trees; the fire may devour a building, a block, aye, even a city, as once and again we have seen in recent years, and men's hearts remain unchanged. Nothing can reach them but "the still small voice" of gospel grace, for in that especially Jehovah speaks. It were well, therefore, that we had less faith in noise, and more in that which is the most God-like thing on earth, namely, a character molded after the example of Christ, and created and sustained by the agency of the Holy Ghost. It were well that the voices among us were less loud, and the deeds were more pronounced. Life is more potent than words; and character, though quiet, is more influential in the long run than any immediate sensation that flares up and crackles like a blaze of thorns, and, like that blaze, dies down after a brief season. Better a star than a meteor, however brilliant for the moment it may seem; better a steady beacon, like the light on yonder headland, than a dancing marsh-fire. And if Christians generally would seek to act out the principles of the Sermon on the Mount leaving all *ad captandum* and self-seeking devices alone, they would soon fill the land with an influence which would do more for its evangelization than all the other agencies put together would effect.

II. But, in the second place, the lesson which we have deduced from our text, taken with its surroundings, reminds us that the force of love is always greater than that of sternness. Every one has heard of the old fable which tells how the sun and the wind strove with each other, which of them should first make the traveler divest himself of his cloak. The more fiercely the wind blew the more firmly the wayfaring man gathered his outer garment about him. But when the sun shone warmly upon him he speedily threw the weighty covering from his shoulders. So antagonism creates antagonism. If you attempt to drag me by force, it is in my nature to resist you, and I will pull against you with all my might; but if you try to attract me by kindness, it is equally in my nature to yield to its influence, and I will follow you of my own free will. What the hammer will not weld together without fiery heat and prolonged labor, the magnet will bring together and hold together in a moment. So in dealing with men, the mightiest influence is love.

But there had been little of that in Elijah's dealings with his fellows. Indeed, his intercourse with them had been but fitful and infrequent. His history is one of sudden appearances and mysterious hidings; and up to the time of this vision, at least, though he had been thoroughly faithful, he had shown but little tenderness to his countrymen. Evermore he had come with denunciation on his lips, so that even the good Obadiah was terrified by his appearance; and if that were so with him, we cannot wonder that Ahab and his partisans were roused by him into more furious animosity. There had been enough of the terrible in the past. Now he must go back and try "the still small voice"; and especially he must initiate a successor, who should be not the similitude but rather the complement of himself, and should go about in love and fellowship and helpfulness among the people of the land.

But, striking as is the illustration of the truth that terror of itself cannot move men to repentance which is furnished by the history of Elijah, we see the other side of it in its highest manifestation in the work of Christ. By love the Lord attracts us to himself at the first, and by love he keeps us with him to the last. Law and terrors do but harden the heart, but love melts it and makes it impressible. See how this came out in the Saviour's dealing with the woman whom her accusers dragged rudely before him as taken in the very act of sin. Her soul was chafing under their harshness. She was in a mood to be defiant. Angry words had no doubt been the first upon her lips, and she might have spoken bitterly to her tormentors. But when she saw his benignant countenance and heard his gracious words, the frown passed from her face, the passion disappeared from her eyes, and the determination to vindicate herself went out of her heart. Thus she was not injured by his kindness, for her sin never seemed so hideous to her as it did when he said to her, "Neither do I condemn thee"; and she never judged herself so severely as in the moment when she received his forgiveness. When sternness has had its Carmel victory, Jezebel is as defiant as ever; but when love succeeds, the woman of Samaria becomes a preacher of the gospel. Sternness would have said to Nicodemus: "You are a coward; when you come to me in the open day and say in the hearing of all men what you have spoken to me in secret, then I will instruct you": and that, most likely, would have driven him away for ever. But love told him of God's gift of his Son to the world, that whosoever believeth in him should not perish but have everlasting life; and the result was seen that day when, at the foot of the cross, whence ten of the very apostles had fled, Nicodemus was found made great by the Redeemer's gentleness.

Now, here again we have a word in season to many among ourselves. If the pastor is "under the juniper tree," and bewailing his want of success — wondering why inquirers rarely come to him, and crying like Isaiah, "Who hath believed our report?" let him examine and see whether he has not been attempting to move men by sternness rather than by love. Let him ask himself whether he has not been dealing in side subjects away from the great center, and forgetting the attraction that is always in the cross. Let him inquire whether he has given due prominence in his discourses to the love of God, and whether he has not been going about among his people cold and stern and repulsive, rather than tender, affectionate, and winsome in his gentleness. Who has not heard of the great mistake committed by the first Moravian missionaries to Greenland—how they began their labors by seeking to instruct the people concerning the being of God and the evidences of Christianity, and the future state of reward and punishment, and wondered why they saw no fruit, and how they were at once enlightened and reproved by perceiving the effect produced upon the minds of some of the natives by their hearing—or rather, I should say overhearing, for it had not been intended that they should hear—the reading of the account of the sufferings and death of Christ? "What is that you read?" they said. "Read it to us again." And then there began a great movement among them, which resulted in the conversion of multitudes. Ah! yes, does not the temptation of the modern pulpit take it just here? The preacher wishes to be intellectual, original, eloquent, and chooses his themes so that he may be able to make manifest these qualities. But God is not in these, for, though they may awaken admiration, they are, after all, cold, stern, marbly things and do not reach the heart. Nothing will touch that but "the still small voice" that tells of Jesus and his love. That is the only instrument the Spirit will employ in changing a man's nature. Let the pastor, therefore, get back to that, and preach it with a love corresponding to that of Jesus in his own heart, and he will never lack results. Well said the good Angel James—and from his own experience he had a right so to speak,—" Raise me but a *barn* in the very shadow of St. Paul's Cathedral, and give me a man who shall preach Christ crucified with something of the energy which the all-inspiring theme is calculated to awaken, and you shall see it crowded with warm hearts; while in the statelier building hard by, if the Gospel be not preached there, the matins and vespers shall be chanted to the statues of the mighty dead." Let the desponding pastor heed these words, and let him try the "still small voice" telling of the love of Christ upon the cross; and though the Jew may call it an offense and the Greek pronounce it folly, he will find that it is the power of God unto salvation to every one that believeth.

I say the same thing to the Sunday-school teacher who is sad at heart because he seems to see his scholars indifferent, yea, even perhaps antagonistic, to all his appeals. Have you tried them, my brother, with the "still small voice" of gospel love? Perhaps you have been dealing too exclusively in the whirlwind, the earthquake, and the fire. Have they ever felt your gentleness? Do they know you love them? and have you ever told them of Christ's love to them? Have you ever laid you hand in pleading affection upon them, and let them see that you are in earnest for their salvation? We have lesson helps nowadays in abundance. Every religious newspaper has some learned man at work to simplify, illustrate, and enforce the meaning of the passage that is to be the theme for the week, and that is all well so far as it goes. But never forget that the best teaching help is a loving heart; and if you desire that you must keep yourself in close personal contact with the Lord. If I wish to make steel magnetic I must bring it to a magnet, and, in like manner, if I would win men to Christ by love I must first have the love of Christ in my own heart. He must magnetize me before I can myself become a vehicle of his magnetism. As Sister Dora said, "Be very full of the glad tidings, and you will tell others." Oh, my fellow laborers, let us always remember that all the other matters without that will avail nothing; but that, even without many of them, will be made powerful by God. Learning is good, illustration is good, accuracy of interpretation is good; but love is best of all: therefore, with all our getting, let us get love, and let us avoid continually severity and sternness.

Need I add here that the same principle applies to parents in the training of their children in the nurture and admonition of the Lord? Are you disappointed in the results of your labors with your sons and daughters? Then let me beg you to examine whether you have not been trusting in the whirlwind, the earthquake, and the fire, and forgetting the "still small voice"? You say you have tried everything. Let me ask you if you have tried gentleness; and let me beseech you to make the experiment of that. Do not rudely drive your children from you, but open to them the arms of your affection. Make home attractive to them, and then you may discover that there is more power in love to win them to yourself than there is in terror to repel them from the evil against which you have hitherto been so sternly warning them. A happy home is the best safeguard against the prodigality of children.

III. But, in the last place, the lesson which we have deduced from our text, taken with its surroundings, reminds us that the apparently insignificant is oftentimes really the most important. The "still" voice was also "small." It was little in comparison with the whirlwind, the earthquake, and the fire, but it moved Elijah himself more than they all. He was at home with the raging elements. He laid his hand even upon the lightnings and they came at his bidding, saying, Here are we; and so none of these terrible things moved him. But the small voice bowed him down, "for it was so when he heard it that he wrapped his face in his mantle and went out, and stood in the entering in of the cave." So sometimes, yet, the man who is unmoved by the most awful expostulations and the most desolating judgments is subdued at last by the prattling pathos of a little child. We must not undervalue agencies because they seem to be insignificant. It was said of the Lord himself, "Can any good thing come out of Nazareth?" and the first apostles were despised as "unlearned and ignorant men." Yet though God used only "the weak things of the world," he did confound with them "the things which are mighty." The big trees in California have sprung from seeds each of which is no larger than a grain of wheat; and the river which at its source is a tiny tinkling rill over which a child may stride, is at its mouth broad enough and deep enough to bear a navy on its bosom. Let us not, therefore, "despise the day of small things," or say of any agency "Is it not a little one?" A few drops of water rightly used may raise a heavy weight; and even a little child may, by the help of God, be the means of lifting up some sinner from his degradation and bringing him at once to his Saviour and himself. One does not need to be some great one to do good service for the Lord. The clarion voice of the great Reformer indeed rung out in "half-battle" words over Europe, but it was first that of the poor miner's son singing for bread upon the open street; and the pen of a tinker has written a book which has gone into many languages and many lands as the power of God to souls unnumbered. Thus often the "small voice" of the obscure believer of whom men have scarcely heard has inaugurated a movement that has blessed a multitude. Let no one say, therefore, that he can do nothing, for still the promise holds, "One man of you shall chase a thousand; for the Lord your God he it is that fighteth for you as he hath promised you." And, again, "A little one shall become a thousand, and a small one a strong nation. I the Lord will hasten it in its time." This touches us all, for, no matter how circumscribed our sphere, or how limited our resources, we may have some little thing that we can do which, in its place, will correspond to this "still small voice." The uselessness of many is perfectly accounted for when we say that because they cannot do something great all at once they will do nothing at all. Here, again, the love of sensation makes its appearance; and it is forgotten that those agencies which are now the greatest, and which have in them most of the elements of permanence, had their beginnings in the smallest things. Each was first a faintly stirring thought in the heart of some humble disciple; then the thought grew into desire, and the desire stimulated to a beginning with such things as he had, and then "the handful of corn upon the top of the mountains" grew up into a harvest which "shook like the cedars in Lebanon." Wesley never dreamed of anything so great as the Methodism of to-day when he began his work; and if we will examine it well we shall discover that almost every one of those institutions that are now radiating blessings round them had its commencement in something which, as contrasted with the high-sounding pretensions of earthly grandeur, was as insignificant as the still small voice of my text after the whirlwind and the earthquake. Courage then, my brethren! Let each go forth and do the little that is at his hand with all his might, and God will make that little great. Say not that you have no influence, for the tiniest child has a power which no human arithmetic can reckon. Do not affirm that you have no resources, for if you can call God your own you have the wealth and power and wisdom of the Infinite behind you. Forth then, and begin your work! It is work which only you can accomplish. It is work which the world needs. It is work for which the Saviour calls. It is work which shall have results stretching into eternity. Wait not for some great opportunity: the golden year is now; the accepted time is to-day; the appointed sphere is where you are. Do not quarrel with your call as Moses tried to do, or begin to make excuses about your weakness and inefficiency. Here is the answer to all these objections: "Certainly I will be with thee." Go then, like Gideon, in this thy might, and the strongholds of Satan will fall before thee in a manner as unaccountable to the men of the world as was the crash of the walls of Jericho at the blast of the rams' horns. May God add his blessing. Amen.

FEBRUARY 12, 1882.

THE PLEASURES OF SIN.

Hebrew xi. 25. Choosing rather to suffer affliction with the people of God than to enjoy the pleasures of sin for a season.

In this chapter, which is devoted to the heroes of faith, no paragraph is more worthy of study than that which refers to Moses. It sets before us the motive principle of the sublimest life of which ancient history can boast, and if I were minded to enter biographically upon its exposition I should call you to observe particularly the following points, viz.: that the choice of Moses was not blindly made in the impulsive ardor of boyhood, and while yet he knew not what he was required either to suffer or to sacrifice, but maturely, when he was come to years, and was in the full vigor of his powers; that it involved the forfeiture of the grandest position in the world, and the endurance of privation and hardship; that it was made from a regard to truth and with firm belief in the rightness of God's moral administration and in the certainty of a future recompense; and that it resulted in the attainment of a nobler sort even of earthly grandeur than he could otherwise have reached, with the added advantages of the favor of God and eternal glory. But for the present my purpose is more limited. As by the powerful lens you gather the sunlight into one burning spot which sets anything inflammable on fire, so this morning I wish to focus the lessons of this passage upon the one expression which I have selected as my text, if, by any means, their concentrated influence may, through the help of the Holy Spirit, kindle in your hearts the fire of piety. My words will, I trust, prove salutary to those of all ages, but I earnestly bespeak the attention of the young. You, also, my beloved friends, have a choice to make; nay, whether you are conscious of the fact or not, you are already in the actions of every day making a choice whose issues stretch throughout eternity. It is, therefore, of the deepest importance that you have clearly before you the nature and consequences of those things between which you have to make your election. I will endeavor to make those apparent to you this morning, and I beseech you to weigh well, in the balance of a calm and candid judgment, the statements which I shall make.

Let it be conceded, then, in the outset, that sin has pleasures. This must be true, otherwise men would not commit it. In every instance, at least in the outset of the sinner's career, he is drawn toward iniquity by the belief that in some way or other it will minister to his enjoyment. Sometimes he may have no higher aim than the gratification of a prurient curiosity. At other times his sin may begin in the impatience of restraint and the pleasure which is felt in overleaping the barriers which authority or affection may have placed before him. Sighing for self-forgetfulness one may flee to the maddening cup to secure that object; while another may seek only the wild throb of sensual delight. Thus sin, at first, is indulged in for pleasure, and doubtless there is a kind of enjoyment in its commission. I do not deny that, for it would be both irrational and absurd to do so; neither do I ignore it. I admit it in the frankest and fairest manner; but my question is, What are the characteristics of such pleasure? Take it at its best, and suppose you have the greatest joy that it is possible for sin to furnish, of what sort is it, and what is it worth? My answer is that its value is what mathematicians would call a negative quality—it has the minus sign before it; that is to say, "it costs more than it comes to"; in the equation of life it does not add to, but rather takes from, the sum total of your happiness, and leaves you less truly yourself than you were before you enjoyed it. That you may judge for yourselves I will give you the data from which I have worked out this result, and that you may better remember them I will put them in the form of a few simple propositions:

I. In the first place, then, take note that the pleasures of sin are short-lived. In the expressive symbolism of Scripture, they are like water in a broken cistern which speedily runs out; or like the blaze of thorns which crackle and flame up for a little and then die down into a heap of ashes; and the experience of all who have indulged in them will corroborate this statement. There is in them, at best, only a temporary thrill which vibrates for a moment and needs to be reproduced again and again. They are not joys forever. They do not live within a man, sounding a ceaseless undertone of happiness in his "secret soul" wherever he may be. They cannot be said to give pleasure save for the brief season that the excitement lasts. Take intemperance, for example. There must be some kind of exhilaration in the state of intoxication, even though it should be produced by the dethronement of reason and conscience for the time; but how long does that ecstasy continue? Ask those who know best from their own experience, and they will tell you that even when they have seemed to secure it their joy has passed away from their embrace and they have been left in deeper misery than before. Nor is this true of that sin only. It holds alike of all. The pleasure of iniquity in any form is confined to the moment of indulgence in it. It is not a thing which you can catch and keep for any length of time. You have, if I may so express it, to manufacture it anew on every occasion, and each time it will be found to be as volatile as before. You can only recall the enjoyment by repeating the sin; and with each repetion the same discovery of the fleeting nature of the joy is made. It is not a fountain sending ever forth its sparkling waters; but it is a leaky pitcher which is empty before we can drink out even that which it at first contained. Do not suppose that this is an exaggeration, or that I am straining my very utmost to make out a case, and so representing the matter unfairly. You suspect the preacher, perhaps, of undue prejudice against these enjoyments, and in spite of all his protestations to the contrary, you are inclined to take a large discount from his words. Listen, then, to another witness, whose testimony I give in lines which are not more exquisitely beautiful than they are strictly true:

> "Pleasures are like poppies spread—
> You seize the flower, its bloom is shed;
> Or like the snow-fall in the river—
> A moment white, then melts forever;
> Or like the Borealis race
> That flit ere you can point their place;
> Or like the rainbow's lovely form
> Evanishing amidst the storm."

Now these are the words of a man who had no great liking for ministers of the gospel, and who, on occasion, could hold them up to merciless scorn and lash them with the scorpion-scourge of his stinging satire. You cannot, therefore, suspect him of any bias in favor of their way of putting things. They are, besides, the expressions of one who spoke from personal experience. He had indulged in the pleasures of sin; he had taken from them all they had to give, and yet this is his testimony regarding them. But why need I call up the shade of that gifted poet here? I make my appeal to yourselves. Have you got that amount of pleasure out of sin which you expected from it when you began to yield to it? You know you have not. Think not to say within yourselves that though your little indulgence in it has brought you only disappointment, a greater would give you satisfaction. Can you change the character of sin by adding to its enormity? Depend upon it, the greater the sin the greater will be the disappointment. Seek not, therefore, permanent happiness where it can never be found. Over every sinful pleasure you may write the Lord's own words: "Whosoever drinketh of this water will thirst again." It is only when we come to Christ, and find pardon and peace in him, that enduring happiness can be obtained. And we receive it from him because he works a change upon our inner nature. Sin sends us out of ourselves for joy. Jesus gives us enjoyment by coming into us and supping with us and we with him. Hence the true Christian carries over his pleasure within himself. It does not depend on external things; but, itself an internal thing, it sends itself out throughout all his life. It is not an experience separate from everything else in his consciousness so much as an element entering into and pervading all his actions and emotions. As the stop in the organ is not itself a separate note, but gives its own peculiarity to every note which the player sounds for the time, so Christ in the heart is not there dwelling apart in a secluded shrine, but entering into all the experiences of the soul, elevating and ennobling them all. Weigh well this contrast, and I think you will have no difficulty in deciding which you will choose. Pleasure in sin is external and evanescent. Christian happiness is internal and permanent. The one springs from what the sinner is at the moment doing, and disappears when the deed is done; the other results from what the believer is, and is enduring as his own character; the one is galvanic and spasmodic, lasting only while the sin-battery works, the other is calm and natural; the one is like the lightning—a brief gleam enduring but for a moment; the other is like the light, not only beautiful in itself, but bathing everything in its own loveliness. Surely there need be no hesitation here. Surely, with these facts before you, the choice of Moses will be repeated by you and you will forego the pleasures of sin.

II. In the second place, take note that the pleasures of sin leave a sting behind, and will not bear after-reflection. There is guilt in them, and there never can be happiness in contemplating that. Yet when the brief hour of joy is fled the guilt is the entire residuum of the joy. Have you ever entered a banqueting-hall the morning after some high festival had been held in it, and while yet everything remained precisely as the guests had left it at the midnight hour? The candles burned to the sockets, the floor covered with the evidences of the night's hilarity, the dishes piled confusedly upon the tables, and the decorations which looked so gay in the brilliant lamplight now all withered and disheveled! You can scarcely believe it is the same place as that which a few hours before resounded with mirth and song, or re-echoed with the applause of some orator's address. It is deserted; nay, it is repulsive; and you turn away from it to moralize on the passing glory of all earthly things. But such an external contrast is nothing to that which is furnished by the history of the votary of pleasure when you compare what he is in the moment of indulgence with what he feels in the hour of reflection. Follow him to his chamber. Visit him in the morning, as he is compelled to confront himself. See his bloodshot eye, his quivering hand, his starting, timid, nervous movement at every sudden sound. Go in, if you can, into his inmost feelings, and what is there left after the momentary happiness of his indulgence? He will not look into his heart to describe himself to you. He dares not do it. There is no companion he more fears than himself; there is no sound to him half so painful as silence; and so he flees back to the society of his companions, and seeks in the noise of revelry renewed to drown "the still small voice" of conscience. But it will not be always hushed. Sometimes, even in the midst of merriment, its upbraidings will come as the ghost of Banquo intruded at the royal feast; and often mid the darkness of the night they will drive sleep from his pillow. The great dramatist, in that most weird and yet most instructive tragedy to which I have just alluded, has shown us how sin " doth murder sleep," and that the stain upon the conscience will not " out," though washed by all the waters of the ocean or sweetened by the perfumes of Arabia, but we must beware of supposing that his representation is true only of such unscrupulous ambition as leads to murder. What saith the wise King about the ruby cup? " Look not upon the wine when it is red, when it giveth its color in the cup, when it moveth itself aright; at the last it biteth like a serpent and stingeth like an adder." At the last! at the last! Oh, that men would learn to forecast the future in this way, and to think of what must be "at the last!" Remember that the day is coming when you must look back on all you have done and enjoyed. But what a retrospect is that of the man of pleasure! Is there on this earth a sadder sight than that of him who has lived a life of sinful indulgence looking back upon the guilty past and saying: "It had been good for me that I had never been born"? His time wasted, his talents abused, his energies prostituted, his conscience crying out with a power that gives him only too sure a foretaste of the pangs of hell—where is there in this wide world a more horrible experience than that? And yet that is what the pleasures of sin come to even on earth—at the last. And what beyond? Even in that lowest deep there is a lower deep still opening to devour him; but I will not attempt to portray that. In the powerful picture of Noel Paton, which he has styled the "Dance of Pleasure," you see a motley multitude of young and old, and rich and poor, and men and women, rushing madly after the queen. They care not for each other. In the fury of their selfishness they strike against each other and trample each other down; yet still they follow on, and she is decoying them to the brink of an awful abyss, over which each at length must fall. But the painter shows only its dark and rugged edge, leaving suggestion to preach the warning. So I would only lead you to the border of the unseen state, and leave conscience to testify to the dreadful perdition which is the end of sin.

How different from all this is is the experience of the Christianly good man. His happiness will bear reflection. It will stand cross-examination. His yesterdays look backward with a smile, and do not, Parthian-like, wound him as they fly. He has had his struggle and conflict. Yet, in the happiness which he has enjoyed, there has been nothing to give him pain. He had pleasure in the experience at the time, and he has even more now as he looks back. I do not know if there be on earth a more beautiful thing than the old age of a Christian who in youth dedicated himself to God, and has spent his life in keeping that holy resolution. His conscience is peaceful, his heart is happy, his future is glorious. Which way he looks there is beauty. Behind him his whole life seems gilded with the purple splendor of the setting sun; around him his children are clustering in holy affection; before him Christ is preparing him a welcome in his Father's house; above him there is a crown, incorruptible, reserved for him to wear. The traveler in Switzerland sees few more lovely sights than that which is associated with the descent of the Great Scheideck through Rosenlaui to Meyringen. The pathway runs now through thickets, and now through green pasture-land, inclosed by forest and enlivened by châlets and herds of cattle. As you move downward you see little or no splendor, and are hemmed in on every side with perpendicular walls of rugged rock; yet, ever as you turn to look behind, you are transported with the scene that meets your view. In the forefront the pine forest, swayed by the breeze, seems bowing its head in lowly reverence to the great Monarch of all; while in the background rise the snowy peaks of the Wellhorn and the Wetterhorn, tinted with the blush of sunset, and forming a battlement of mountain grandeur scarcely surpassed by the range even of Mont Blanc. Such a valley, I think, is the life of the Christian on the earth. As he descends the way seems commonplace enough. The yodel of the herdsmen and the lowing of the cattle are in his ears, and he sees nothing that is remarkable; but when he looks behind the retrospect is full of grandeur, and the grandest thing about it is that its gilded summits point him to the higher glories of the heaven that is awaiting him. Which, then, will you choose? You cannot altogether escape pain on earth; but, in the case of sinful pleasures, the joy is for the moment, the pain is permanent; in the case of holiness, the pain is for a time, while the happiness is everlasting. I speak as unto wise men. Judge, therefore, whether you should not, from this hour, forswear the pleasures of sin.

III. In the third place, take note that the pleasures of sin are such that the oftener they are enjoyed there is the less enjoyment in them. There is a wonderful harmony between God's moral law and the physical, intellectual, and moral nature of man; for every violation of its precepts does, in the end, evoke the protest of all our powers. Sinful indulgence either palls upon the taste, or, by its reaction on the system, destroys the very capacity for continuing in it, in which case the craving remains, while the ability to satisfy it is gone. This is a part of my theme which might be illustrated in a very harrowing manner; I prefer, however, to suggest it thus to you in the simplest way, leaving you to think it out for yourselves. The confirmed drunkard has not now the pleasure which he had at first in the flowing bowl. The enjoyment has gone, and only the slavery remains. But it is so with every other sin. Each time such guilty pleasure is felt, a portion of the sensitiveness is destroyed, and it takes more to produce the same excitement again, until at last it is impossible to produce it by any means whatever. But with the joys of holiness it is quite different. The oftener we enjoy them they are the higher. The longer and better a man knows Christ the more happiness does he derive from him. This is a joy which never cloys; this is a pleasure which never palls; this is a delight which, so far from destroying the capacity to receive it, only increases that the more, so that, at the close of his career, the believer can say to Jesus what the governor of the feast said at Cana, "Every man at the beginning doth set forth good wine, and when men have well drunk then that which is worse; but thou hast kept the good wine until now.' Here again, therefore, I offer you the materials for coming to a wise decision in regard to this momentous matter. I am persuaded that the longer you think out the point which I have now rather hinted to you than amplified before you, the more will you be convinced of its truth. Why, then, will you choose a pleasure which will burn out of you the very power to reproduce itself and reduce you to a helpless slavery? Turn, I pray you, to the Lord Jesus, and through faith in him and obedience to him you will enter upon the enjoyment of a happiness which shall grow upon you as the sun waxes to its meridian height, and which has in itself the elements of the blessedness of heaven.

IV. Finally, I would have you to take note that the pleasures of sin are most expensive. Here I refer not to money, though that is by no means unimportant; and when men are inclined to say that they can not afford to be Christians, I would like them to sit down and calmly reckon up how much their sins cost them. But I speak now of the expense of the man's own nature. The word of God says, "Bloody men shall not live out half their days"; and notwithstanding the existence of a few exceptions, I am persuaded that, in regard to vicious men generally, this will be corroborated by observation and experience. The sinner is old before his time. His physical power is gone. The least illness proves serious to him. He can make no such drafts on his strength as he was wont to do, or if he attempt to do so his life is the forfeit. His intellect has lost its freshness. It needs to be whipped up by stimulants; and when their influence is removed it sinks into lethargy and weakness. His will has become powerless. He is swayed one way or another entirely by outward influences. His conscience has become seared. In a word, he is a wreck. Did you ever look upon that wild sea-piece of Stanfield's which he has called "The Abandoned"? The sky is dark and lowering, with a forked flash of lightning shooting athwart it; the ocean is angry, and all over it there lies a dreary loneliness that makes the spectator almost shudder. The one solitary thing in sight is a huge hull, without mast or man on board, lying helpless in the trough of the sea. The men who stood by her as long as it was safe have been picked up by some friendly vessel now entirely unseen, and there that battered, broken thing floats on at the mercy of the winds and waves. That is sad enough; but what is it after all in comparison with the condition of an abandoned man, abandoned by friends, abandoned by himself, abandoned, it may be, even, like Saul, by God, and drifting on the ocean of life all dismantled and rudderless, tossed hither and thither by every wind of appetite or impulse, and soon to disappear beneath the waters! And what then? I dare not trust myself to speak of that. Muse on it yourselves for a moment, and then say if you can calculate the cost of the pleasures of sin? Far otherwise is the experience of the Christian. His pleasure is not expensive. A little goes a great way with him, and the more of Christ he knows the more does he learn to use his body as a temple of the Holy Ghost, his intellect as an instrument of serving God, and his will in choosing to run in the way of the divine commands. His faith brightens his mental powers, not at first, indeed, but through the stimulating influence of the truths which he believes. His love strengthens his will, and his steadfastness in well-doing softens the sensibility of his conscience, making it as quick to the presence of evil as the apple of the eye is to the least particle of dust. Christian faith, indeed, will not make a genius out of a dullard; but it will make the man nobler, physically and mentally as well as morally, than without it he would have been. So far from wasting his energies it economizes them, and haloes them all with the joy of its own happiness. Perhaps you imagine I have overdrawn the contrast! Let me, therefore, fortify my assertion by a suggestive contrast taken from real life; and that you may have every justice, I summon to testify before you one who had ample riches at his command, who wore the coronet of a peer, and who beside was dowered with heaven's own gift of brilliant genius which secured him world-wide renown. He had everything the world could give, and yet ere he had finished his thirty-seventh year he wrote thus of himself:

> "My days are in the yellow leaf,—
> The flower, the fruit of life are gone:
> The worm, the canker, and the grief
> Are mine alone."

Now, on the other side, let me call an English nonconformist minister in the time of his old age. He was gifted with an eloquence which has rarely been equaled and endowed with a loftiness of intellect that enabled him to grapple with the mightiest themes, but all through life he was a martyr to the most distressing physical anguish, so that he had scarcely a moment that was free from excruciating pain. Yet amid all this he contrived to put into his career some of the noblest work which his generation saw, and he had a quiet happiness, and sometimes even a brimming humor, that were quite remarkable. Returning in his later days from spending the evening with some friends, his daughter said to him, "Father, you did not enjoy yourself much to-night, I fear." "Yes," was the reply, "I enjoy everything. I enjoy everything"; and no man who knew Robert Hall could doubt that he spoke the truth. Here again, then, my dear friends, I place before you the materials for coming to a decision on this great question. If you wish your lives to resemble the course of the sun, rising in beauty, going forth in power, and shining more and more unto the perfect day; if you would have your death resemble his setting; if, like him, you would go down in a sea of glory and set only to shine on in the firmament of the world beyond, then cling to the cross of the Lord Jesus Christ and cultivate that soberness of mind which he enjoys: but if you desire to waste your strength, to paralyze your intellect, and to destroy your soul eternally, you will give yourself to the constant pursuit of "the pleasures of sin." There was once a king in Jerusalem who sounded every "depth and shoal" of pleasure, and drank of every cup of human joy. If there be any element of permanent satisfaction in life apart from

God he might have found it, for with every possible advantage he made a deliberate search after it, and still returned with this melancholy result: "Vanity of vanities, all is vanity and vexation of spirit." Listen to him, my young hearer, if you will not hearken unto me; listen to him, as, worn and weary and wounded too, from his lifelong pursuit, he cries back to you, half in mocking irony and half in deep, painful, solemn earnestness: "Rejoice, O young man, in thy youth, and let thy heart cheer thee in the day of thy youth, and walk in the ways of thine heart and in the sight of thine eyes, but know that for all these things God will bring thee into judgment with him."

FEBRUARY 28, 1875.

AFFLICTION AS RELATED TO LIFE.

Isaiah xxxviii. 16.—O Lord, by these things men live.

The song from which these words are taken was stricken out of the heart of Hezekiah by a remarkable personal experience. Just after the destruction of the host of Sennacherib which had been laying siege to Jerusalem he was prostrated by a dangerous malady, the result, most probably, of the fatigue, excitement, and anxiety which came upon him in connection with the defense of his capital from the Assyrian invader. At first it would seem that he had little apprehension as to the issue of his illness, but when the prophet Isaiah told him that his disease was mortal, and bade him set his house in order, his heart sank within him. He had just escaped a great peril; the Lord had given him a marvelous, yea, miraculous, deliverance, and so he might naturally conclude that there was still before him an earthly future in which he might do much for the consolidation of his kingdom, for the revival of religion among his people, and for the honor of Jehovah. But now all these hopes were dashed to the ground; the cherished purpose of his heart was apparently frustrated; his work was to remain forever unfinished; and as he thought on these things he "turned his face toward the wall, and prayed unto the Lord and wept sore." He could not understand God's dealings with him. Why had he been delivered from Sennacherib if he was thus and now to be removed? To what end had been his inauguration of spiritual reforms among his subjects if he was to be cut down before they could be carried through? It was as if the bird should be shot in the middle of its song; or as if the fabric of the weaver should be taken from the loom before the pattern which he was working had been finished; and so his plaint shaped itself into an individual solo in that great dirge of Ethan the Ezrahite: "Wherefore hast thou made all men in vain?"

But as he lay thus tearfully communing with his own heart and with God, Isaiah returned to his chamber with a message of healing assuring him that he should go up to the temple on the third day, and sealing the prediction by the wonderful sign of the going back of the shadow ten degrees on the sun-dial of Ahaz.

So it all came about through the use of the means which the prophet had prescribed; and Hezekiah improved the first hours of his recovery for the writing of this song, which, after pensively rehearsing his musings while he lay looking death in the face, breaks forth at length into glad thanksgiving for his restoration to health, and for the addition of fifteen years to his earthly life. Yet sincere as the song is, he did not conceive that the chanting of that was all the gratitude he owed, for he recognized that through his experience he had received a new ideal of life, and he made it his deliberate resolution to keep that before him in all his after conduct. This is the thought that lies beneath the words of my text. They refer primarily, indeed, to God's promises to Hezekiah while he was in affliction, and their performance to him in his restoration to health; but they indicate, also, that from this time on life had become a nobler, grander, more important thing in his view than it had ever been before;

and they carry in them the unexpressed purpose that he would thenceforth seek not mere existence, but that service of God in which nothing is lost, but everything that seems to us fragmentary and temporary finds its ultimate completion and its sure permanence. Thus the sentiment of Hezekiah is akin to that of the words with which Christ repelled the first temptation in the wilderness, "Man shall not live by bread alone, but by every word of God;" and he made the discovery of its truth through the discipline of his illness and recovery.

But he is not by any means singular in this respect, for wherever affliction has been truly sanctified to a man he can say precisely what is here expressed; and that aspect of the subject is important enough to furnish the theme for our discourse to-day. The conception and quality of life as affected by the discipline of any form of trial—that is the topic for the morning.

Let us take first the conception of life as a whole, and see how that is modified or altered by experiences like those through which Hezekiah passed. I enter not here into scientific theories of the nature or the origin of life. It is my privilege from this place to view the matter in a moral and spiritual light, and, so regarded, I do not fear contradiction when I affirm that they who have had no such critical experience in any form have never fully awakened to the difference which there is between mere existence and life. In sleep there is as real existence as when we are awake; but what a paltry thing life would be if it were to be a constant sleep! Yet there are those among us in whom, though their time may be busily occupied and though their intellects may be keen and vigilant, the spirit slumbers; and who know as little of life in its noblest sense as if their years were passed in unconsciousness. They are like the land-owner on whose estate there is an undiscovered silver mine, who is no richer for his hidden wealth, and who cannot be said even to possess it. Nothing has come to reveal them to themselves, or to give them any vivid sense of the existence of God and their relationship to him. Nothing has opened their eyes to the possibilities of life that are yet undeveloped in them. One day has been to them like another; and the unbroken monotony of their experience has fostered in them the expectation that things will always continue with them as they have always been. Thus they verify the psalmist's words, "Because they have no changes, therefore they fear not God." But when something like that which came to Hezekiah comes to them, then there is a thorough, if also a rude, awakening, and they discover that they have yet to begin to live. One may easily see this exemplified in the votary of pleasure. He has merely vegetated through existence. The pampering of his tastes, or the gratification of his appetites, or the enjoyment of society, constitutes for him the chief good, but when an arrest is laid upon him by disease, and he is prostrated in helplessness and compelled to look God and eternity in the face, he is made to feel that he has nothing to show for his existence, and that he must stand before the awful judgment-seat with not even so much as a handful of leaves instead of that which ought to have been the fruitage of a life. Ah! with what earnestness from such an one does Hezekiah's prayer ascend: "O Lord, I am oppressed, undertake for me"; and how he discovers at length that in all these things is the life of his spirit; nay, if he desires recovery, it is, like the Jewish king, that he may be made to live indeed. At such a time there comes to him a revelation of the hollowness of worldly pleasure like that which was given to Mrs. Winslow in the ball-room when the words of the catechism were flashed into her soul—"Man's chief end is to glorify God, and enjoy him forever": and that is for him the birth-hour of a new life.

Or take the case of him whose object in existence has been the accumulation of wealth. He has thought of nothing but how he may increase his hoard. Success has continually attended his exertions, and perhaps, like the fool in the parable, he was saying to himself, "Thou hast much goods laid up for many years: eat, drink and be merry," when God's hand was laid upon him, and he discovered that he could take nothing of his property with him into the world beyond. Then he found out that true wealth consists in what a man is and not in what a man has; then he saw the relation of the life that now is to that which is to come as he never did before; then he found that his occupation in the past had been as foolish as that of him who neglects the body for the sake of the raiment, and he arose with a new ideal for his life—adding his attestation to the truth of the words of my text, "By these things men live; and in all these things is the life of my spirit." In how many instances has a serious illness, or a terrible business humiliation, or a trying domestic bereavement, when the world seemed going from beneath him, and he was left alone "in the blank and solitude of things" to face eternity and God, brought a man to revise his theory of life! He has risen from his couch to seek forgiveness for the past from God in Christ, and to consecrate himself to the service of his generation by the will of God. He has come to regard this earthly life as but the portal to the life immortal. He has rectified the perspective of his existence, and has been led to value the now for its bearing on the hereafter; the present for its motherhood of the future; and if sometimes, as in the case of a Loyola, the issue has not been all unmingled blessing, still it has aroused to thoughtfulness; it has changed existence from spiritual somnambulism to waking earnestness; it has turned the attention from external accumulation to internal character; it has opened the ear to the voice of the Eternal, and stirred the heart with ambitions that rise to those things which are above, where Christ sitteth at God's right hand; and if that be true, we may surely say—By these things men live.

II. But passing now to the quality of the life, we may see how that, also, is affected by such experiences of affliction. And here so many features of that which we call character are either evoked or developed by trial that all I can do is to make a selection from them, and illustrate what seem to me the more important. There is, for example, the element of strength, whether in its passive exercise as patient endurance, or in its active manifestation as persevering energy. The poet has caught the truth which now I mean to emphasize when he bids his readers "learn to suffer and be strong." He who has known no affliction is easily worn out. A little thing puts him out. The child, who has had small experience of the world, is discouraged by a tiny difficulty, and depressed by a light affliction. A little trouble seems tremendous to one who has known nothing but prosperity. The old sailor who has been all but shipwrecked is not dismayed by a summer squall, for he says, "I have been in worse than this;" neither does he give up even in extremities, for he remembers that he has been brought through before, and he is energetic to the last. Now it is the same with life as a whole. You will find the strongest characters always among those who have been most sorely afflicted. In the home where sudden and alarming illness enters it is usually the healthiest and hardiest who are the most upset; and not unfrequently they are so distressed as to be practically useless in the emergency. They have lost their balance for the time. They have no readiness in resource; no quietness of spirit; no presence of mind; no control over themselves or others. But if there be one there who has herself passed through the fire; who has herself been, it may be, for days of suspense on the very borderland between the two worlds; she is equal to the occasion; she knows where to look for succor; and placing her hand in God's, she is at once steadied and upheld for duty. With inflexible resolution she commands herself into control; sees what is to be done, and has it accomplished while others are indulging in the luxury of tears. Her face is a benediction to the sufferer, and her silent energy is stronger for work and for helpfulness than the ruddy health of him whose emotion has overmastered him, and showed how weak he is despite his physical muscularity. So it is, also, in business. The man who has passed through one panic keeps a level head in the next. He knows that loss of fortune is not the greatest calamity that can come upon him, and he sees through the storm to the calm that is beyond. He has fathomed the experience, and looked the worst in the face, and that gives him the composure and the collectedness which enable him to grapple successfully with the difficulties of the hour. But the same thing holds in spiritual matters. Luther was wont to say that his three great teachers were prayer, study, and trial; and any reader of his life can perceive that if he had been required in the early part of his career to face some of the dangers which menaced him at a later date he would have faltered in his course. But through the minor experience he gained strength for the severer ordeal; and so it came about that what would have appalled him at the outset made almost as little impression on him at the last as "the whistling of the idle wind that he regarded not." If, then, strength of character be a desirable thing we ought to be reconciled to the afflictions by which alone it can be developed. They are to the soul what the tempering is to the iron, giving it the toughness of steel, and the endurance, too; and if that be so we may surely say regarding them—"By these things we live."

Then, again, we can see that experiences like this of Hezekiah have a great influence in producing unselfishness in a man. I distinguish here, however, between a short, sharp, critical illness which brings a man to the brink of the grave, and out of which he is raised almost as if from the dead, and a long life of feebleness. I admit that in some cases of the latter description there is a tendency to the development of selfishness. Every one in the house so habitually ministers to the comfort of the confirmed invalid that he is tempted to regard such service as a thing of right, and is prone to consider himself as the great center of the home, who should be thought of before all others. I know, indeed, that this is by no means universal; for I have seen those who, while chained to their couches for long periods by helplessness, have been lying planning hour by hour for the good of others. But I acknowledge that there is a danger of selfishness incident to such a condition. When, however, a man has been in the very grip of the last enemy, and has recovered; or has been within a little of losing all he had, and has escaped, you can understand how such an experience sends him out of himself. It intensifies for him the idea of life as a stewardship for God, and he sees the folly of making all the streams of his effort run into himself. He reasons thus: "What if I had died? these possessions would have been no longer mine. They cannot, therefore, be mine in the highest sense at all, for that which is mine by inalienable ownership must be mine throughout eternity. But if they are not inalienably mine, then they must be intrusted to me by God, and I must use them for God;" and forthwith he begins to think of others, and of others as having a God-given claim upon himself.

What is true thus of possessions, he extends to other things; and so it has come that an experience like this of the Jewish king has shaken many a man out of himself and set him to think of living for the good that he can do to others. Howard's life of benevolence was the outcome of a critical illness; and of multitudes more than of him it can be said that they sloughed off their selfishness in the crucible of trial; while, again, your habitually healthy and comfortable man who has known no crisis gives little heed to his fellows, and leaves their misery unrelieved. If we knew the former histories of all the men who, like the priest and Levite, pass misery by on the other side, we might discover that they had never known a serious affliction, and had never been brought face to face with God; while the good Samaritans who bring the needed succor have been, it may be, oftener than once at the very portals of that world into which nothing but character enters, and where a cup of cold water given to a disciple for the sake of Christ shall in nowise lose its reward. The man who has really seen death comes out of that experience, if at least it has been sanctified to him, disenchanted with himself, and feeling that his very life is itself a trust which God has given him for the service of his generation. Thus, affliction of some sort seems to be requisite for the production in us of thoughtfulness for others; and recognizing the value of that element in character we may say that men who have not known affliction have not yet truly begun to live.

But is only a broadening out of this last remark when I go on to affirm that sympathy is born out of such experiences as those of Hezekiah. He who has passed through trial can feel most tenderly for those who are similarly afflicted. This is so true that the inspired writer has said even of Jesus, "In that he himself hath suffered being tempted, he is able also to succor them that are tempted;" and, indeed, in one aspect of it, the very necessity for the Incarnation is found in the principle which I have just enunciated. To have a sympathizing God we must have a suffering Saviour, and there is no true fellow-feeling with another save in the heart of him who has been afflicted like him. Nay more, the having suffered like another impels us to go and sympathize with him. Those of us who have lost little children feel a prompting within us to speak a word of comfort to every parent who is passing through a similar experience. Indeed, it was in connection with an affliction of that sort that my attention was first drawn, some twelve years ago, to the text of this discourse. I had just a few weeks before buried a beloved daughter, the light of the household, and the darling of all in it, and had gone to attend a meeting of Synod where an honored minister, who had been through the same trial oftener than once before, came up to me and took me by the hand, and said to me, with a reference to my sorrow, "By these things men live." That was all, but each successive year since then has given a new verification of his words, for oh! how often in the interval have I been enabled to comfort others with the comfort with which I have been comforted of God, and the efficacy of the consolation lay largely in the fact that it was offered by one who had proved its value for himself. We cannot do good to others save at a cost to ourselves, and our own afflictions are the price we pay for our ability to sympathize. He who would be a helper must first be a sufferer. He who would be a saviour must somewhere and somehow have been upon a cross; and we cannot have the highest happiness of life in succoring others without tasting the cup which Jesus drank, and submitting to the baptism wherewith he was baptized. Every real Barnabas must pass to his vocation through seasons of personal sorrow,—and so, again, we see that it is true that "by these things men live." The most comforting of David's psalms were pressed out of him by suffering; and if Paul had not had his thorn in the flesh we had missed much of that tenderness which quivers in so many of his letters.

But this train of thought leads naturally up to my last remark here, namely, that experiences like Hezekiah's have much to do with the usefulness of a man's life. Usefulness is not a thing which one can command at will. It is, in most cases, the result of a discipline; and is possessed by those who in a large degree are unconscious that they are exercising it. It depends fully more on what a man is than on what he does, or, if it is due to what he does or says, that again, is owing very much to what he is, and what he is now has been determined by the history through which he has been brought. You see that in the case of a physician. His experience goes far more to the making of him than his college training has done. That, indeed, if it has been worth anything, has mainly taught him how to utilize his experience; and the difference between one medical man and another depends very largely indeed on the history and practice of each. Now it is so, also, in spiritual things. The helpfulness of another to us in the prosecution of the Christian life is determined more by his personal experience than by his intellectual pre-eminence, and thus it happens often that an humble and largely disciplined disciple, or what we call an "exercised" Christian, may be more useful to us than an eloquent preacher. Here, too, as it seems to me, is the secret of the difference between one man and another in the matter of pulpit power. Few things, indeed, are so humiliating to those of us whom God has called to public positions in his church as to hear anatomical critics ask, "What is the secret of his power?" One will say that it is in his voice; another that it is in his manner; another that it is in his aptitude of illustration; another that it is in his personal appearance; and still another that it is in his literary taste and simplicity of style; while some, perhaps, will resolve it all into that vague thing which they call magnetism, and some into his earnestness. But scarcely one will think of the history that is behind the sermon, or of the experience out of which it has been born: but there, in the discipline through which God has brought him, and which no other man can acquire by any effort, is the hiding of his peculiar power; there is the root of his spiritual usefulness. The discourses which find others are those which have been struck out of him by the crises through which God has brought him; and that same discipline having sent him into his own soul has given him in the knowledge of himself a key to the hearts of others, so that before they know it he has entered them and taken possession of them for his Lord. When one reads Robertson of Brighton's life he comprehends the power of his discourses; and this is a power which no theological seminary can develop, for it is conferred by God through personal discipline. It is the power of the heart rather than of the head; the power of character rather than ability; the power of experience rather than of rhetoric. Ezekiel was made a sign to the people through the loss of his wife; and the usefulness of many men, both in the pulpit and out of it, has had its roots in similar discipline. Ah! it is a costly price, and yet " by these things men live."

But, not to dwell longer on the effect produced by such experiences on different qualities of character, I must add one word of caution. It is not every affliction that works out such results; and whether any trial will do so or not depends entirely on the spirit in which it is borne. Only they who, like Hezekiah, turn to God under it receive blessing through it. A man may be sent to Jabbok, and feel himself in uttermost solitude, but unless while he is there he wrestles with the Lord it will not be to him Peniel, and he will go away from it less serious and spiritually impressionable than he was before. One cannot be, after such a crisis, precisely as he was before it came upon him. If he turn to God under it, he will be the better of it, for it will give for him a new significance to life, and work out in him some quality of character in which before he was deficient. But if he is not the better for it he will be the worse. If he does not apply to God for deliverance out of it or grace under it he will be hardened by it, and be more indifferent to the great spiritual realities than ever. When, therefore, I say as the outcome of our morning's meditation not only that an experience like this of Hezekiah is a blessing, but also that the absence of such an experience in a man's history is the greatest of all misfortunes, my words are to be taken with the qualification that under it he draws near to God. That is the hinge on which it all turns. An affliction so borne will always bring forth fruit in giving a new quality to our character, and a new power to our life; but if we refuse to acknowledge God in such a crisis we shall come out of it cold, callous, impassive, and mayhap defiant; and it will be a curse to us, and not a blessing.

April 18, 1880.

OPPORTUNITIES AND THEIR LIMIT.

JEREMIAH xviii. 3, 4. 3 Then I went down to the potter's house, and, behold, he wrought a work on the wheels.

4 And the vessel that he made of clay was marred in the hands of the potter: so he made it again another vessel, as seemed good to the potter to make *it*.

JEREMIAH xix. 1, 2, 10, 11.—1 Thus saith the Lord, Go and get a potter's earthen bottle, and *take* of the ancients of the people, and of the ancients of the priests.

2 And go forth unto the valley of the son of Hinnom, which *is* by the entry of the east gate, and proclaim there the words that I shall tell thee.

10 Then shalt thou break the bottle in the sight of the men that go with thee.

11 And shalt say unto them, Thus saith the Lord of hosts: Even so will I break this people and this city, as *one* breaketh a potter's vessel, that cannot be made whole again: and they shall bury *them* in Tophet, till *there be* no place to bury.

THE chapters from which these two texts are taken should be read and studied together if we wish to get a complete view of the one subject of which they both treat. They should be set also in the framework of the history to which they originally refer, in order that through the interpretation of them which that supplies we may discover the principles of permanent importance which underlie them, and of which the case to which the prophet applied them was only a single illustration. Some little attention may be required to secure this intelligent apprehension of these, I fear, too sadly neglected portions of sacred Scripture, but the result will be fraught with instruction and admonition to us all, and will more than repay any effort that may be needed for its attainment.

In the former of the chapters Jeremiah tells us that at the suggestion of the Divine Spirit he went to a potter's house and saw a workman moulding a vessel upon the wheels. Even as he was looking, something went wrong with the clay that was under the potter's hand. It was "marred." He discovered something in it which made it unfit for the purpose for which he had originally intended it; but he did not throw it aside on that account, for it was still soft and plastic to his touch, and so he made it into another sort of vessel—less honorable and less valuable, it may be, but yet useful—into which his practiced eye saw that it might still be turned. Here we have, therefore, a work still in process—still, as I may say, in the clay—and the suggestion is that so long as that impressionable condition lasts, if the result first aimed at is not gained, another, though perhaps a lower, may yet be attained.

In the latter of the chapters the prophet narrates that he was commanded to take a potter's bottle—not now, you observe, in the formative and easily-molded state of clay, but fully baked and hardened—and break it in pieces in the sight of certain persons whom he was to lead out to the valley of Hinnom that they might be witnesses of his action. We have here, therefore, not a manufacture in process, but the destruction of a finished article which had proved to be a failure. The clay had been made into a bottle, and the bottle had been hardened in the fire. Its quality as a vessel was irrevocably fixed; and as it had turned out to be good for nothing, it was broken in pieces. It was no longer possible to make it into something else, and therefore no further pains were taken with it, but it was shivered into fragments which were cast on the refuse heap that had accumulated in the unclean Tophet.

When we put these two symbolical messages of the prophet together thus, it is impossible to evade the conclusion that there is a most intimate connection between them, and we begin to get a glimmering of the spiritual truth that is beneath them. But when we take the application which Jeremiah makes of each, there is no longer any room for doubt upon the subject. Listen to these words connected with the first : " O house of Israel, cannot I do with you as this potter ? saith the Lord. Behold, as the clay is in the potter's hand, so are ye in mine hand, O house of Israel. At what instant I shall speak concerning a nation, and concerning a kingdom, to pluck up, and to pull down, and to destroy it ; if that nation against whom I have pronounced turn from their evil, I will repent of the evil that I thought to do unto them. And at what instant I shall speak concerning a nation, and concerning a kingdom, to build and to plant it ; if it do evil in my sight, that it obey not my voice, then I will repent of the good wherewith I said I would benefit them." Then take the following in relation to the second : " Thus saith the Lord of hosts : Even so will I break this people and this city, as one breaketh a potter's vessel that cannot be made whole again ; and they shall bury them in Tophet, till there be no place to bury." Now put these together and you get the inference that the clay in the one case and the bottle in the other represent the house of Israel—each, however, in a different stage of development. The clay denotes the educational period, when the national character was as yet only in process of being formed ; the bottle symbolizes the hardened determination into which that character ultimately settled; while in the making of the clay into another vessel and in the breaking of the bottle, we have set forth the difference of the divine treatment of the people in these two conditions. But (as I have often reminded you, when expounding other symbolical passages of the word of God), we cannot get a simile that will hold in every particular, and here there is one important distinction between the material emblems and the moral beings whom they are used to typify which must never be overlooked. Clay is an unconscious piece of matter, and a bottle is a dead, senseless, irresponsible thing. But the Israelites were spiritual and responsible beings, dowered with free agency, and having liberty to choose what they would make of themselves. The marring of the clay in the hands of the potter, therefore, must not be misunderstood. Literally, that is not a thing for which the clay is responsible; nor would any one blame a bottle for being worthless. But as here employed these things are to be taken as denoting results produced by the perversity of the people represented by the clay and the bottle. The marring of the lump upon the wheel signifies no mere unavoidable accident in the history of the nation, but rather a deliberate purpose on the part of the people to throw off their allegiance to Jehovah. They could never do that in any degree without correspondingly injuring their ultimate future. But if, through the expostulations of the prophet, they repented, and submitted themselves in willing obedience to the Lord's commands, then they would still remain plastic as clay; and though the higher ideal had been lost by them, God would shape another future, lower yet still useful for them, as it pleased him, and something good would yet be made of them for his glory and for the welfare of men. On the other hand, if in spite of all entreaty they hardened themselves into defiant and stubborn rebellion against Jehovah, they would thereby pass from the soft, yielding, and easily moldable condition of clay upon the wheel into the hard, fixed, and unimprovable state of a fully-baked vessel which did not answer its purpose; and as nothing else could be made of them, they would be cast out as worthless, and consigned to irremediable destruction.

Such seems to be the significance of these two symbols; and this view is entirely corroborated by the history to which they were primarily applied by Jeremiah. The Jewish nation was at this time in a most deplorable condition. Originally intended by Jehovah to be a peculiar people, an holy nation, a kingdom of priests, and the witness of truth to the world at large, it had refused to rise to that high vocation, and had chosen to become like the neighboring states, in idolatry, in sensuality, in covetousness, and in unrighteousness. The clay "was marred upon the wheel." It had, therefore, to be subjected to another treatment. Never, indeed, could it fill in the noble outline which had at first been marked for it; but still there might be yet an outcome of good if the people would but submit themselves to God and return to him. And many of them—indeed most of those who were carried into captivity to Babylon—did thus return to him. They were the "soft ductile clay," and God "made it another vessel." The nation, indeed, never was again as it had been in its palmy days, or as it might have been if its citizens had been true to God all through. Its kingly power never again emerged; the ark of the covenant was no longer in its temple; much of the old glory was hopelessly gone. Virtually it had to begin anew and on a lower level. But, though it did not attain the lofty rôle which had at first been intended for it, there was still a great future in store for it, for the returned exiles raised a platform on which at length Messiah was to appear, and the story of the struggles of the people under the Maccabees was to be full of inspiration to multitudes in every after generation. But there were others among the people who would take no advice and heed no entreaty. These were they who sided with the rebels against Babylon, and would not accept God's discipline. They were hardened in their obstinacy and stubborn in their impenitence. They were the misshapen vessel of earthenware, for "they had rejected God's loving chastisement, had refused his mercy, and persisted in their sins." So upon them came the frightful calamity of the siege of Jerusalem, described in this nineteenth chapter of Jeremiah's prophecies, when God "broke them with a rod of iron and dashed them in pieces like a potter's vessel."

Nor were these the only illustrations furnished by the Jewish nation of this law of the divine administration. We see the same thing repeated in connection with the Saviour's personal ministry in Palestine. All through these three years and a half, the clay, though marred, was still upon the wheel, and if there had been any repentance among the people, or any willinghood among them to receive Jesus as the Messiah, they might have been formed into yet another vessel, and risen once more into prominence among the nations. But they elected to reject Jesus and put him to death upon the cross, and thereby they turned the clay into a worthless piece of pottery too vile for ornament, too ill-made for use, and too hard to be remolded,—only fit, therefore, to be cast out and broken into fragments.

But now, having a firm grasp of the meaning of these two symbolic prophecies in their primary relation to the Jewish nation, let us distill from that the principles of permanent importance which it contains. They are the following: First, that there is a divine ideal possible for every man under the gracious providence of God; second, that this ideal is attainable by him only through implicit faith in God, and willing obedience to all his commandments; third, that if this faith and obedience are refused by a man, his history is marred, and it is no longer possible for him to become what otherwise he might have reached; fourth, that if the man should repent and return unto the Lord, he may still, through the rich forbearance of God, rise to a measure of excellence and usefulness which, though short of that which was originally possible to him and intended for him, will yet secure for him the approval of the Most High; and, fifth, that if the man harden himself into persistent rejection of God, and show stubborn impenitence, there comes a time when improvement is impossible, and there is nothing for him but "everlasting destruction from the presence of the Lord, and from the glory of his power." The mere repetition of these propositions is enough to show you that they carry us into that region of mystery which enshrouds the great questions of God's sovereignty and man's free agency. But I do not propose at this time to enter into that domain. These two truths are the ultimate boundaries of human thought on all moral questions. We cannot get rid of either, and though to our finite minds they seem utterly inconsistent with each other, yet we must hold them both in apparent antagonism, believing that full knowledge, if it could be attained by us, would discover their harmony. No matter where we begin in our cogitations we shall, if only we go far enough, come up against one or the other of them, and then all farther progress is arrested. If we confine our attention to the divine side, we shall find ourselves at length hemmed up by the purpose of God; if again we restrict our thoughts to the human, we shall reach our ultimatum in the free agency of man. This is the inevitable result of our limitation as creatures, for only God can fully comprehend God. But while that is most true, the principles which I have deduced from the two symbolic prophecies of Jeremiah are exceedingly valuable as serving to show us that there is nothing in the human freedom that subverts the divine sovereignty; and that there is nothing in the manner in which God's sovereignty is maintained that destroys human freedom, or weakens human responsibility. God is superintending and overruling all, as the potter is manipulating the clay. Yet man has the choice whether or not he will submit himself to God, even as the Israelites, who were symbolized by the clay, had the liberty to determine whether or not they would serve Jehovah; and it is to me a most interesting thought that the question "O house of Israel, cannot I do with you as this potter?" was put by God not to terrify the people by the assertion of his power to destroy them, but rather to encourage them to repentance by assuring them that if they returned to him he could still make something valuable out of them, even as the workman framed a serviceable vessel, after all, out of the clay which had become marred and unfit for his original purpose. But leaving all abstract discussions, let us attend briefly to each of the propositions which I have enunciated.

I. There is a divine ideal possible for every man. God has not made any man simply for destruction. I know that there are many who so misrepresent him; but there is no countenance given to any such view in the sacred Scriptures. He has an archetype or pattern before him, which it is possible for each man to reach. What that is may be, indeed must be, different for each. There was one ideal possible for Egypt, another for Assyria, and another for Babylon, with their respective privileges and opportunities, and quite another for Israel, with its pre-eminent advantages. These other nations were not required to be everything that the Jewish people ought to have become. God is not unrighteous to demand equal attainments from unequal gifts. He gives to one five talents, to another two, and to another one; but he does not look at last for ten from each of them. And what is true thus of nations is true also of individuals. He has one ideal for those who, like ourselves, are favored to the full with gospel blessings; and another for such as have not our original advantages. But there is a possible result that shall be worthy of L'. approval for each; and that each may reach that, has been his original and primary design in the creation of each. I enter not now into the question why there are these original inequalities in the case of men, for I do not think any one can solve that, and I content myself with simply marking their existence, as connected with the ideal that is possible for each. That ideal is not the same for all, but it is in each appropriate to and in correspondence with the environment in which he is placed.

II. This ideal is to be attained by a man only through implicit faith in God and willing obedience to his commands. It was a profound saying of a great philosopher in regard to physical things that "we command nature by obeying her." He meant, for example, that by complying with the requisite conditions in electricity, we can command that agent to do our work. And similarly we may affirm that we command God by obeying him. I should hardly have dared, I confess, to use that expression if I had not found in the writings of the ancient prophet such words as these, "Concerning the work of my hands command ye me." But you are, I hope, in no danger of misunderstanding my meaning. By obeying God we secure his approval and co-operation with us and in us by his Spirit for the attainment of that which he has designed to make us. Here again, however, we are to bear in mind that the commandments of God do not mean the same for all men. Those who as yet have never received the books of revelation have still certain commandments, or what Paul calls a law, written in their hearts; and if they obey these they will rise to the divine ideal for them. Whether any of them have ever done so I dare not affirm, but that it is possible for them to do so seems to me evident: and if they do, they will be judged according to their light, and approved for what they have accomplished. But we, who have in our hands the living oracles of God, need not spend time in speculation about them. It would be much more profitable for us, and becoming in us, to improve our own opportunities. Now here we are told that we shall reach that which God has designed for us through faith in the Lord Jesus Christ, and implicit submission of our intellects, and hearts, and wills, and lives to him. The great question for us, therefore, is whether or not we have thus given ourselves up and over to his service, for only thereby can we rise, each in his own place and after his own pattern, to what Paul has called "the measure of the stature of the fullness of Christ." Ah! when we try ourselves by this test, must we not all admit that we have fallen below the divine ideal for us, or, as the great apostle has expressed it, "that we have come short of the glory of God," that is, that we have come short of giving such an illustration of the wisdom and love of God in the fashioning of our characters as otherwise might have been seen in us?

III. This brings me to the third proposition, formerly enunciated, namely, that if such faith and obedience are refused by a man, that man's history is marred, and it is no longer possible for him to become what otherwise he might have been. That is seen by us every day in common life. The youth who trifles through those years which ought to have been devoted to education, may possibly, as the saying is, "take himself up" in after days, but he can never attain such a position as might easily have been his if he had been diligent all through the formative period of early life. And the same thing holds morally. Sin mars the divine ideal for a man. It deprives him of the full advantage of the skill and help of God in the development of his character. It is no longer possible even for God, in consistency with the moral nature of his government, to make of him all that was originally attainable by him. Look, for example here, to such men as Balaam, and Saul, and Judas, and you will see how true it is that sin mars the realization of a noble and possible future. What a character Balaam might have become, with his prophetic insight and his poetic soul, if only he had kept true to his convictions! but the clay was marred, and the man who might else have been a noble example, now serves only as a beacon of warning. How possible, too, it was for Saul to have been almost a model king! He had great kindness shown him by Jehovah. Samuel, also, was drawn in quite a wonderful manner to him, and as we read the history of his prowess in the matter of Jabesh-gilead, we feel that he only just missed becoming great, and missed it because he preferred his own way to God's. And Judas, too: what might he not have been as an apostle, with all his privileges and opportunities? But the clay was marred under the divine potter's hands, and because he chose the things of the world in preference to obedience to Christ, he who might have been a son of consolation became the son of perdition. Ah! how many among us are at this moment, by their characters and positions, living illustrations of the truth that if we refuse to obey God's commands and receive Jesus as our only Redeemer, Lawgiver and King, we make the loftiest life impossible for us! God help us to lay this solemn thought to heart.

IV. But now, fourthly, if the man should repent and return to the Lord, he may yet, through the rich forbearance of God, rise to a measure of excellence and usefulness, which, though short of that which was originally possible to him and intended for him, will secure the approval of the Most High. This is the gem thought of these two chapters. If, having discovered the cause of our failure in our sins, we turn from these and give ourselves up to God, he will yet make something out of us worthy of himself and full of joy and encouragement to ourselves. Observe again, I beseech you, that question, "O house of Israel, cannot I do with you as this potter?" and remember it was meant to encourage the people to go back to God, with the assurance that it was still possible for him to make something good out of them. But they said (look at the 12th verse of the 18th chapter): "There is no hope; but we will walk after our own devices, and we will every one do the imagination of his evil heart." Ah! that is a true word of Paul, "We are saved by hope." These Jews had no hope, and therefore they went farther and farther down. Jeremiah tried to rekindle hope in them by this illustration of the potter, but it was in vain; they refused to receive his message, and hardened themselves into uttermost obstinacy,—and then came destruction. Now let me hold up, clear and distinct, this hope to sinners before me this morning: There is no need to despair yet. If you are willing to return to God in Christ, he is able to work out in you and bring out through you something of nobleness and holiness. There will always be in you and about you, indeed, the marks of your former lives; but God has you yet upon the wheel, and he will make you "another vessel as it pleases him." Think here of such a case as that of Manasseh. The son of the good Hezekiah, he might, had he walked steadily in his father's footsteps, have become one of the noblest of Jewish monarchs. But he gave himself up to idolatry and sank into the most debasing sins. At length the judgment came and he was carried off to Babylon. There, in thought and prayer and penitence, he returned to God; and the Lord, making another vessel of him, restored him to Jerusalem and his throne. He never became what had been at first possible for him, but he did become another and a better man; and his name stands out on the historic page as a striking proof that even although one has gone far astray he may yet, through God's grace and by returning unto him, become a worthy man and be finally accepted. But why need we go so far back as Manasseh's days for illustrations of this truth? We may find many in our own generation. Probably, even as I speak, each of you has some such case with which he is acquainted recalled vividly to his remembrance. There may even be some here whose personal experience confirms my words. I think of John Newton in the pulpit, doing a noble work for God and men in spite of his early sins and shameful habits. He was never such a man as he might have been had he been all through his days truly devoted to his God, but he was a good and useful man after all, saved by grace through faith in Christ and repentance unto life. I think of some, not far away from us, who, after years in prison, have found their way through Christ back to God, and are now—though the mark of the old life may be seen yet very clearly stamped upon their countenances—living earnestly for the glory of God in the salvation of men. I think of others, long enslaved by intemperance, and even yet feeling degraded at the thought of what but for it they might have been, but now emancipated from the thraldom of habit, by the power of the Holy Ghost, through faith in Jesus, and living mainly "for the good that they can do." And with such cases before me, I proclaim the willingness of God to save all who penitently turn to him, and to make them vessels of mercy which he will "prepare for his glory." Let no one go away saying there is no hope. If there is the least prompting within you to return—though it may be faint as the spark in the smoking flax, or feeble as the strength in the bruised reed—that is an evidence that you are not yet hardened into impenetrability; and if you yield to its impulse there is One who will receive you and renew you, and make you yet noble and honorable before him, a trophy of his grace; aye, it may be—let me carry out the figure of my texts—a cup in which he will hold the living water of his refreshment to the lips of many weary ones among your fellow-men. Return, then, O return to him, and he will " form you all anew."

V. Our last proposition is that if the man harden himself into persistent rejection of God and show stubborn impenitence, there comes a time when improvement is no longer possible, and there is nothing for him but everlasting destruction from the presence of the Lord and the glory of his power. The clay that was plastic was made into another vessel; but the bottle that was burned into hardness and was found to be worthless was broken into pieces and cast out. So when impenitence is perversely persisted in there comes a point at which the heart is so hardened thereby that repentance is neither thought of, nor prompted to, nor desired, and the man is abandoned to perdition. And where, do you ask, is that point? I answer that I cannot in every case precisely tell. It may be even in the present life, in some instances. It was so, I cannot but think, in the case of Saul, for when, having finally given up God, he went for help to the cave of Endor, and Samuel appeared to him, as much to the alarm of the woman as to his own, he heard only words of doom. He had gone to the wrong resort. Had he but turned to God, we may be sure that there would have been something in the future for him still. So again in the case of Belshazzar, when Daniel came in haste to decipher the writing on the wall he read out only words of condemnation.

He spoke nothing now, as before he had done to Nebuchadnezzar, of the duty of breaking off sin by righteousness, but merely said, " Thou art weighed in the balances and found wanting. God hath numbered thy kingdom and finished it." With these cases in mind, therefore, I must affirm that this point of transition between the ductility of the clay and the hardness of the burned bottle may be passed by a man even in this life, though, I must also add, that it is not yet passed by any one who has a prompting to repentance within him, and a desire to return to God and become other than he is. But if I may not speak with certainty concerning this life, if indeed I must speak with caution regarding the point on which I have just touched, I have no hesitation regarding the end of this probation for all, for, as I read the Scriptures, the whole trend and tenor of their teaching go to prove that after death there is no possibility of changing character, for then the clay is no longer on the wheel, and the God-given opportunities are ended. Then the vessel is taken to its place of honor in the heavenly palace, or cast out to its place of dishonor and destruction in the abysmal Tophet. I know that there is a great deal of very loose thinking current in these days about what is called " probation after death." But the Bible has nothing in it which seems to give the least countenance to any such thing. And the course of thought along which we have travelled this morning cuts at the root of the reason plausibly assigned by many for their advocacy of this opinion. It is said that every man must have a probation somewhere, and therefore that those who have had no probation on earth are entitled to it after death. But who are they who have had no probation on earth? Are they infants? Then, if they are to be put on trial, and therefore in jeopardy, after death, millions of bereaved parents' hearts will leap up in indignant protest at such an idea, and each will say, "My gathered lambs are folded in the Good Shepherd's arms: I want none of your speculations that shall speak as if they were still in danger." Nay more, if, without personal probation, they suffered death because Adam sinned, I want to know why without a personal probation they may not enjoy eternal life, since Jesus Christ died for them and rose again? The same principle applies to idiots. We are, therefore, restricted to the heathen. But are we quite sure that they have no probation before death? Is the presentation of the gospel necessary to a probation? If that be alleged, then I want to know on what authority the statement is made? I find nothing of that here in Scripture. On the contrary I find that, as I have already said, the ideal for each man is different, and that the ultimate character of each will be gauged by his opportunities and what he has made of them, such as they were. "They that have sinned without law" shall not be judged by a law of which they knew nothing: but they shall be judged none the less according to the light which they possessed; and what is that but saying that this life is for them also a probation? No man, therefore, has a right to affirm that any human being, come to years of discretion, on the earth, has not had a probation here. All have not equal privileges. That is true even in places where the gospel is enjoyed; and it is more largely true, of course, when we take in the race as a whole. But equal opportunities for all are not essential to a probation for each. If they were, then no one of us here could say that we have even now a probation, for there are inequalities in the talents given to each of us, and in the opportunities afforded us for their improvement. Thus we see that the assumption that some men have no probation here lies at the root of this modern heresy; and that, as I have shown you, is an assumption of what is false. Therefore do not let your soul be drugged by this opiate. Do not dream of probation after death. Even if it were true that such a thing were to be given to the heathen, there would still be no hope for you. And so, while you may, before the day of grace ends and the door of opportunity is shut, return to the Lord by faith in Jesus and in obedience unto him.

I conclude with a word of exhortation especially addressed to the young. I have tried to show you this morning that the marring of sin will prevent you from reaching the highest excellence of character in life, and I have pointed out also that, though you may afterward turn to God, the result, at last, will be short of that which otherwise you might have gained. How important it must be, therefore, to give yourselves to God in Christ, with the first dawnings of your moral intelligence! Keep away, I beseech you, from all youthful follies and early sins; for, even if you should repent of them afterward, you will suffer either some positive evil or some negative privation in consequence. Depend upon it, God will make you, in some way, to possess the sins of your youth. Preserve, I implore you, the first freshness of your early innocence, and seek to maintain your young sensitiveness of conscience, for if you once lose these, you will never in the future be what otherwise you might have become. You may have pardon through the blood of Christ, and sanctification by the Spirit of Christ, and usefulness, too, by the grace of Christ, but you will find that something has gone forever from you, and that some other things are forever unattainable by you. When you pluck a flower in the summer morning all sparkling with dewdrops, if you shake these off you will never form them again. You may pour water on it a thousand times, but never again can you put back on its opening leaves those " bright orbicular diamonds " as they sparkled so gloriously in the early sunbeam. So, if you go into youthful sins, you can never regain all that you have lost thereby. Another vessel, by God's grace, may yet be shaped upon the wheel, but it will be lowlier and less honorable than that which you have marred. Therefore, give yourselves now to Christ and become early adherents of that religion of which one of the characteristics is that it keeps itself "unspotted from the world."

December 10, 1883

THE HARVEST OF RETRIBUTION AND REWARD.

GAL. vi. 7, 8. Be not deceived. God is not mocked; for whatsoever a man soweth, that shall he also reap. For he that soweth to his flesh, etc.

IT is one of the characteristics of Paul that he enforces the commonest duties by the highest motives. When he urges the Corinthians to make a contribution for the poor saints at Jerusalem, he drives home his appeal by these words: "For ye know the grace of the Lord Jesus Christ, that though he was rich, yet for your sakes he became poor, that ye through his poverty might be rich." When again he vindicates himself from the accusation of fanaticism which his enemies had made against him he says: "Whether we be beside ourselves, it is to God; or whether we be sober, it is for your cause, for the love of Christ constraineth us; because we thus judge that if he died for all, then these all died; and that he died for all that they which live should not henceforth live unto themselves, but unto him which died for them and rose again." His habit thus was to run up the separate actions of his life to great principles, by which they were dominated, and in accordance with which they were regulated. The poet has reminded us that in the material universe,

> "That very law which molds a tear
> And bids it trickle from its source,
> That law preserves the earth a sphere
> And holds the planets in their course;"

and much in the same way the apostle shows that the great fact of our redemption by Jesus Christ should affect the little things of our benevolence and our manner of speech as really as the great things of our life-aim and our bearing at certain crucial and decisive turning points in our history. The background of his life was the cross of Christ, and from that every action, whether to human view important or the reverse, drew its inspiration and acquired its momentum.

But if the Cross was the background of his life, the future state was its environment. That enswathed it, as the sky enswaths the landscape. This earthly existence was for him "rounded" with eternity, and he had learned to view the conduct of 'now' in its relation to the great hereafter. So he was continually referring to the future as a warning, or a test, or an encouragement in the present. The two great facts in the world's history to him were the first and second comings of the Lord Jesus Christ. The two great doctrines on which, to him, all others depended, and which, in his view, stood equally related to all our actions, though in different ways, were redemption and retribution. In the midst of his sufferings he found support in looking back to the obligation under which he lay to Christ, and solace in looking forward to the time when he should be clothed upon with his house which is from heaven. Again, when he was dealing with those who had fallen away, the saddest aspect of their guilt was, in his eyes, that they were the enemies of the cross of Christ, and the most awful thing about their destiny was that their end is destruction. Thus these doctrines, as he held them, were not mere dry, dogmati estatements, but rather omnipresent and all-pervading motives which influenced everything he said, or wrote, or did.

Accordingly we are not surprised to find that the words of my text stand in immediate connection with the command that ministers of the gospel should be liberally supported by those whom they instruct. That is a commonplace duty, but it is lifted by Paul into eternal importance, when he links it on, as here, directly and immediately to the doctrine of retribution; for then we are reminded that in the way in which we deal with it we must sow either to the flesh or to the spirit, and reap either corruption or everlasting life. Now, though my business this morning is mainly with the doctrine itself, I cannot help showing you thus, in the very outset, how it is to be applied to all things in that conduct which, according to a recent writer, is "three-fourths of life." Paul's faith in a future state of rewards and punishments did not lie dormant in his soul, like a forgotten article of furniture in a dusty attic. It was a living and active principle. And his life, as a whole, was not "a fortuitous concourse" of actions, but the outcome, in individual details, of those two great truths which he held in the grasp of a firm and intelligent belief, namely, that "we are bought with a price" and that "we must all appear before the judgment-seat of Christ that every one may receive the things done in his body, according to that he hath done, whether it be good or bad." Behind him always was "the cross of Christ"; before him always was "the judgment-seat of Christ." He never forgot either; and every portion of his conduct was affected by them both. It was not, therefore, an exceptional thing with him to enforce such a common and ordinary duty as the support of a minister, by such an overwhelming motive as that which is furnished by the doctrine of retribution. Rather we may say that the importance of the doctrine, in his view, is attested by this incidental application of it. He is not here systematically and argumentatively reasoning it out. It is to him one of the most absolute of certainties, not more nearly bearing on ministerial support than on other duties, but bearing on that as really as on others; and so his reference to it here is a proof of the fact that the present life, and all in it, was for him the germ of eternity, and was invested thereby with an infinite significance. Leaving, then, the duty in connection with which the words of my text were originally written, let us attend to the doctrine which they teach.

I. And in the first place they declare that the relation between our life here and our condition hereafter is that which exists between seed and the crop that springs from it. What that is it might be very difficult for us scientifically to explain; yet even the youngest among us knows something of its distinctive peculiarity. There is in everything that can be rightly called a seed a certain germinant quality, so that when it is put into, or "sown" in, appropriate soil, it begins to sprout, and, under favoring circumstances, ends in the reproduction of itself, not alone as a unit, but manifold. An acorn and a stone differ from each other in many respects, but the fact that the one when planted in the earth produces an oak-tree and other acorns, and that the other, though subjected to the same treatment, undergoes no change, but remains simply and only a stone, marks the one as a seed and the other as not a seed. Moreover, as Paul reminds us in his well-known argument on the resurrection, God "has given to every seed its own body," that is to say, each produces its own fruit. A fir-tree does not spring from a chestnut, neither a beech-tree from a pine-cone. If you sow corn you do not expect to reap wheat; and if you plant an orchard with apple-trees you do not look to see plums upon their branches. Or, as the Lord himself has put it, using the analogy, however, for another purpose, " Of thorns men do not gather figs, nor of a bramble-bush gather they grapes."

There is here a great unchanging and unchangeable law. Each seed produces its own body, because God has so ordained. That which we reap from off the fields of nature is always of the same kind with that which we have sown. No sane man, even if he should be the most unquestioning believer in the transmutation of species, would expect a crop of valuable grain from an inclosure which he had sown with tares; and every husbandman when he plants his corn does so in the confidence that, according to the uniformity of nature's operations, he will have a harvest of the same. He has no manner of doubt about it. There may be sometimes a question in his mind during a long drought as to whether he shall have a larger or smaller crop, possibly even as to whether he shall have a crop at all; but he knows that if he have any crop, it shall be of the same kind as that which he has planted. On the plane of material nature, then, every one understands, admits, and acts upon this principle as an absolute law admitting of no exceptions—"Whatsoever a man soweth, that shall he also reap."

Now, with these facts before us, we are in a position to understand what is meant when it is said that our life here bears to our condition hereafter the same relation which seed does to that which springs from it. For one thing it means that our thoughts, words and actions here have in them a seminal and germinating principle. They are not like a handful of gravel which, scattered over the earth, remains gravel and nothing else; but they are seeds which, wherever dropped, are falling into a soil whereon, at length, there shall appear a harvest that shall be of the same kind as themselves. Have you ever thought of this, my hearers? There is a principle of life and reproduction in everything that the soul within you does, and in the harvest of the future you must reap that which has sprung up and ripened therefrom. We may not be able quite to realize, at first, all that this implies. But there are experiences in the present life which may assist us to arrive at a more adequate conception of its solemn import. Thoughts tend to reproduce themselves. He who admits a holy suggestion into his mind will find that ever more in the pauses of life, and sometimes, too, even in its bustle and business, things allied to that sacred meditation, and indeed developed by it, will steal into the current of his consciousness and fill his soul with their refreshing influence. Indeed it is just in this way that the devotions of the closet come at length to hallow the entire day; the seeds sown in that hour so quickly germinate that the life is perfumed by the fragrance of their blossoming. But the same thing is true on the other side. Let a man take in an evil thought, and it will constantly reproduce itself within his mind, and either torment him with its ever-recurring loathsomeness, or draw him away with its seductive influence. The sight of an impure painting; the reading of a bad book; the hearing of a song in which the witchery of music is wedded to the vice of sensuousness, will keep returning to the memory, either as something to be battled with, or as an influence that will finally conquer us—and this is all owing to the fact that thought is seminal and reproductive. So in regard to words. They are not dead things—like counters in a game, to which some have compared them. In a very holy sense the Lord Jesus has said in his parable, "The seed is the word," but it is no less true that every word is a seed. It reproduces itself either in blessing or in curse. Do you want an illustration? Then, take the case of the profane swearer, and you will see how from the root of his first oath all his black blasphemy has sprung until he is so much a slave to his evil habit as hardly to be conscious of the utterance of those things which send a shudder through the hearts of his hearers. While again, on the other hand, the speech of the good man increases in attractiveness with his constant practice of reverence.

What, indeed, is the great law of habit, when you come to think it out, but just another form of the principle of my text, "Whatsoever a man soweth, that shall he also reap"? And that question may fitly introduce us to the thought that our actions, as well as words, are reproductive. You know how true that is in the case of the victim of strong drink, and the votary of gambling. But these cases are only *large type illustrations* of what is seen, if we care to look for it, in other actions. That which we have done recurs to us either to haunt us as remorse, or to bless us in the approval of conscience and of God. We have by our first commission of it so sown it that it shall bear fruit, either to upbraid us for being its creators, or to bless us for having called it into being. No article of our conduct ever stands alone. It may pass from our memory, indeed, for a time, even as the seed in the soil decays and dies; yet, at length, in the reproduction of it we shall be made to think of it and to connect it with its fruit. What a graphic illustration of this we have in the case of Joseph's brethren! They sold him into slavery, and when they had palmed their lie upon their father they thought no more upon their guilt. They had rid themselves of an inconvenient reporter of their evil doings, and so all was well. But when that which they had sowed in the captivity of their brother was reaped by them in the shape of their own imprisonment, *then* they said one to another, "We were verily guilty concerning our brother: when we saw the anguish of his soul; when he besought us and we would not hear; therefore is this distress come upon us." And can we help seeing how the lie which Jacob told to Isaac bore fruit to Jacob's own misery in the falsehood of his sons to himself? Thus, either in our own enlarged and habitual commission of it, or in the being compelled to endure it at the hands of others, sin is ever, by its own reproduction, the punishment of sin. And whether we think of it or not, in all our thoughts and words and actions we are sowing seeds of which we shall have to reap the harvest by-and-by.

But the same thing is seen, very often, in the relation of one segment of our life upon earth to the remainder of that life. It is one of the commonest of commonplaces that youth is the seed-time of life. If that be improved as it ought to be, the rest of the earthly existence will be noble; but if that be wasted, the remainder will never be what it might have been and ought to have been. The man may receive regeneration, indeed, through repentance unto life, and in some aspects of his later history there may even be good brought out of the former evil; but never can he be what he might have been if he had not to reap in his age the harvest from the seed he sowed in youth; and if he do not repent at all, the life as a

THE HARVEST OF RETRIBUTION AND REWARD. 177

whole is a seed from which the ultimate harvest must be terrible. There is a way of speaking on this subject, indeed, which would lead us to suppose that the "sowing of wild oats," as it is called, is merely a necessary stage in the development of a young man, and that if, after that has been gone through, he can be led to settle down, no great harm will come. But, not to say that there is a tremendous uncertainty in that *if*, we must bear in mind that from every seed planted there is and must be a growth, and that in some way or other God will make a man possess the sins of his youth. The sowing is to be followed by a reaping, and the crop will be of the same kind as the seed; so that after all there are few things in life so expensive and so absolutely insane as this same scattering of wild oats, at which so many foolishly make mirth as if it were a thing of course. Young man! remember it: you shall have to reap all that you sow. It may not be this year, or next year, but you *shall* reap—for as the French lady said to the great ecclesiastic, "My Lord Cardinal! God does not pay at the end of every week, but at the last he pays!"

Now, with these experiences in the present state of existence fresh in our remembrance, we can better apprehend the truth regarding future retribution which is taught by my text. Just as individual thoughts, and words, and actions are seminal; just as one part of our earthly life is a seed-time for another; so our life on earth, as a whole, is the germ from which our eternity shall spring. Retribution is the reaping of the harvest from the seeds which all through our earthly existence we were sowing. The sinner will be given up to his sin—left to it and in it; the saint will rise to higher holiness, and find happiness and reward in the things which most he delighted in on

8*

earth. There is nothing arbitrary here. I have no doubt, indeed, that in heaven there will be a special bestowment of reward; and in hell a positive infliction of judicial punishment; but still, as one of my revered instructors has remarked on these verses, "It surely deserves notice that in very many passages of Scripture the misery of the irreclaimably impenitent is represented as the native necessary result of their own conduct. The whole economy of God's moral government would need to be altered; the constituent principles of man's nature would need to be changed, before those who live and die 'carnal' can be really happy in another world." * That which a man has fostered here in himself will be the source of his blessedness or the fountain of his woe hereafter. In a word, *himself* will be his reward or retribution, and that self he is making now, by the thoughts and words and actions in which he is indulging. So as he is sowing now he shall reap hereafter; nay, more explicitly, *that* which he is sowing now he will reap hereafter. It is as absurd to suppose that if we are wedded to sin here we shall be holy, and therefore happy, in the future life, as it is for a man who has planted thorns to expect from them a return of grapes. And if we delight in the Lord after the inner man, and find our joy in serving Christ on earth, we may as rationally look for heaven in the state beyond as the farmer who sows barley may anticipate that he shall reap the same. To expect anything else is to "mock God" by disregarding the law which he has written as clearly on our moral constitution as that of fruit bearing after its kind is written on the vegetable kingdom. Here then are the two things that underlie the figure of my text,

---

* John Brown, D.D., in exposition of the Galatians in loco.

—the present life is the seed-plot of the future state; and the harvest which we reap in eternity is the same in character and quality as that which now we sow.

II. But the second thought suggested by the words before us is that there are only two kinds of seed which we can sow in our earthly existence. The apostle mentions sowing to the flesh, and sowing to the spirit—these are all; and each of us is doing one or the other. There is no third alternative. It behooves us, then, to make very sure what these two are. The "flesh" is Paul's term for unrenewed human nature. And if you look at the section of this epistle to which the text belongs you can be at no loss to discover what he means by the phrase "he that soweth to his flesh." For thus he writes: "The works of the flesh are manifest, which are these, adultery, fornication, uncleanness, lasciviousness, idolatry, witchcraft, hatred, variance, wrath, strife, seditions, heresies, envyings, murders, drunkenness, revelings, and such like"; and lest anyone should imagine that only very heinous sins, which rank in the eyes of men as crimes as well as vices, come under this classification, he has still further indicated the scope of the term when he says, "Let us not be desirous of vainglory, provoking one another, envying one another." Nay, as seems to me very plain from the verse immediately preceding the text, he includes the stinginess which witholds suitable maintenance from the Christian minister under that "sowing to the flesh" of which the result is corruption. And as he has declared that "they that are Christ's have crucified the flesh with the affections and lusts," it is also perfectly clear that all who are not Christ's, and who have not crucified the flesh, are sowing to the flesh. On the other hand, the "spirit" throughout this passage is most naturally taken to mean not the Holy Spirit, but that which is the proper antithesis to unrenewed human nature, namely, the renewed man.

Thus, then, we get the result that the unregenerated man is "sowing to the flesh," and the regenerated man—he who is in Christ and therefore a new creature—is "sowing to the spirit." So it comes to this, that if we would make the best of the present life as the germ of the future state, we must be born again; and the evidence that we are thus regenerated will be furnished by our manifestation of the fruit of the Spirit " which is, "Love, joy, peace, long-suffering, gentleness, goodness, faith, meekness, temperance." Nay, more, as in the natural world that which we take for seed has already grown and is itself a fruit, so these virtues which are themselves in one sense the fruit of our regeneration are in another the seed of the Spirit from which are yet to spring up the blessedness and reward of heaven. My brethren, these are great principles. They have a tremendous sweep; and yet they bear down with all their force upon each individual among us. They tell us that unless through faith in Christ and the agency of his Spirit we have been born again we are and must be sowing to the flesh. I dare not make any exceptions here, and so the question for each of us—a question whose answer carries the whole color and complexion of our eternity in it—is, "Have I been born again?" Oh! if it be that a soul here is still unrenewed, may God the Holy Ghost use the truth which I have now brought before you in quickening that soul to life in Christ!

III. But, in the third place, the text suggests that

in the case of both sowings the harvest will be an increase. Usually the crop is a multiplication of the seed. As the parable has it, in some it is thirty-fold, in some sixty-fold, and in some an hundred-fold. So, too, it is always the case that the quantity reaped is proportioned to the quantity sown. "He that soweth sparingly shall reap also sparingly; but he that soweth bountifully shall reap also bountifully." There shall be degrees in retribution and reward. The ragged urchin in our city streets, who has not had the opportunities of a Christian household, will not have to gather such a harvest of suffering from his sowing to the flesh as will he who has sinned against light and privilege of the highest order. The heathen, who have not heard of Christ, will not have the same future as those who, having had the Saviour preached to them, have defiantly rejected him. The Lord said unto Capernaum: "It shall be more tolerable for the land of Sodom in the day of judgment than for thee." So, in the matter of retribution the condition of each will be proportioned to his guilt. But the same principle holds in reward. There shall be degrees of glory as well as of perdition. He who creeps in at last to the kingdom through the fast closing gate, and by a death-bed repentance becomes regenerated, shall not have a place like that of the man whose entire life has been devoted to the Lord Jesus. He who made the one pound into ten received in the parable authority over ten cities. He who from the one gained as much as made it five was set over five cities. All this goes to show that while it is wholly of grace that reward is granted to any believer, yet the reward itself is graduated for each according to the magnitude of the service. We all admit that in the matter of reward; but we too often forget that the same principle holds in respect to punishment; and I cannot but think that if more prominence had been given to that aspect of the subject there would be less difficulty felt in accepting that doctrine which has been such an offense to many modern inquirers.

But though there is thus a proportion in quantity between the seed and the crop, the harvest is always an increase on that which was sown. From the seed of the flesh the ripened result is corruption, which is flesh in its most revolting state. From the seed of the spirit the full ear is life everlasting, which is eternal holiness with its concomitant of endless happiness. And what can I say to make these ideas more clear and forcible than this simple presentation of them is? Corruption! The delirium tremens of the drunkard, and the living death of the sensualist whose sin has found him out here on earth, may help us to understand something of what that must mean in eternity, and for the rest I must ask Byron to help me out. For these are his words describing even earthly desolation of heart:

> "It is as if the dead could feel
> The icy worm around them steal,
> And shudder, as the reptiles creep
> To revel o'er their rotting sleep,
> Without the power to scare away
> The cold consumers of their clay."

But enough of that! I turn rather to the other side, and bid you remember that the highest happiness of the Christian's experience on earth will be but like as the faint light of early dawn is to the meridian day, when it is compared with the blessedness of heaven. The harvest is always an increase. We plant a single grain, we pluck a full ear; we sow in handfuls, we reap in bosomfuls; we scatter bushels, but we gather in rich granary stores. The remorse of earth is but the germ of the despair of hell. The holiness of the present is only the bud from which will blossom that vision of God which is the full-flowered beatitude of heaven.

Now, if all this be true, see how it invests the present life with infinite importance. It used to be said by the apostles of infidelity, under the name of secularism, that belief in a future state unfits men for the performance of the duties of the life that now is by fixing their minds on that which is as yet in the distance. But the course of thought which we have followed this morning utterly falsifies such a statement. It were just as rational to allege that the husbandman by looking forward to the harvest incapacitates himself for the work of the spring-time; or that the youth by setting his ambition on after success is thereby disqualified for the prosecution of his early education, as it is to affirm that faith in the future life prevents us from performing the work of to-day. The truth rather is that it intensifies the importance of the present by focusing upon it the issues of eternity. It makes us all the more careful to do the work that lies at our hands, not in the fleshly manner of the unrenewed man, but after the spiritual method of the regenerated soul. Every thought we think, every word we speak, every action we perform, every opportunity of service neglected or improved, is a seed sown by us the fruit of which shall multiply either into untold miseries or myriad blessings in the eternity into which we go. That is the teaching of the word of God, and who shall say that such a view of the case does not magnify, rather than diminish, the significance of the present? In the stirring history of English martyrology we read of an eminent victim that on one occasion he was taken from his dungeon to a chamber which was hung round with tapestry; that there he was being gradually drawn into a conversation regarding himself and his companions when in a moment of quietness he heard the sound of the nib of a pen moving upon paper, as if some one were writing behind the arras; and that immediately thereupon he became silent, for well he knew that by a thoughtless word he might bring upon both himself and his brethren the severest suffering. But, my hearers, the actions in which now we engage are seeds whose fruit shall be eternal, and when we know and believe that shall we be less careful of them than he was of his speech? It is told of a famous painter that he was remarkable for the careful manner in which he went about his work, and when one asked him why he took such pains his answer was: "Because I paint for eternity." Beloved, shall this be so in the case of one who is trying to secure a lasting earthly fame, and shall we not be considerate in all our ways, knowing that what we are doing now shall have an eternal effect upon our character and condition? Every day we live we are treasuring up for ourselves wrath against the day of wrath and revelation of the righteous judgment of God, or we are laying up for ourselves treasures in heaven, "where neither moth nor rust doth corrupt." What need, then, that we should daily consider what shall be the end of these things, and whether we are sowing to the flesh or to the spirit? Let the thoughtless among us be startled into earnestness by this solemn consideration; and if there be those here who are seeking prayerfully to sow to the spirit, but in their battle with discouragements are filled with despondency lest at length there should be little result, let them take courage; they *shall* reap. It may not be immediately, but they shall reap in due season, if they faint not. It is to "mock" God to think otherwise, and when I put it so, my Christian brethren, you, I know, will be the last to incur any such guilt as that. Hold on, then, though your sowing should be in sorrow. Here is a song for your inspiration. Sing it, and as you honor God by the faith which it breathes you will acquire new strength for the work which you are carrying through. "They that sow in tears shall reap in joy. He that goeth forth and weepeth, bearing precious seed, shall doubtless come again with rejoicing, bringing his sheaves with him."

FEBRUARY 27, 1881.

DEBTORS.

ROMANS I. 14. *I am debtor both to the Greeks and to the barbarians: both to the wise and to the unwise.*

THE Greeks styled "barbarians" all those who did not speak that polished language of which they were so justly proud. In the mouth of a Jew, therefore, the phrase "Greeks and barbarians" included all Gentiles. So, when Paul affirms that he is "a debtor both to the Greeks and to the barbarians, both to the wise and to the unwise," his meaning is that he is under obligation to Gentiles universally without respect to race or culture; and in the text he gives that as a reason why he was so anxious to visit Rome—because that was the place where he was most likely to meet representatives of all existing nationalities and of all grades of intelligence. The language is commercial, and yet the obligation which it acknowledges is not precisely that which a merchant commonly understands by the words. Debt is that which a man owes to another for something which he has bought from him on trust, or received from him as a loan. But Paul was not in any such way indebted to the Gentiles. He had never bought anything in their markets without paying its price. They had not lent him any sums of money on interest. No human being had any pecuniary claim against him. He was, in that sense, the most independent of men, for he owed no one a penny.

Neither did he owe the Gentiles any gratitude for favors which he had received at their hands, for in almost every city in which he labored he had encountered persecution, and suffered wrong. It was not therefore, on the ground of anything which he had obtained *from* the Gentiles that Paul acknowledged himself to be their debtor, but solely on the ground of that which he had received from another *for* them. At his conversion to Christianity he had been commissioned to the Gentiles " to open their eyes and to turn them from darkness to light and from the power of Satan unto God, that they might receive forgiveness of sins, and inheritance among them which are sanctified"; and so he regarded himself as "the apostle of the Gentiles." Just as at a far later date John Wesley declared that the world was his parish, so Paul looked upon himself as a bishop whose diocese included all the Gentile nationalities. "The glorious gospel of the blessed God" had been "committed" to his "trust" for their behoof; he had been "allowed of God to be put in trust with the gospel" for their benefit, and, therefore, that he might be a faithful steward of the mysteries of God, he was exceedingly desirous of preaching the truth as it is in Jesus to men of every nation, and of every degree. He could not honestly hold it back. It had not been given to him for himself alone, and if he had attempted to keep it from his fellow-men he would have been false to the trust which had been committed to his care, and could not have vindicated himself either at the bar of conscience or at the bar of God.

The case stood thus: On the one hand he had himself been signally blessed by the Lord Jesus Christ. When he was ignorantly rushing on in a career of antagonism to the truth, and had become a persecutor and a murderer, he was apprehended by the mercy of the Most High, and at the very moment when his eyes were opened to the discovery of his guilt he received the assurance of his forgiveness. Henceforth a new life began in him. Everything was changed to him; and in recognition of the love which had been shown to him he placed himself soul, body and spirit at the disposal of the Lord. Had it pleased the Saviour so to employ him, he would probably have preferred to remain at Jerusalem and work in his service there; but it was not for him to choose, and when he was specially commissioned to go to the Gentiles, he went with his whole soul to do his Master's bidding. Underneath this obligation, therefore, in the heart of Paul there lay all his gratitude to the Redeemer for his own salvation, and he sought in this practical way, by laboring for the benefit of others, to show the magnitude of his appreciation of all that he owed to Christ.

Then, on the other side, there were the clamant needs of the Gentile world. The vision of the man of Macedonia crying, "Come over and help us," was, indeed, a special divine indication to him of what the Lord would have him to do; but it came to him in that form and at that time, because it was already in the line of all his aspirations, and desires, and purposes. He knew the hollowness of the idolatries of the Gentiles; he had seen the degradation to which their worship led; and having learned the value of his own soul at the cross of Christ, he was eager to be the means of communicating the same revelation, and conveying the same life to them. This was the spontaneous prompting of the new nature which he had received from Christ by the regeneration and in-dwelling of the Holy Spirit; but that yearning of his own was intensified, and made no mere spasmodic emotion, but an abiding principle of action, in him by the reception of his commission as the "apostle of the Gentiles." For that commission made him personally responsible for their becoming acquainted with the gospel of the Lord Jesus, and so, wherever he came into contact with them, he could not rest until he had preached it to them. Whether they should accept it or not rested with themselves. That was a matter of their own choice. But as for the proclamation of it to them, he had no alternative; for necessity was laid upon him, and he felt that it was at his peril if he should hold his peace.

How that motive operated in him is seen in a very peculiar manner by his course at Athens. He was in that classic city alone. He had not intended, so far as appears, without the support of companions, to do anything publicly there; but when he saw the state of things among the people his spirit was so stirred that, in defiance of all the dictates of prudence, and at the risk of scorn and persecution, he could not but speak. And when we get thus up to the fountain-head of motive in his heart, it becomes easy for us to understand how it came that Paul was enabled to do so much both for the church and for the world. He was always on the outlook for opportunities of paying this debt both to the Greeks and to the barbarians; both to the wise and to the unwise. He was not afraid to speak to men like Sergius Paulus, or Festus; and yet he was not above seeking the salvation of a runaway slave like Onesimus. He was equally earnest in the little prayer-meeting of women at Philippi where Lydia was converted, and upon the summit of Areopagus where he was surrounded by the proud philosophers of Athens; for he was in debt to both alike, and he sought to have himself clear from the blood of both. He could not rest under this obligation, but went in obedience to it from city to city until he reached Rome at last; and even there, when he was an "ambassador in bonds," he found a congregation large enough for his ambition in the soldier that was chained to his right arm. He never saw a man without remembering that he had a debt to pay to him, and so, not more for the benefit of the stranger than for the exoneration of his own conscience in the manifestation of fidelity to the trust which he had received for him, he sought his highest welfare. Unlike the dishonest debtor who flees from land to land that he may escape his creditors, Paul was ever on the move that he might fairly and honestly meet the obligations that rested upon him, and might have new opportunities of coming into contact with those for whom God had appointed him trustee. Brethren, when I put it so, I cease to wonder at the unwearying assiduity of the great apostle, while at the same time I am filled with shame at the poor, paltry littleness of our modern Christianity when compared with his. For, while there was undeniably a specialty in the case of Paul, inasmuch as he was distinctly and divinely commissioned to be the apostle of the Gentiles, the obligation to which he here refers is general and rests on every individual believer. In him it came to a distinct and definite head, and took an individual and peculiar direction under the articulate command of the Lord. But his was only a specific instance of a generic principle, and that principle holds to-day for us as really and powerfully as it did for him.

Now what is that principle? It is this, that personal possession of any peculiar privilege is of the nature of a trust, and involves the obligation that the privilege shall be used by the individual not for his own pleasure or profit merely, but for the welfare of those who are not similarly blessed. What I have that another has not is to be used by me not for my own aggrandizement, but for the good of that other as well as for my own. It is not mine in the sense of its being simply for my own enjoyment. I may not say regarding it: "Is it not lawful for me to do what I will with mine own?" for I do not hold it as of absolute possession. It is committed to me as a trust. I hold it merely as a steward holds that which is another's; and I am to use it not for myself alone, but also with a view to the benefit of those who have not the same privilege as has been conferred on me. The greatness of exceptional endowment, of whatever sort it may be, carries with it an obligation to similar exceptional greatness of service. The highest of all, by virtue of his very elevation, is to be the servant of all. The power of the strong is, shall I say? divinely mortgaged in the interests of the weak; the sufferer whom I have the means of relieving has a God-given claim upon me for that relief; and the ignorant, whom I am able to instruct, is by God entitled to that instruction at my hands. He who has, is in debt to him who has not. This is clearly the true interpretation of such a parable as that of the good Samaritan; and indeed it is the true and proper outcome of the gospel itself.

I know that it seems to run counter to the common modes of thought of the world; but it is not the less surely the Christian view of the matter because of that. Selfishness would repudiate all such indebtedness. The man of power says he has won his position, and that he has a right to use it as he will, no matter what may become of others in the process. The man of wealth thinks that the merit of his acquisition is all his own, and that to talk of his being in debt to others because he is so wealthy is a ridiculous absurdity. The man of education is apt to become proud of his learning. Has he not amassed it all by his own efforts? May he not therefore keep it to himself? or if he wishes to diffuse it may he not do so on his own terms, and so as to minister to his own profit? And so with all other possessors—each in his own measure is prompted to say of his property like another Nebuchadnezzar, "Is not this great Babylon that I have built for the house of my kingdom and for the honor of my majesty?" and so each has become, by virtue of his possessions, just so much the more an oppressor and an affliction to those who are beneath him. That has been the world's way.

But Christ has inaugurated a new dispensation and reversed all that by introducing the principle on which I am now insisting, and already we see indications of its operations among us. Take power, for example, and how readily now men understand and assent to the statement that it has its duties—and that is only another word for debts—as well as its prerogatives? The chief magistrate of this Republic is presumably the most powerful individual in it, yet he may not use his power simply for his own ends. True, he is limited by the Constitution, but still outside of the Constitution altogether, and in the public opinion of the country, there is the feeling that in numberless ways which no written constitution could enumerate he owes it to the community to exert his power for the public welfare, and not either for personal or party purposes. It may be difficult to enforce that obligation in any legal way, but still it is there, assented to by his own heart as well as required by his fellow-citizens. Then as to wealth: the conviction is becoming stronger among us that riches bring obligations with them, and that the man who is blessed with them owes certain duties, that is to say, is himself a debtor, to the community of which he is a member. No civil statute, indeed, could define precisely what these duties are, and no legal tribunal could enforce them; but still they are there, and the obligation to perform them is not the less imperative or important because the measure of obedience to them is left in each case to the impulse of the individual heart. The rich man who makes himself a great Dead Sea into which all the streams of his effort run, and from which nothing flows out, is despised; while every one honors him who uses his money for the good of the people. That shows how thoroughly this principle that possession implies trust has permeated our modern life. The same is true of education, and of all the other things which become the property of a man, whether by inheritance or through God's blessing on his own exertions. True, we are a very long way yet either from a universal or from a full recognition of this principle in general society. But it is making its way; and what I am anxious that you should observe is, that it has had its origin in the gospel; and that in the measure in which it advances it will diminish the perils that are, I fear, incident to our modern civilization.

It has had its origin in the gospel, for, until Christ came, men cared little for anything outside of themselves. The question of Cain, "Am I my brother's keeper?" gives the key to the explanation of all the enormities of the ancient civilizations; and after a survey of the history of the world before the advent, one might employ the preacher's words: "So I returned and considered all the oppressions that are done under the sun; and behold the tears of such as were oppressed; and they had no comforter; and on the side of their oppressors there was power, but they had no comforter." But Christ brought the power of the highest to the help of the lowest; and he taught his followers to look "not every man on his own things, but every man also on the things of others." He condemned the selfish and complacent policy of passing misery, or sorrow, or want, or oppression "by on the other side," and commissioned all his followers—as really as he commissioned Paul to be apostle of the Gentiles—to use all the resources at their command for the mitigation of the sufferings and the removal of the ignorance of their fellow-men, so that each of them might say, "I am a debtor both to the wise and to the unwise."

And this principle, thus introduced by the gospel, furnishes that which is needed to meet the perils of our modern civilization. The tendency of the times is to increase the separation between different classes in the community. We continually hear it said that the rich are becoming richer, and the poor are growing poorer. The gulf which has long yawned between employers and employed is widening; and the distance between the avenues and the tenement houses is constantly becoming greater. Now some of that is no doubt inevitable. We can never have a dead level of absolute equality. It is as natural for society to divide itself into classes as it is for the tree to diverge into branches. And though there be no aristocracy so-called among us, the divisions are just as clearly though it may be not so strongly marked in this land as they are in some European countries. The truth is that such divergence is everywhere unavoidable, although, in these days, even the very triumphs of modern machinery have helped to make it worse than perhaps otherwise it might have been. And the thing has to be accepted. We cannot get rid of it, and we must not seek by any factitious means, far less by any violent means, to remove it. What we have to do is to bring the gospel principle of my text to bear upon it with more force. For see how it takes the poison out of all this diversity of condition among men. It makes the powerful man the trustee for the weak ; the rich man the guardian of the poor ; the learned man the teacher of the ignorant, and the free man the emancipator of the enslaved. Thus by so much the more powerful one becomes, by so much the better it will be for the weak beneath his protection ; by so much the wealthier the rich man is, by just so much the better will it be for the poor to whom he is a debtor ; and so with all other possessions. When his followers disputed among themselves which should be greatest, the Lord, instead of seeking to uproot ambition, gave a new definition of greatness as service, and bade them be ambitious of that, thereby transmuting that principle which had been the blackest curse of humanity into a means of richest blessing. And in precisely the same way here, the gospel, far from blotting out all distinctions in society, as the communist would do, makes the very privileges which mark the distinction between a higher class and a lower the basis of obligation, so that the one is the debtor of the other, and the obligation increases with the increase of the privilege. In this regard it is a solemn thing to be the possessor of a special blessing, for while it is a boon it always brings a responsibility, and makes its receiver a debtor to others who are less fortunate than himself. That is the Christian principle ; and when men generally accept and act upon it, the millennium shall have begun. Meanwhile it is ours, each in his own place, to carry it fully and faithfully through, and so to supply what in us lies of that wholesome and corrective influence that is needed to counteract the selfishness that is seeking to disintegrate society.

But if this principle introduced by Christ is thus making its way in the world, we should expect to find its highest manifestation in the Christian church. And here, though it has not yet attained anything like its legitimate development, we are not entirely disappointed, for it has put the heroism and self-sacrifice into our religious life. It has originated and sustained the great missionary enterprise; and though the church as a whole has not yet anything like come up to the level of Paul, not to speak of that of his Divine Master, still there have been individuals who are not unworthy to be compared even with the great apostle of the Gentiles. While we here at home are enjoying our privileges with self-complacency and satisfaction, and thinking that we perform our part by giving a small annual donation to the American Board, the men whom that Board has commissioned are laboring with devoted heroism to carry the gospel into benighted lands. Only two days ago I received the account of the pioneer work in 1881 of those noble men who have gone to begin a mission in West Central Africa, and as I read the thrilling narrative of patience and self-sacrifice, of long journeying cheerfully undertaken and severe sickness meekly borne, I felt ashamed of myself, and recognized that I am not worthy to unloose the latchets of their shoes. The people around them will have it that they have gone to trade. They insist upon it that they must have gone to receive. They cannot understand that they have gone to give. They look upon them with wonder when they learn their purpose; and the day is coming when they shall be spoken of as among the Pauls of this nineteenth century. These men have no gain to seek of an earthly sort. They have gone like the apostle to pay a debt—your debt and mine; and their example ought to quicken and stimulate us to similar self-denial here in our own city. For there is a sphere here also at our very doors for the operation of this principle, that every privilege is of the nature of a trust.

We all admit that the possession of spiritual blessing involves responsibility, but in making the admission we think almost exclusively of responsibility for ourselves. We feel that because we *have* so much, therefore we ought to *be* so much. Because we have the Bible and the sanctuary and church ordinances, and the like, therefore we ought to make the best and the most of these for our own individual sanctification. Our holiness ought to be the result of our privileges. And so far so well. That is all true, and no one can gainsay it, but it is not all the truth; for we have these privileges that we may pass them on to others. Remember, the principle of my text is, that he who has, is debtor to him who has not. If we have the Bible and others are without it, then we owe the Bible to those who have not yet received it. If we have a church edifice, and others have no place wherein they may gather for the worship of God, and no means to rear one, while we have the power to help them, then we owe churches to those destitute ones. If we have a minister whose words on the Lord's day are full of inspiration and strength to us, and others have no stated ordinances, then we owe it to these others that men shall be commissioned to preach unto them the word of life, and to gather them into Christian communities for mutual edification and for the further extension of the gospel of Christ. Yes, I say we owe it to them, for the plea here is not to our generosity but to our justice, and unless we honor it, we must stand forth at last before God and the world as defaulters, and that in a department where the loss from our unfaithfulness is one that cannot be computed in dollars and cents, but must be reckoned in the souls of immortal men. Ah! if we who profess and call ourselves Christians did but feel the full force of this obligation as Paul felt it, how soon would the world be converted unto Christ? How easy then would become the solution of that problem which presses so heavily upon the heart of every faithful minister in this city, How shall the great population round about us be thoroughly evangelized? There are Christians enough in all our churches to do the work if each of them would say with Paul, "I am a debtor" to all around me who know not the gospel of the Lord, and would realize that he has received the glad evangel as a trust for those who have not yet heard its message of mercy. My brethren, when I put the matter thus I am overwhelmed with the sense of the obligation that I am seeking to enforce, and am constrained to cry for myself as my own shortcomings rise up before me: "Deliver me from blood-guiltiness, O God, thou God of my salvation." We execrate the deed of her who, having received a ring from the imprisoned nobleman under the promise that she would take it and let it plead for him with his queen, held back the token and allowed him to go unforgiven to the block. We loathe the treachery of those who, having in their hands a reprieve for the brave old Covenanter, kept it to themselves and sent him to the scaffold. And we! God help us! we, with the gospel that proclaims mercy to mankind in our hands, let multitudes go down undone to an eternity without telling them the good news or seeking to lift them from their degradation! Yet, let us be thankful, we are doing something—would that it were more—but we are doing something, and to-day you are asked to give your contributions to keep up the work. The Bethany Mission makes its appeal to you once more. It asks you for the means of carrying on its operations for another year. Give it in full, and let the offering of to-day be the prophecy of a yet larger liberality when you shall be requested to rear for them a building of their own.* We are debtors to those seven hundred children and to those one hundred and twenty church members, because we are debtors to the Lord Jesus Christ. May he help us now in some degree to meet the obligation!

February 26, 1882.

---

* It is gratifying to be able to state that since this discourse was preached the new Bethany Church, on Tenth Avenue near Thirty-sixth Street, has been built by the Broadway Tabernacle Church, at a cost of $58,000, of which about three-fourths has been already paid.

THE REVELATION AT THE BUSH.

DEUTERONOMY xxxiii. 16. The good-will of him that dwelt in the bush.

In recent days there has been much debate among critics as to the authorship of the book of Deuteronomy, and many have supposed that its date must be fixed far down in the history of Israel. The grounds on which such an opinion is advanced seem to me far too slender for the support of so sweeping a conclusion. The objections to it are so serious as to be utterly insurmountable save by evidence of the clearest sort; and the different views which have been substituted for that commonly believed among us are so inconsistent with each other as to be mutually destructive. For all these reasons, therefore, I am constrained, in spite of the learned dissertations of the so-called higher critics, to rest in the conviction that, with the exception of the last chapter, and some few editorial additions here and there which can be easily distinguished even by the English reader, the book, as a whole, is, as it purports to be, the work of Moses himself.

But, however the case may stand with the work as a unit, the words of my text are decisive as to the authorship of the blessing of which they form a part. Every jurist is familiar with the story of the judge who upset the argument in favor of the antiquity of a document by holding it up between him and the light, and revealing in the water-mark of the paper itself a date far later than that which had been claimed for the writing upon it. Now, such a water-mark is the phrase before us; only in this case it goes to establish the antiquity rather than the recentness of that of which it forms a part and into which it is inwoven. For the reference in it is to a personal experience. It was, therefore, quite natural that Moses should make it, and just as improbable that it should be made by another. The force of this consideration becomes all the stronger when we reflect that, unusual as the experience alluded to undeniably was, there is not a single reference to it in the whole compass of Hebrew literature but this. None of the writers at any one of the different dates which have been fixed upon by the higher critics for the production of this book has said a word that even hints at the vision which was given to Moses at the bush. Neither in the psalms nor in the prophets, whether before or after the exile, do we find the slightest mention of it, and so if an unknown author in any one of those eras had been seeking to personate Moses, it is in the highest degree unlikely, judging by contemporary documents, that he would have sought to put these words into his mouth. So far as appears from the other books of the Hebrews, and however unaccountable to us it may seem, the revelation made by Jehovah at the bush had been very largely lost sight of by them, or, at all events, it was not a thing usually referred to among them, and therefore it would have been unnatural for any one writing then, in the name of Moses, to speak in this casual and incidental way about it. But, on the other hand, how perfectly natural such an allusion is in the mouth of Moses himself! For he could never forget that day in Horeb. Beautifully has Matthew Henry said in this connection: "Many a time God had appeared to Moses, but now [that] he is just dying, he seems to have the most pleasing remembrance of that which was the first time, when his acquaintance with the visions of the Almighty first began, and his correspondence with heaven was first settled; that was a 'time of love' never to be forgotten." So it was quite artless and unpremeditated in Moses to speak here of "the good-will of him that dwelt in the bush," and the reference is what may be called a water-mark which proves the authenticity of the tribal blessings of which it forms a part. It is a little thing, such as no pretended Moses could have thought of, but perfectly natural for Moses himself to say; and by all the laws of evidence the very littleness of the thing makes it just so much the stronger as a proof.

But, leaving this matter of criticism, let us go on to inquire what we are to understand by "the good-will of him that dwelt in the bush." You are familiar with the history. After forty years of shepherd-life in Midian, during which, by communion with God amid nature's wildest solitudes, Moses had wrought himself clear of that self-confident rashness which had marked his earliest attempt at advancing the cause of the Hebrews in Egypt, he was startled with the sight, in the desert, of a bush which seemed to be on fire and yet was not consumed. As he turned aside to look upon the strange spectacle, he heard a voice which he instinctively recognized as that of God commanding him to put off his shoes from his feet, because the place whereon he stood was holy ground; and then, after long conference, he was constrained to accept a commission to deliver his kinsmen from the cruelty of the oppressor. There was here, therefore, a revelation both in symbol and in word. These two ran parallel to each other, or, rather, they were not so much two as one, and when Moses speaks of "him that dwelt in the bush," he must be understood as referring to the sum total of that truth regarding God which he received both from what he saw and from what he heard on the memorable occasion to which he refers. To get at that, therefore, we shall have to consider both, that we may read each in the light of the other; and when we do so, we shall discover not only that they mutually supplement each other, but, also, that they have a wondrously precious significance for us.

I. Let us take, first, the revelation through the symbol. Moses saw a bush apparently aflame, and yet unburned. The fire did no injury to the acacia branch, but only made the greenness of the leaves more conspicuous by the contrast. Now what was the meaning of this emblematic representation? It has commonly been regarded as a figure of the Israelites in Egypt subjected to the fiery ordeal of persecution at the hand of Pharaoh; and yet only multiplying the more the more they were oppressed. The church of God, so it is said, is here shown to be indestructible; and this is proved by the martyrology of the ages. In perfect harmony, therefore, with this traditional interpretation of the symbol the Church of Scotland has taken for its seal a representation of the burning bush with the motto, " Nec tamen consumebatur " (" yet it was not consumed "). Now that is truth, and very important truth; it is truth, too, which in any case will come to be included in a full exposition of the meaning of the symbol; but still, though I put it forth in my discourses on the life of Moses as the chief thing taught by this divine object-lesson,* I have come to the conclusion, on mature reflection, that such an

---

* See Moses the Law Giver, p. 47.

interpretation proceeds upon a wrong principle. It makes the fire represent the furnace of affliction in which the Hebrews were then burning; but if that be so, where is the emblem of the divine presence which made holy the place in which it was manifested? If God were there under a visible symbol at all (and we must believe that he was, for does not Moses here speak of him as "dwelling" in the bush?) then he was there invailed in the fire. Under the whole Mosaic economy, God was partially revealed and partially concealed in the glory flame-cloud which as vapor by day and flame by night hovered over the encampment of the tribes in the wilderness, and which at length settled into the Shekinah that dwelt between the cherubim in the holy of holies of the tabernacle. It is, therefore, much more thoroughly in harmony not only with the verbal communications made by Jehovah at the time to Moses, but also with the whole tenor of the Mosaic system, to take the fire here as the form under which Deity for the moment had made Himself visible rather than as the emblem of the furnace to which the Hebrews were exposed in their house of bondage. We have here, in a word, the first appearance of the Shekinah which ultimately overshadowed the mercy seat; and in the command, "Draw not nigh hither," we have the forerunner of the vail which shrouded the innermost sanctuary from view, and kept all irreverent intruders from entering the place which was open only to the high priest, and to him only when he went in with the blood of the atonement. The fire, then, is the visible token of the divine presence.

But what of the bush? The answer is already furnished by our interpretation of the glory flame. It is that in which the presence of God was dwelling, and so we regard it as the emblem of him in whom the true Shekinah abode; in whom the Word became flesh; in whose humanity alone deity could reside without consuming it as it would certainly have consumed any other humanity, and whose glory as of the Only Begotten of the Father men beheld "full of grace, and full of truth." And we may, perhaps, see a corroboration of the truth of this view in the predictions of a later day which spoke after this fashion, "Behold the man whose name is the Branch!" "Behold I will bring forth my servant the Branch." Even as afterwards in the tabernacle one of the great meanings of its symbolism was Incarnation; so we have the same thing here in the bush; and thus the theophany then vouchsafed to Moses takes its place in the line of those anticipations, as I may call them, of the advent, of which we have so many in the Old Testament, and especially reminds us of the appearance of the Peniel angel to Jacob, and that of the Captain of the host of the Lord to Joshua. These were all alike the forecast shadows of him in whom God was "manifest in the flesh," and each had its own light to shed on the wondrous Incarnation for which they were all preparatory. This view of the matter is confirmed by the expressions used in the history to which my text refers, for there we read, "the angel of the Lord appeared to him in the flame of fire out of the midst of a bush"; and "God called unto him out of the midst of the bush," so that no created angel can be meant, but indeed "the Angel of the Covenant," who is the fellow of the Almighty, and who for us men and for our salvation became Incarnate in the Son of Mary.

But God in Christ is thereby also in the church, which is the body of Christ, and as such he is the source of its indestructibility. Here, therefore, we get at the thought which has commonly been connected with this revelation at the bush; but it is subordinate to the main teaching, and indeed an inference from it; and it may be carried still farther, since God in Christ is thereby also in every individual believer, for is not the Christian a temple of the Holy Ghost at once purified and protected by the flame of the indwelling Spirit? Now, if all this be true, the goodwill of him that dwelt in the bush is, in New Testament phraseology, "the grace" or favor "of the Lord Jesus Christ," or, which comes to the same thing, of God in Jesus Christ.

II. But now let us look at the conference of this divine angel with Moses at the bush, and see how this view is confirmed. In reading over these two chapters of Exodus—the third and fourth—we are impressed with the following things concerning the mysterious One who spoke to Moses out of the midst of the bush:

1. In the first place, he calls himself by the incommunicable name. When Moses, shrinking from the magnitude of the task laid upon him, wished to know what he should say if the people to whom he went should ask, Who sent you? what is his name? this answer was given him: "I AM THAT I AM. Thus shalt thou say unto the children of Israel, I AM hath sent me unto you." I AM—it is the expression of independent self-existence—appropriate to none but Deity, whose consciousness is an eternal present. The thought is overwhelming; yet, overwhelming as it is, it is also steadying and comforting in its influence, and I do not wonder that years after Moses had heard these words at the bush, and when he saw his fellow-men falling in death by his side, he found his consolation

in the truth which it revealed, and said in his psalm: "Lord, thou hast been our dwelling-place in all generations. Before the mountains were brought forth, or even thou hadst formed the earth and the world, even from everlasting to everlasting, THOU ART—God." But what I am more concerned to show you now is that in the New Testament we find the same claim advanced by the Lord Jesus Christ; for when the Jews said to him: "Thou art not yet fifty years old, and hast thou seen Abraham?" he replied: "Before Abraham was born I AM." And indeed, as I have more than once showed you,* we have in the fourth gospel a series of similar I AMS, whereby Jesus revealed himself to those around him as the Jehovah of the Old Testament dwelling in human nature, even as here the glory flame abode in the bush. You remember them well. They are such as these: "I AM the bread of life;" "I AM the light of the world;" "I AM the Good Shepherd;" "I AM the door;" "I AM the resurrection and the Life;" "I AM the way, the truth and the Life;" "I AM the true vine;" and the time when, through these announcements, a soul perceives the Deity of Jesus is for that soul the supreme moment of its existence when, like Moses here, it receives its commission to its proper life work. So again, in the opening chapter of the Book of Revelation, we have the Lord speaking of himself in the like fashion, thus: "I AM Alpha and Omega, the beginning and the ending, which is, and which was, and which is to come," while the author of the Epistle to the Hebrews has crystallized the same truth into this dogmatic statement: "Jesus Christ, the same yesterday, to-day, and forever.". So here

---

* See "The Limitations of Life and Other Sermons," p. 23.

again we find that the I AM in the bush is the anticipation of the Jesus whom we know and worship as our Redeemer, and whose " good-will " is that favor in which is life.

2. But, in the second place, we find from this conference at the bush that the divine angel who spoke with Moses there is the covenant God, for he said: "I am the God of thy father, the God of Abraham, the God of Isaac, and the God of Jacob." In his reasoning with the Sadducees of his day, the Saviour drew from these words an argument for the resurrection of the body; for as God is not the God of the dead but of the living, it must follow that Abraham, Isaac, and Jacob were still in existence when God so described himself, and as such would yet have their humanity perfected and glorified. The Sadducees grounded their objection to the resurrection of the body on their rejection of the immortality of the soul, and the Lord answers in this way the underlying heresy of his antagonists, leaving it to his own resurrection to prove the falsity of that which they had built thereon. My business now, however, is not with that aspect of the words, but rather with the covenant relation which they express; and we know that on a memorable occasion Christ startled his hearers with the assertion that many should come from the East and from the West, and should sit down with Abraham and Isaac and Jacob in the kingdom of heaven—words which clearly imply that the kingdom which he founded, and of which he is the head, is the carrying out of the covenant made with the old patriarch, so that he claims to be the God of Abraham, Isaac and Jacob. To the same effect are Paul's words in the Epistle to the Galatians, when he says : "They which are of faith are blessed with faithful Abraham,"

implying that Abraham's faith in Jehovah, as revealed to him, is the same in its nature, its object, and its effects as our faith in the Lord Jesus Christ; that is to say, that he who revealed himself as the God of Abraham is he whom we now know as the Lord Jesus Christ.

3. But in the third place we find from this conference at the bush, that the divine angel who spoke to Moses is the omniscient God who knows all his people's troubles and comes to their deliverance. He said: "I have surely seen the afflictions of my people which are in Egypt and have heard their cry by reason of their taskmasters; for I know their sorrows, and I am come down to deliver them out of the hand of the Egyptians." Pharaoh had long oppressed them, making their lives bitter with hard bondage, and there seemed to be no divine protest against his procedure. It looked almost as if God had forgotten the Hebrews, and for generations they were cruelly maltreated. But he was not unmindful of them, and in the fullness of time he sent Moses to be their emancipator. Now, have we not here in miniature, and on a small scale, the very same thing which we see on the wider area of the world, and in the ampler scope of human history as a whole? For centuries God allowed the Pharaohs to grind the Hebrews in slavery. We cannot understand his silence. His forbearance with evil and injustice is to us incomprehensible. Yet it is a precisely parallel case to his treatment of the human race as a whole, only for "centuries" there we must read millenniums. For long he allowed sin to be apparently triumphant. He did not interpose to check it among the nations generally until the advent. As Paul said to the philosophers at Athens, "the times of this ignorance God overlooked,"

and it was not until the fullness of the time that he came to deliver men from its curse. We cannot understand the delay; but it is in the case of the world no more incomprehensible than it was in that of the Hebrews. True, in the latter the years of the delay were not so numerous, and the people affected were not so many, but the principle in both is the same, and if the Hebrews did not reject their deliverance because it was so long in coming, why should we refuse salvation because Christ did not come to the world sooner with its blessings? More especially as, when he did come, he came with a compassion identical with that expressed for the Hebrews at the bush. Listen to these words: "The Son of Man is come to seek and to save that which was lost." "The Son of Man came not to be ministered unto but to minister, and to give his life a ransom for many." "I am come that ye may have life and may have it more abundantly." Are they not all in harmony with this? "I am come down to deliver them out of the hand of the Egyptians." May we not infer, therefore, that they came from the same heart, and that the Jehovah of the bush is the Jesus of the cross?

4. But, in the fourth place, we see from this conference at the bush that the divine angel who spoke to Moses there is the long-suffering God who bears with the waywardness of his people. How tenderly he treated Moses on that occasion! From the extreme of rashness the son of Amram had recoiled to that of timidity; and he who, forty years before, attempted to run without being sent, now seeks to decline his commission altogether. He is profuse in excuses, such as that he was unworthy of the honor which was offered him; that he was unable to answer the Israelites if they should ask him "Who sent you?": that

even if he went the people would not believe him; and that he was not eloquent, but slow of speech and of a slow tongue. These were the pretexts which he put forward in order, if possible, to evade the duty that was laid upon him, but out of them all God nourished him into such strength that he went at length, and became the leader of the Exodus. Now, it is scarcely possible for any one to read the account of this conference without being reminded of our Lord's training of his chosen apostles; how he bore with their weaknesses and waywardnesses, teaching them as they were able to receive it, and bringing them up, at last, to such a point that Peter had to say, "We cannot but speak the things which we have seen and heard," and Paul had to declare that necessity was laid upon him, yea, woe was unto him if he preached not the gospel! In this conference, in the desert of Midian, we have thus, I make bold to say, an anticipation and synopsis, under Old Testament forms, of the whole training of the twelve by Jesus for their work, as it is recorded in the four gospels, and so the inference is inevitable that the Jehovah of the bush is the Jesus of Nazareth.

5. To mention only one point more, this divine angel is the God who promises to be with his people in all their history. When Moses said, "Who am I that I should go to Pharaoh?" the voice out of the bush answered, "Certainly I will be with thee." So, after Jesus had said to his followers, "Go ye, therefore, and disciple all nations, baptizing them in the name of the Father and of the Son and of the Holy Ghost; teaching them to observe all things whatsoever I have commanded you"; and when, perhaps, he saw on their countenances an expression of consternation at the magnitude of the charge which he had

given them, he added, "And lo! I am with you alway, even unto the end of the world." A large promise which only Deity would dare to make, and which, in its likeness to the words addressed to Moses—"Certainly I will be with thee"—indicates that it came from the same divine source. Thus, whether we look at the significance of the symbol in itself considered, or at the conference which was carried on in connection with it, we are warranted, I think, if not required, to come to the conclusion that the Jehovah of the bush is the Jesus of the New Testament, of whom it is written that "he shall save his people from their sins." "The good-will of him that dwelt in the bush" is, therefore, equivalent to "the grace of our Lord Jesus Christ"; and so, every time the apostolic benediction is pronounced, the pastor supplicates for his people precisely the same spiritual blessing that Moses here requested for the descendants of Joseph, along with, and supplementary to, the temporal prosperity on which he dwells so lovingly and long. For worldly wealth is of little value if we have not the divine good-will with it. If we are poor that good-will is of itself an ample portion; and if we are rich, it will make our riches harmless to us, by teaching us to turn them into means of blessing to others; while, on the other hand, if we despise the favors of our covenant God, and seek only the wealth of earth, we shall ultimately lose both, and find ourselves at last, like the descendants of Ephraim and Manasseh, hopelessly captive in the grasp of our destroyer. Above everything else, therefore, and along with everything else, let us seek this favor by faith in and faithfulness to the Lord Jesus, and we shall discover, as we go on, that he is true to us in every emergency and through every vicissitude.

For I must not neglect to add that in the mouth of Moses the words "The good-will of him that dwelt in the bush" had, in this blessing of the tribe of Joseph just before he died, a far richer significance than they could have had on then when, after having seen the great sight and heard the great words, he turned away from the desert of Midian, and took his journey into Egypt. He went on there in faith, but now he could look back upon a rich experience. Between the bush and the plains of Moab lay forty years of the fullest realization of all that Jehovah had promised, and so he commended Joseph's children to one whom he knew to be faithful to his word. Had he not been to Egypt and brought out his people into freedom? Had he not enjoyed closest fellowship with God as a man talketh with his friend? Had he not been directed by him in every difficulty and provided for by him in every strait? Whom he had proved, therefore, they might trust. The Lord who had with him stood the strain of the Exodus, and the test of the wilderness wanderings, would not fail them in their time of need. He had been with him, and he would be with them. And is not this true of our Jesus yet? Whom has he failed? When has he broken his word? Who dares to say that he has gone to him and been cast out? Is it not the unvarying testimony of his people in all generations that they never found him wanting? Come, therefore, and prove his good-will now to you. For, while there is so much that is parallel to the gospel in this conference between Jehovah and Moses at Midian, there is in one point a marked difference between the two. The Jehovah of the bush said, "Draw not nigh hither," but the Jesus of the cross says, "Come unto me, all ye that labor and are heavy laden, and I will give you rest." But that is just the great distinction between the old dispensation and the new, and it was rendered necessary by the circumstances of the times. In those ancient days the world was not ready to receive the gospel invitation. There needed yet a long education before men would listen to it either with patience or appreciation, and so the truth, while preserved among them in the figurative system of Judaism, needed also to be protected from them by the restrictions which hedged that system round. These restrictions were like the horn framework of the lantern through which the light shone, no doubt, only dimly, but by which, also, it was kept from being extinguished by the rude blasts of idolatry and immorality. Now, however, they have served their purpose and are no longer needed. The vail of the temple has been rent asunder; the temple itself has disappeared; and, instead of the "draw not nigh," we may hear the "come unto me"; "for in him we have boldness and access with confidence by the faith of him." "Whosoever will," therefore, let him come and claim this divine good-will. Any one may get it through faith in Jesus, and he who secures it "has chosen the good part which shall not be taken from him." Did not the multitude of the heavenly host sing in the hearing of Bethlehem's shepherds, "Glory to God in the highest; peace on earth, and good-will to men?"—to men, not to the sons of Joseph merely, nor to the Hebrew nation alone, but to men. Come, then, O burdened one, whatever thy load may be, whether sin, or sorrow, or perplexity, or want, or whatever else, come and claim thy share in this blessed benison for humanity, and then thou shalt realize how much is meant by "the good-will of him who dwelt in the bush."

MARCH 5, 1882.

TRUE GREATNESS.

MATTHEW xx. 26, 27, 28. Whosoever will be great among you, let him be your minister, and whosoever will be chief among you let him be your servant, even as the Son of Man came not to be ministered unto, but to minister and to give his life a ransom for many.

AMBITION is natural to man. The desire of greatness is inherent in every human spirit, and even the schoolboy's heart throbs with responsive enthusiasm when he reads the Homeric hero's injunction to his son, "always to be the best and superior to all others." Depravity, indeed, has turned this principle to evil account, but it was implanted in us for the noblest purposes, and it is, even in our present state, a witness to the immortal progress for which we were originally designed. Next to the having of a wrong ambition, the worst thing that can befall a man is to have no ambition at all, for then the mainspring of his soul is broken, and his energy and elevation are at an end. It will not do, therefore, to indulge in wholesale and indiscriminate denunciation of this desire. It belongs to man as man, and what we have to do with it is not to seek its extirpation, but to give it a spiritual character, and turn it into a direction that will benefit others rather than ourselves. Just thus, indeed, it is that the Lord Jesus deals with it. He does not seek to destroy anything that is of the essence of our humanity. His design in his redemptive work is to purify man's nature as a whole; and therefore, far from uprooting ambition, he transfigures it by making it the spur that stirs us on, not to self-aggrandizement, but to holiness and beneficence.

To see that this is a true statement of the case you have but to look at the incidents in connection with which the words of my text were originally spoken. The mother of James and John, instigated apparently by her sons, requested of the Lord that when he came to his kingdom these two disciples might sit, one on his right hand and the other on his left. To this he replied, not by directly refusing the petition, but by showing that from the nature of his kingdom they could pass to its high places of honor only by drinking of the cup which he had himself to drain, and submitting to the baptism with which he was himself to be baptized. But the mere making of such a request on their behalf by their mother wounded the pride of the other ten disciples, and so to make his meaning still more plain, and restore harmony among his followers, he went on to say that in that spiritual system of which he was the head it was not to be as it is among the kingdoms of the earth, in which the measure of a man's dominion over his fellows is the measure of his greatness. His kingdom was not to be of this world in any respect, but its special and peculiar feature—marking its radical difference from the monarchies of earth—was, that whereas in them greatness was a thing of rule, under him it was to be a matter of service. His words may be thus paraphrased: "There needs be no strife between you on this point; indeed, if you rightly understood my kingdom there would be none; for even if I were to exalt James and John to the posts of honor which have been asked for them, they would be so exalted not to exercise dominion over you but to be your servants, for that is the principle of my administration. The highest is the highest because he ministers to the lowliest. You have called it my kingdom, and you have said well, for it is mine; yet even I am here, not to be ministered unto, but to minister, and to give my life a ransom for many."

Now observe what all this amounts to. The Saviour does not say that is a wrong thing to desire to be the chief, or to wish to be great. He does not seek to eradicate ambition, but rather to show what its true function in regenerated manhood is to be. He takes that passion which, in the breasts of such men as Nebuchadnezzar, Xerxes, Alexander and the Cæsars, had covered the earth with misery, and he transmutes it into a principle by the operation of which, in the hearts and lives of his followers, the world would yet be blessed "from the rising of the sun to the going down of the same." He defines what true greatness is, and bids his disciples be ambitious after that. He substitutes the greatness of love for the love of greatness; and to those who are eager for power he preaches the might of service; while with a sublime egoism, to be explained only by his consciousness of deity, he holds himself up as the brightest exemplification of his words. Let us meditate a little upon these striking sayings, and we may find in them some wholesome hints as to the nature, the model, and the motive of true greatness.

I. They have something to tell us, in the first place, concerning the nature of true greatness. What is greatness? Scarcely two persons among us would give the same reply to that question. All would admit that it denotes pre-eminence, but each would have his own preference as to the department in which it was to be manifested. Some would associate it with power, some with courage, some with eloquence, and some, perhaps, with wealth; yet each would think of it as conferring an advantage on its possessor, and so putting others at a corresponding disadvantage. Here, however, it is connected with that love which works not for its own, interest but for the benefit of others. Still, that we may not be one-sided in a matter of so much importance, we must remember that as Jesus used the word "service," holiness was combined with the love out of which it sprung. So we come to the result that the really great man is he whom holiness and love combine to inspire for the service of his generation by the will of God. How different such a definition of a great man is from that commonly current among us must be evident to every one. I willingly admit, indeed, that now men's judgments on this subject have been considerably affected by the principles of the gospel; but still the prevalent idea of greatness is very far from being identical with that which I have deduced from the Saviour's words before me. We crown the man in whom we behold intellectual power that has won the success of position or of wealth, but we too rarely think of goodness as being the highest form of greatness. Now, though Christ does not ignore intellect, or even riches, he yet regards these things, and all things like these, as but instruments, and he is, in the gospel sense of the word, the greatest who uses all such gifts or possessions in the service of mankind. "He that will be greatest among you, let him be your servant."

If, then, this view of the case be correct, one or two inferences of importance follow from it.

1. For one thing, it is evident that he who wins this greatness does not attain it at the expense of others. Many run after the prizes of the world, and not unfre-

quently those who bear them away have succeeded in doing so more by scheming to keep others from getting them, than by fair and honest establishment of their own merits. Men rise very often by pushing others down. Here, however, the prize is won by helping others up. Intrigue, oppression, "*coups d'état*," are alike unknown in such a rivalry as is here suggested, for he who is exalted on this principle to the place of honor has already won the gratitude of those above whom he is elevated, and is where he is with their highest approval. The pursuit of great things, when these are sought simply for one's self, leads not seldom to the violation of the principles of truth and justice and benevolence, and ends full often in bitterest disappointment; but the ambition for the greatness that consists in service stimulates to deeds of self-sacrifice, and has at last the reward of that charity which is twice blessed, because " blessing him that gives and him that takes."

2. It follows, further, from what has been said, that we may win this greatness anywhere. The poet musing in the country churchyard speaks of some as slumbering there who, had the way been opened to them, might have become famous in their country's annals; and it is plain that even in a republic which proclaims that all men are born equal, the paths to worldly honor are greatly circumscribed. Everybody has not the intellect of a Webster or the genius of a Henry as his birth capital, conferred by God. The poet is born, not made; the same thing is true of the orator; and unless some war should break out, which God prevent! there can be no field for military glory. But here—in service—is a department always open; open also to the poorest and the wealthiest; to the least intelligent and the

most intellectual; to the youngest and the oldest; open in the family and the church; in the neighborhood and in the world; yea, whoever a man may be, wherever he may go, and whatever may be his resources, he may be always the means of helping others, and by that may win at last the commendation and the crown. To bid you aim after merely worldly positions would be to entail certain disappointment on many of you. The peripatetic orators who visit our public schools and tell the boys before them that there may be future Presidents of the Republic among them, forget that such an honor can fall at most on only eight men in a generation. Very few of those who begin the study of the law, fired with the ambition which the thought that "there is always room at the top" inspires, ever reach the top. Not every one who has sought after wealth—though that is perhaps the easiest thing of all to get—has obtained it; and in the race of life you may see multitudes lying on the course exhausted and forlorn, having given up all hope of reaching the goal. Thus, in all these departments, multitudes are sure to be disappointed. But we may all get this gospel greatness. Opportunities for winning it lie all around; and so in urging you to seek for it I am starting you out on no uncertain quest, nor sending you to chase a deceitful marsh-fire. You may attain that which I set before you, and you will attain it, if only your thoughts are set on serving others and your hearts are filled with love.

3. But it follows, thirdly, that this greatness is satisfying to its possessor. Literature is full of the sighings of successful men over the disappointment which even success has brought to them. The enjoyment of life, on the world's plan, is in the

pursuit. When the prize is won it ceases to charm. That which, in the distance, seemed goodly fruit, crunches in the mouth like ashes. No abiding happiness can be found either in literary fame or political position, or stores of wealth, in themselves, but there is always satisfaction in serving our generation; and he who, by the grace of God, seeks to make the world the better for his presence will from that effort have the holiest joy. He may, indeed, be misconstrued by his fellows; he may be ridiculed as an enthusiast; he may be reproached for what others call his improvidence; and while he has been thinking of serving Christ in his people, some will affirm that he has been only the more cunningly aiming for his own advancement, but he will have within him the testimony of a good conscience, and above him the complacency of an approving God; and the day will come when his worth shall be recognized and his title to men's gratitude and affection conclusively established. This greatness bears investigation. There is nothing in the means by which it has been acquired to create remorse, while the happiness of him who has won it is redoubled by that of those in whose service it has been gained. What a drawback to the conqueror's joy is the appearance of the battle-field after an engagement? And who among us has not felt his eyes grow dim as he has read of the great captain saying, as he walked among the dead and dying on the night after his most brilliant success, "Alas! alas! next to a defeat, the saddest thing is a victory at such a cost." But there is no such shadowing sorrow attendant on the greatness to which Jesus summons us. Its achievements are in the way of saving men, not of destroying them; and in the promotion of their highest interests it finds its abiding joy. Here, therefore, is an ambition that is free from the evils that commonly accompany the workings of that natural principle. It rises without thrusting others down; it finds its field of operation in every department of life; and it seeks its own enjoyment in promoting the happiness of others. Be it ours, my brethren, to aspire after the greatness which the Lord has here described. Let others have the prizes of the world if they will, choose ye this crown of never-fading glory! The highest commendation one can earn is this—"He hath done what he could"; and the noblest life record is that which comes nearest to his of whom it was said that "he went about doing good." That is fame, though no earthly herald may trumpet it abroad, for Christ shall proclaim it on the day of days before the assembled universe.

II. But the text has something to say to us, in the second place, about the model of greatness: "Even as the Son of Man came not to be ministered unto, but to minister, and to give his life a ransom for many." In one point of view the greatness of God is that of service. All things depend on him. He holds the planets in their orbits. He rules the changing year. "In him we live and move and have our being." He gives us breath, and food, and raiment. The tiniest insect fluttering in the sunbeam is upheld by him, and a sparrow cannot fall to the ground without his care. He is thus, in a very true sense of the word, the servant of the creatures whom he has called into being and sustains. Yea, when we come to think it out, we shall see that the greatest inventions, even of recent days, in the way of applied science are just so many new methods in which we may avail ourselves of God's service, and take advantage of his ministry. I speak it reverently, yet it is most true, that every power in nature is in the last resort the power of God, and so in steam, electricity, etc., we are but in different ways taking advantage of God's goodness as a servant. Thus the highest of all is the servant of all. But, striking as the nobleness and the divinity of service appear when we look thus at the universal ministry of God, we have a more impressive illustration of the same thing in the mission and work of the Lord Jesus. In creation and providence God lays nothing aside. He has made no sacrifice in either of these. He has not—if I may so express it—put himself about to serve his creatures. Everything in nature is done with ease. Nothing is difficult to omnipotence. But in redemption it was different. To deliver man from the guilt and power of sin it was needed that the Son of God should become a man, and, after a life of obedience, should submit to a death of shame; and *there* was sacrifice; *there* was a giving up of that which even Godhead felt to be infinitely valuable, and when that was done Jehovah rendered the highest service to humanity, and gave a pattern of the loftiest greatness.

It deserves to be remarked, however, that though the point of the reference made here by Jesus to his death lies in its power as an example, he uses language concerning it which clearly implies that it was redemptive and sacrificial. It was the "ransom" or price which had to be paid for the declaration of Jehovah's righteousness in the forgiveness of believing men; and the use of this term here as it were incidentally, when allusion is specially made to quite another side of the subject, is a valuable testimony from his own lips to the substitutionary nature of his death. But, indeed, the same thing must come out even when we regard the giving up of his life as an example; for if there were no righteous necessity for his dying as a means of saving men, then it becomes a mere display of sentiment, a throwing away of that which, without detriment to any interest, might have been kept; and that could be no proper model of any sort for men. When, however, we reflect that only by his giving himself up to death in the sinner's room could any one be saved, then we see in his voluntary surrender of himself to the cross the noblest act of service of which the universe has been the scene. Christ came into the world to die, and in his death he served us more effectually than others could have done by their lives. But it must not be forgotten, either, that his death was but the climax and consummation of a life of ministering —the last and greatest act in a series of the sublimest services ever rendered by one person to others. He was continually ministering. He was always at the call of weakness, or of suffering or of want. Every one of his miracles was benevolent. He never thought of his own case, or allowed regard for himself to stand in the way of the manifestation of his love to others. "Even Christ pleased not himself." He sought no personal aggrandizement. He coveted no gold or silver. He desired no earthly glory. But wherever a sick one needed healing, or a weak one required strength, or a weeping one sought solace, there he was to be found doing appropriate service. When he sat exhausted on the well of Sychar, he denied himself both repose and refreshment that he might guide an erring woman back to the way of holiness. When with his twelve apostles he went for retirement to the eastern shore of Genesaret, he did not allow consideration for himself to keep him from instructing the multitudes that persistently followed him; and he added to that kindness the working of a miracle for their feeding. Nay, even when the darkness of Calvary was closing over him he forgot his own agony as he heard the prayer of the penitent who hung beside him; and in those words of answer, "To-day shalt thou be with me in paradise," we have one of the sublimest instances of self-abnegation which even his history contains. This is the model of the highest greatness. Be not appalled, I pray you, by the purity of its perfection, but seek day by day to come nearer to the height of its ever ascending ideal. Lay aside all inferior standards. Seek to imitate no meaner ensample. We dwarf our efforts by consenting to accept less exalted models. Let us, therefore, keep ever "looking unto Jesus," and, like Paul, make this our motto: "This one thing I do: forgetting those things which are behind and reaching forth unto those things which are before, I press toward the mark for the prize of the high calling of God in Christ Jesus." It may entail upon us the drinking of many a bitter cup, and the enduring of many a fiery baptism, but if we press forward in this holy quest, then, at the end, for us, too, as for Paul, there will be "the crown of righteousness which the Lord, the righteous judge, shall give us at that day."

III. But this text has something to say to us finally about the motive to true greatness. We are to seek it for the sake of him who gave himself for us. I do not find, indeed, any distinct expression of this thought in the verses before us. Jesus does not say in so many words, "Serve one another, because I have served you;" but still the reference which he makes to his death, as an example, brings before every Christian's mind the magnitude of the obligation under which Christ has laid him. He died for us. But for his death our deliverance would have been impossible. Through his sacrifice our salvation has been secured. Thus we owe everything to him. Our present privileges and our future hopes all center in him. If he is anything to us at all, he is to us "all and in all." And the great question of our hearts, in view of his services to us, is "What shall I render unto the Lord for all his benefits?" Now, his answer to that inquiry is virtually this: "By love serve one another. He is the most deeply grateful to me who is the most self-sacrificing minister to the temporal and spiritual necessities of others. Wherever you see another standing in need of your assistance as much as you were needing mine when I came to help you by dying in your stead, help him, and that will be thanking me, for 'inasmuch as ye do it to one of the least of these ye do it unto me.'" We are, thus, to see Christ's image in every sick and sorrowful and suffering one; and we are to show our gratitude to him for his death in our behalf by laboring to serve them in the most self-denying manner. Thus gratitude is the source of greatness, and so this Christian ambition, alike in its root and in its fruits, is transfigured and becomes a totally different thing from that which is commonly so called. Behold how it showed itself in Paul. I call him, all in all, the greatest man whom the Christian church has yet produced. For activity, for self-sacrifice, for constant devotion to the good of others, he stands unrivaled among the sons of men, and if you ask him to explain it all, he will reply in these autobiographic words: "I am crucified with Christ, nevertheless I live, yet not I, but Christ liveth in me, and the life which I now live in the flesh, I live by the faith of the Son of God who loved me and gave himself for me;" or these: "Alway bearing about in the body the dying of the Lord Jesus that the life, also, of Jesus might be made manifest in my body." Now, if we would emulate his greatness, we must follow the same plan. We must begin by receiving Jesus Christ into our hearts as our Redeemer, and we must go on by maintaining our love to him and our confidence in him until at length self shall be swallowed up in him, and our one absorbing, overmastering ambition will become that we may reproduce, as far as we may, Christ's own self-sacrifice on our lowlier level and within our more limited area.

I have seen a picture which, by the genius of the artist, told at least one chapter of the story of a poor man who was confined for years in a cold, dark dungeon. There was but one little opening in the wall, and through that a sunbeam came for but a few minutes every day making a white patch of light on the opposite side of the cell. Often and often the lonely man gazed on that little spot which was thus daily illuminated, and at length a purpose to make something on it grew within his soul. Groping on the ground, which was his only floor, he found a nail and a stone, and with these for chisel and mallet he set to work on that bright little patch for the brief time of every day that it was kissed by the sunlight, until at length he brought out upon it in sculptured relief a rude representation of Christ upon the cross! Let us imitate that prisoner! Our sphere may be circumscribed; our life-chamber may be dark; our surroundings may be dreary; yet if we be truly set on following Christ, we shall discover some tiny chink through which the sunshine of his guiding providence shall come; and on the spot where its directing light shall fall, let us, with such means as we find at our hand, hew out, not in cold stone but in living love, the likeness of the sacrifice of Christ. Thus shall we attain that loftiest greatness whereof Jesus has to-day been speaking to us!

> "For he before whose scepter
>   The nations rise or fall,
> Who gives no least commandment
>   But come to pass it shall,
> Said that he who would be greatest
>   Should be servant unto all.
>
> And in conflict with the evil
>   Which his bright creation mars,
> Laid he not aside the scepter
>   Which can reach to all the stars?
> Of the service which he rendered
>   See on his hands the scars!"

May 15, 1881.

THE SEAL AND EARNEST OF THE SPIRIT.

II. Cor. i. 22. Who hath also sealed us, and given the earnest of the Spirit in our hearts.

It is, I fear, too true of us Christians in these days, that though we are living under the dispensation of the Holy Spirit, we make far too little of his operations, alike in our thoughts, our discourses and our prayers. The place of that divine agent in the economy of salvation is equally important with that of the Father and the Son, and yet in our meditations and experience he has too largely dropped out of our consideration. Many treatises have been written on the love of the Father, scarcely one has been devoted to the love of the Spirit. We are never weary of extolling the work of the Son, and prayer is made to him continually; but little is said, comparatively, about the Holy Ghost, and few petitions are presented unto him.

The hymnology of the church, which is an unerring witness to the quality of Christian experience through all the centuries, attests that while many of those sacred songs which are most popular show forth the praises of the Father and the Son, there are but few which worthily express our obligations to the Spirit. A learned editor in this city has compiled into a large volume entitled "Christ in Song" a great number of the finest lyrics which tell of Jesus and his work; but a similar collection by another hand under the name of "The Holy Ghost in Song" reveals that in this department our praise has been meager in its volume, and for the most part only medium in its quality. Of the four hundred and twelve hymns contained in Lord Selborne's "Book of Praise," only fifteen are arranged under the heading of "God the Holy Ghost," and even of these there are five which have no special reference to the Spirit, and might as well have been placed under some other division. In our own hymn-book—which in this regard may be taken as a fair sample of our praise-books generally—out of thirteen hundred and fifty-seven hymns only forty-six are marked in the index as being either addressed to the Holy Spirit, or having any reference to his work.

This may be to many a startling statement, but it is the simple truth; and it seems to me to indicate the quarter in which the source of that which must be deplored by all of us as an evil is to be found. For hymnology grows out of experience. The church sings that alone which its members have realized as having entered into their own lives, and we take into our lives only that which we implicitly believe. Now if we seek to analyze that which is the common faith of Christians in regard to the Holy Spirit we shall find something like this: there is a general belief in his true and proper Deity; there is a common recognition of the necessity of his agency for the renewal of the heart; and there is, also, though not perhaps so deep and earnest as it ought to be, a realization of the truth that he alone can give power to the preaching of the gospel. When we are longing for conversions, and seeking for such a revival of religion in the city and the land as shall turn many from darkness unto light, and from the power of Satan unto God, we pray for an outpouring of the Holy Spirit.

But there for the most part we stop. We do not deny that it is he alone who can foster and maintain within us the graces of Christian character. We are far from affirming, in so many words, that after we have once been regenerated by the grace of the Holy Ghost we can get on very well without him; or that for comfort, for growth, for security, and for perseverance we are independent of him; but the simple fact is that most of us do not consciously rely on him for these things, do not pray to him for them, and do not give to him the glory when, in spite of our ignoring of him, we are permitted to experience them. This explains the disproportion in our hymn-books to which I have referred, and points to a serious defect in our practical theology. Take the first ten church members whom you may chance to meet; ask them why we need the Holy Ghost; press them to tell you whether they pray for him, and if they do, get them to explain why they have prayed for him; then I venture to say, that most of them will affirm that they wish to see his power manifested as it was on Pentecost, in the awakening and regeneration of men through the preaching of the truth, and that scarcely one among them will allege that he ever thought of asking for him in order that he might himself become purer, more devoted, more Christ-like in his own character and life. Now I have called this a serious defect in our practical theology, and I would have it remedied not by giving less attention to other matters, but by giving more to this. We cannot make too much of the love of the Father, and I would not desire that we should in any degree diminish our appreciation of that. We cannot go wrong in glorying in the Cross of Christ, and anything short of whole-hearted consecration to our divine Redeemer is to be deprecated. Neither would

I have one prayer fewer offered for the outpouring of the Spirit in connection with energizing of men for the preaching of the gospel. But while we do these things we must not leave the other undone. Let us not honor the Father and the Son less; but let us honor the Holy Spirit more, yea, let us honor him equally with the Father and the Son. Let us not make less of the necessity of his agency for giving success to the preaching of the gospel; but let us make more than we have been doing heretofore of the need of his operations in us for our daily spiritual growth; and while we pray as earnestly as ever that he would "baptize the nations" and quicken them into spiritual life let us ask more fervently than ever that he may work in us for the development and ripening of our characters "till we all come in the unity of the faith and of the knowledge of the Son of God unto a perfect man, unto the measure of the stature of the fullness of Christ."

Whatever excuse may be offered for this too common ignoring by us of the work of the Holy Ghost in the sustenance of the individual Christian life, it cannot be said that its necessity is not kept steadily before us in the New Testament. Many of the very names by which he is called set this aspect of his agency very clearly before our eyes. Thus when the Lord Jesus promised to send him as another Comforter, or Paraclete, he taught us to expect him as one who should be our constant helper, as real, as gracious and as powerful as himself. When he is called the Spirit of Holiness, the suggestion is that through his working in us we are to grow in holiness. When he is styled the Spirit of Supplication, we are reminded that all true prayer is the result of his operation in us. When he is spoken of as the Spirit of

Grace, we are led to understand that it is through him Christ's grace is communicated to us and comes to be sufficient for us. And the same truths are suggested to us by the two figures under which his work is brought before our notice in the words which I have taken this morning as my text. Let me endeavor then to unfold to you all that is here implied in order that I may stir you up to ask for the Holy Ghost for yourselves to help you through the daily conflict of your lives, as well as for others that they may be converted unto God by the manifestation of his power.

I. First let us see if we can discover with what fitness it can be said that God hath sealed us by his Spirit. In the verse which I have read, indeed, it is not expressly affirmed that the Holy Spirit is the seal which God has affixed to his people in Christ, but a comparison of Paul's words here with those which he used in his Epistle to the Ephesians when he wrote " in whom, also, after that ye believed, ye were sealed with that Holy Spirit of promise," and again, "Grieve not the Holy Spirit of God, whereby ye are sealed unto the day of redemption," will make it abundantly evident that the same thing was in his mind when he employed the language of the text. In what respects, then, may the Holy Spirit be compared to a seal? The answer is suggested by the uses to which among men a seal has been put. These are three:

1. It has been employed first to authenticate a document or confirm it as genuine. Thus Jezebel is said to have written letters in Ahab's name and sealed them with his seal; and in the book of Esther it is recorded of the decree of the king, " in the name of Ahasuerus was it written and sealed with the king's

ring."* The same usage holds among ourselves, for important deeds are almost always marked with an official seal, and the effect is that all who read them acknowledge them as authentic. So by the Spirit of God the believer has the assurance given to him that he is a genuine disciple of Christ. He has the attestation in him that he is born of God, or, as Paul has elsewhere phrased it, "the Spirit beareth witness with his spirit that he is a child of God." But how is this assurance given to the Christian? Not, I answer, by the administration of any ordinance. The sacraments of baptism and the Lord's Supper have often been called by theologians "sealing ordinances," and there is a sense in which the words thus used may be appropriate, but they do not mean that the reception of these ordinances is indubitable evidence that he who receives them is a child of God. Many who have been baptized have denied the Lord that bought them, and many too who have taken into their hands the symbols of Christ's body and blood have done so only as an empty form and without any spiritual benefit. These therefore are not the means by which believers are sealed by the Holy Ghost. But neither does he impart this authenticating assurance by any direct revelation or through any special communication, as by dream or vision. The Spirit works in a man by working through him. His agency is exerted through the operation of the believer's own faculties. The supernatural acts through the natural, by quickening it into exercise and stimulating it to excellence. Thus it comes that its working is not a matter of consciousness as distinct from the usual operation of the powers of the soul itself. The believer cannot say at

---

* 1 Kings xxi. 8; Esther iii. 12.

THE SEAL AND EARNEST OF THE SPIRIT. 235

any moment in his experience that he feels and knows that there is a power different from his own at work within him. He is conscious only of results. He knows that the Holy Ghost has been exerting his agency within him only when he perceives that the fruit of the Spirit has begun to make its appearance in him. Here, in the word, is the description of that which the Holy Ghost produces in a man—"the fruit of the Spirit is love, joy, peace, long-suffering, gentleness, goodness, faith, meekness, temperance"—and when in his consciousness these qualities make their presence known, he has then the witness of the Spirit in him that he is a genuine believer. In short, when the fruit of the Spirit in the experience of the man corresponds to the description of it which is given in the word, just as the impression on the wax does to the die that produced it, then he is warranted to infer that he is sealed with the Holy Spirit of God, and authenticated to himself as a genuine Christian. This description of the matter is thus equally removed, on the one hand, from that fanaticism which would lead you to expect a direct communication, either by secret revelation or by audible voice, from God, and on the other from that rationalistic naturalism which would deny all reality whatever to the operations of the Spirit in the heart; and I am happy to be able to confirm my statement by the words of such an eminent man of God as Chalmers, who has said: "I could not, without making my own doctrine outstrip my own experience, vouch for any other intimation of the Spirit of God than that which he gives in making the word of God clear unto you, and the state of your own heart clear unto you. From the one you draw what are its promises, from the other what are your own personal characteristics; and the application of the first to the second may conduct you to a most legitimate argument that you personally are one of the saved—and that not a tardy or elaborate argument, either, but with an evidence quick and powerful as the light of intuition." * Thus interpreted, the work of the Holy Spirit in sealing believers is intimately associated with their assurance of salvation, and, therefore, we may see how much we lose by so commonly ignoring his agency.

2d. But a seal was used, in the second place, as a mark by which to distinguish property. When thus employed it was different from all other badges, and was in its nature unique and peculiar. We have something like it in modern times in the trade-mark which a manufacturer copyrights and makes his own, so that wherever it is imprinted one can tell at a glance the ownership of that on which it appears. Just as to-day throughout the British Empire everything that is marked with the broad arrow is at once recognized as the property of the government; so in ancient times, the servants, cattle and goods of a rich man were distinguished by his seal. In like manner believers are recognized as the property of God by the seal of the Spirit; and as sometimes yet with us a seal has an obverse and reverse side, so in the case of believers the seal of the Spirit is at once inner and outer. This is made clear by Paul in these words of his to Timothy: "Nevertheless the foundation of God standeth sure, having this seal"—that is, a seal with these inscriptions on it: "The Lord knoweth them that are his. And, Let every one that nameth the name of Christ depart from iniquity." On the hidden side, visible only to Jehovah, is this inscription: "The

---

* Chalmers on Romans viii. 16. In Lectures on Romans.

Lord knoweth them that are his." He knoweth them not only as his own regenerated ones, but also by their aspirations after himself, by their hidden communion with himself, and by their joy in himself. These things are secrets between him and them. But on the other side, where all men may read it, there is this inscription—" Let him that nameth the name of Christ depart from iniquity." Thus they are distinguished among men as God's property by their departure from iniquity. They are a peculiar people not only in the sense of being God's purchased possessions, but also in that of being different from all others, and that visible difference is in their keeping themselves "unspotted from the world." Hence, just as the authentication of the believer to himself is given in his experience, so the difference between him and others which points him out as God's property is marked in his conduct; and by his non-conformity to the world, which is the result of the renewing of his mind, he is sealed, in the eyes of all men, as belonging to the Lord. I do not say that he is entirely free from sin, but I do affirm that his relation to sin is different from that of other men. They serve sin, but he has revolted from sin, and is departing from it. He falls yet sometimes, but when he does he is overtaken in a fault. He sins yet, sometimes, but when he does he rises out of it and returns to God. When his foot slides it is not like the stumbling of one who is descending deeper and deeper into iniquity; but it is the foot-slip of an eager climber who is panting in his ascent of the hill and if he should fall, he is never content to lie still, but he arises forthwith and renews his toil. His face is in the right direction. His cry is ever Upward, Godward, Heavenward, and he longs to reach the summit, where he shall be like God—for he shall see him as he is. Now this outward character is the badge of Christian discipleship, the mark that a man belongs to God, and it is produced in him by the agency of the Holy Ghost. Hence we may see how near the honoring of the Spirit lies to one of the great necessities of the times. The cry is, and I fear there is good reason for the exclamation, that the church and the world are becoming indistinguishable; that Christians are losing their characteristic features; and that there is little or no difference between them and other men. What is this but to say that the seal of the Spirit is becoming undecipherable; that its sharp relief is worn down; that its inscription is well-nigh illegible? And how is it to be renewed, if not by a new honoring of God the Holy Ghost among us as the author and agent of personal sanctification? Ah! have we not in this worldly conformity among professing Christians the result and Nemesis of our forgetfulness in our prayers and praises of the Holy Spirit?

When the coinage of a country has worn thin and light, so that no one can see the image or read the superscription which once it bore, it is called in, re-minted, and sent forth anew, with a clearly distinct and finely relieved impression from the original die. And so, when our Christian characters are rubbed down by the abrasion of the world to such an extent that the image of the Lord in us has been well nigh effaced, there is all the more need for us to submit ourselves to the reminting of the Holy Spirit, that we may come forth anew and bear unmistakable witness to Christ's royalty over us and property in us.

3. But in the third place a seal was used as a means of security. Thus it is recorded of the stone laid at the mouth of the den into which Daniel was thrust: "The King sealed it with his own signet and with the

signet of his lords, that the purpose might not be changed concerning Daniel," and when Jesus was laid in the grave the Jews made the sepulcher sure, "sealing the stone, and setting a watch." In like manner believers are kept secure in the world by the seal of the Spirit. Now let us clearly understand how this is brought about. The reference here is not to God's almighty protection. Neither is it to the ordering of his all-wise providence. Both of these, indeed, are engaged by covenant for the defence of the Christian, but here the allusion is to something resulting from the Spirit's agency in the believer's heart, by which he is preserved until the day of redemption. And so we come back again to those qualities in the Christian which are wrought out in him by the Holy Ghost, through faith, and we see in them the means of his security.

The characteristics and habits which are acquired by the believer, through the grace of the Holy Ghost, are the means of preserving him from falling before the assaults of his spiritual enemies. Recall again that enumeration of Paul: "The fruit of the Spirit is love, joy, peace, long-suffering, gentleness, goodness, faith, meekness, temperance: against such there is no law." Or that other: "The fruit of the Spirit is in all goodness and righteousness and truth." Then with these catalogues in your memory compare them with the well-known passage which describes the Christian's armor thus: "Stand, therefore, having your loins girt about with truth, and having on the breast-plate of righteousness; and your feet shod with the preparation of the gospel of peace, above all taking the shield of faith, wherewith ye shall be able to quench all the fiery darts of the wicked. And take the helmet of salvation, and the sword of the Spirit which is the word of God, praying always with all prayer and supplication in the Spirit, and watching thereunto with all perseverance." And what result do we get from the comparison? We get this—that the Christian's graces are his armor also; that the very same qualities which are styled the fruit of the Spirit are, in another view of them, the whole armor of God and the means of defence from his soul's adversaries. The virtues to the cultivation of which he is stimulated, and in the development of which he is sustained by the Spirit, are the means by which that Divine Agent secures him from all the assaults of his enemies; and so we see how it comes that the doctrine of the perseverance of the saints, when rightly understood, never can lead to indolence; for the Spirit preserves his people from falling away by the fostering within them of those qualities and habits which are absolutely incompatible with their declension. He seals them by righteousness, not as an objective gift bestowed upon them, but as a character maintained by them, and so that righteousness is a breastplate. He marks them with truth, not as a passive possession, but as an active principle, and so that truth is for them a girdle. And the same is true of all the other items in the catalogue of the Spirit's fruit. Now with these facts before us we can comprehend how it comes that on the one hand believers are said to be kept by the power of God through faith, and on the other it is alleged that he that is begotten of God keepeth himself. Our security is perfect, and yet it is not without our own exertions— for it is effected by the constant manifestation by us of the qualities which are formed and fostered in us by the operation of the Holy Ghost. If, therefore, there be anything like spiritual indolence among us, or if there be frequent cases of falling away among those who were once apparently running well, we may be sure that the root of all such evils is in the ignoring of the agency of the Spirit, whereby we are sealed unto the day of redemption.

II. But I must hasten now to consider with all brevity what is implied in the second figure here employed to illustrate the value of the work of the Spirit in our hearts. "And hath given us the earnest of the Spirit." The term is borrowed from a custom which used to be observed in connection with the transfer of property. It was common in a case of purchase that the buyer received a small installment at once as a sample of that which he had bought and as a pledge that in due season full delivery should be made. This installment or first-fruit was called an earnest, and so when the Holy Spirit in our hearts is styled an earnest, we have these two things implied, namely—first, that the fruit of the Spirit which we here enjoy is the same in kind with the blessedness of heaven, and second, that it is a pledge that heaven in its perfection shall ultimately be ours.

The Spirit in our hearts is a foretaste of the quality of heaven. The life of heaven will differ not in kind, but only in degree, from that of the believer here. "He that believeth on the Son hath everlasting life." Observe, it is not will have, but hath. All that which has come to him through his faith in the Son shall never die. His heaven is begun here, in reconciliation to God, in fellowship with God, in assimilation to God. The quickening which he has here experienced through the agency of the Holy Ghost is the germ of the life of glory. The light which he has here received through the illumination of the Spirit is the beginning of the knowledge of heaven. The happiness which he has here enjoyed, through the work of the Holy Ghost in him, is the commencement of the blessedness of heaven. The earnest is the same in kind with the purchase, and the fruit to which we have this morning so often referred is of the same sort as the inheritance on high.

I say not, indeed, that our present experience gives us any adequate idea of the full glory of heaven. Light is the same in the first streak of early dawn as it is in the splendor of high noon—the same in kind, but how different in degree. Life is the same in its radical nature in the infant on its mother's lap and in the philosopher at his post of observation as he scans the heavens—the same in kind, but how different in degree! So heaven transcends in degree all that we have experienced here on earth. Yet the view which I have now presented, and which I am persuaded is entirely Scriptural, may keep us from falling into foolish and dangerous error regarding the future life. Heaven is not a place of material splendor, any more than hell is a lake of material fire. Retribution is the intensification of that which is known as remorse here; and glorification is the sublimation, the elevation, and the purification of that which the believer has already experienced of joy, and peace, and holiness on earth. The celestial city, with its walls of jasper, and its gates of pearl, and its streets of gold, is a beautiful figure. It is a material symbol for a spiritual reality which will be infinitely greater than anything material can ever be, and that spiritual reality is completed humanity, glorified character, and perfected happiness. Heaven is a state more than a place, a character more than a possession, a happiness more than a position; and we enter into that state, we acquire that character, we taste that happiness here and now through faith in Jesus Christ and by the indwelling of his Spirit in our hearts. How important, therefore, in this regard, that we should keep clearly before our minds the place and the power of the Holy Ghost in the sanctification of our souls!

But our present enjoyment of the fruit of the Spirit is a pledge that the full inheritance of heaven shall yet be ours. "He who hath begun a good work in us will perform it until the day of Jesus Christ." What God commences he carries through; and having done so much in us he will bring it to completeness. This, you observe, is not quite the same as the security which was suggested to us by the seal. That was the pledge that we should be kept for heaven; this is an assurance that heaven shall be possessed by us; and both together are brought before us in the words of Peter, when he speaks of "an inheritance, incorruptible, and undefiled, and that fadeth not away, reserved in heaven for them who are kept by the power of God through faith." Thus the saints are kept for the inheritance, and the inheritance is reserved for the saints, so that there is a double guarantee; and by these two immutable things we may have strong consolation as we pursue our life journey here on earth. Nay, more; both of these guarantees are given by the Holy Ghost in his work within us, and so we see how closely connected with our safety and our joy, our present comfort and our future glory, the agency of the Spirit is. Surely, if we were more thoroughly alive to these considerations we would have a higher appreciation of the Third in the Trinity, and be more frequently found hymning his praise and supplicating his blessing.

But I must conclude. I have, throughout, been speaking this morning to those who have had some experience of the power of divine grace in their hearts, for, as Paul has clearly affirmed, it is only after men have believed that they are sealed by the Holy Spirit of promise. Yet I cannot leave off without saying a word or two to those who have not yet "set to their seal that God is true," by believing in his Son. To them I come to-day as the spies came to Kadesh-barnea, two of them carrying between them the Eshcol cluster of grapes as a sample of the products of the goodly land which they had been to see. I show you in this "fruit of the Spirit" a specimen of the inheritance into which Jesus introduces us. Beware how ye receive our report. Remember what happened to the tribes when they refused, at the word of Caleb, to go up and possess the land, and "take heed lest ye fall after the same example of unbelief." Who among you is willing to set out with us to-day for this celestial heritage? It is true that there is a river to cross before we fully reach it, but in that it only resembles every earthly blessing, for there is a Jordan before every Canaan. It is true that the Anakim are to be subdued, but that is only what we must expect in every enterprise, since nothing worthy of possession ever becomes ours without conflict. But think of your leader; for if you believe in Jesus, then he who erewhile appeared to Joshua as "the Captain of the Lord's host" will guide you on; before him the river will be dried up, and at his advance every adversary will be overthrown. Who, then, is willing to put himself under his leadership? "Come with us and we will do you good, for we are journeying to the place of which God hath said, I will give it you, and the Lord hath spoken good concerning Israel."

JANUARY 8, 1882.

DRIFTING.

HEBREWS ii. 1. Lest haply we drift away from them. (Revised Version.)

THE key-note of this great Epistle is the word "better." It was written to those who were in danger of apostasy from the gospel by reason of their high appreciation of the Jewish law, and its argument is designed to show that inasmuch as Jesus is better than the angels by whom the law was given; more glorious than Moses, who was the mediator of the old covenant; more excellent in his ministry than Aaron, who was its priest; officiated in a nobler tabernacle than that which was erected in the wilderness, and offered a better sacrifice than those which smoked on the altar of burnt offerings, therefore he is the surety of a better covenant, which brought in a better hope, was established upon better promises, and provided some better thing than was known or enjoyed under the ancient dispensation. Such being the case, it would be folly to go back from the gospel to the law, and the despising of the privileges which Christ conferred would entail a much sorer punishment than that which fell on those who perished at the mouth of two or three witnesses for the violation of the Mosaic precepts, and so the solemn close of the whole train of reasoning is this: "See that ye refuse not him that speaketh; for if they escaped not who refused him when he spake on earth, much more shall not we escape if we turn away from him when he speaketh from heaven, whose voice then shook the earth; but now he hath promised, saying: Yet once more I shake not the earth only, but also heaven. And this word, yet once more, signifieth the removing of those things that are shaken, as of things that are made, that those things which cannot be shaken may remain. Wherefore we, receiving a kingdom which cannot be moved, let us have grace whereby we may serve God acceptably with reverence and godly fear, for our God is a consuming fire."

That is the main purport of this magnificent treatise, and the text is the inference which the writer draws from the first section of his argument. Beginning with the fact that God, who had spoken in many ways and in many portions in the prophets, had now spoken unto men in his Son, he strikes what I have called his key-note at the very first, by describing that Son as "being made so much better than the angels, as he hath by inheritance obtained a more excellent name than they;" and after having proved that statement, he sends home at once the inference from it thus: "Therefore we ought to give the more earnest heed to the things which we have heard—that is, heard from the Son—lest we should drift away from them; for if the word spoken by angels was steadfast, and every trangression and disobedience received a just recompense of reward, how shall we escape if we neglect so great salvation which at the first began to be spoken by the Lord?"

It will be seen by you that in thus quoting the words, I prefer the rendering given by the revisers: " lest we should drift away from them "; and this I do because it is a more exact translation of the Greek term, and brings into prominence a truth which is almost entirely concealed by the common version. To let a thing slip is to allow it to pass out of our grasp, or to lose our hold of it; and that could not occur in our experience without our attention being drawn to it in some way. But that is not the precise sort of danger against which the writer guards his readers here. He is anxious to warn them of something which might happen to them before they were aware. He is not so much afraid of their positively "rejecting" the great salvation as of their "neglecting" it, in consequence of their yielding to other influences, or of their being preoccupied with other matters; and his words describe not a direct and deliberate antagonism to the truth, but rather a letting of themselves be carried away from it by forces the operation of which is so insidious and stealthy that they would not notice their existence unless they were to give "earnest heed." This message by his Son is God's final word to men; if it be disregarded, there is nothing more to be hoped for from him, and there is great danger that, even without cherishing any violent hostility to it, you may by certain influences be drifted away from it, and not be conscious of the fact until it has begun,—therefore you must give the more earnest heed that such a danger may be avoided.

Drifted—that is the precise word. The boat is unanchored; it is at the moment in a quiet bay, but by-and-by the tide ebbs, and bears it on its bosom on to the middle of the current, and there it is carried out and away, and, perhaps, if no one has observed its motions, lost. Or, if I may illustrate by a personal reminiscence, take such a case as this: On my first tour through Switzerland I visited the quaint old city of Thun, along with three of my most intimate friends. We stayed at a hotel built on the side of the lake, just at the place where the Aar runs rapidly out of it, and we went to amuse ourselves for a season by rowing about in a little boat. After awhile a difference of opinion sprang up among us as to the direction we should take. One said, "Let us go yonder"; another answered, "No; let us rather make for that other point"; a third had still another suggestion, and we ceased rowing until we should make up our minds; but meanwhile the current was settling the question for us, and unless we had speedily bent to the oars with all our might, we should have been hurried along into a dangerous place, out of which we could only have been rescued, if rescued at all, by the assistance of others.

The influences, therefore, against which we are warned by the words of my text are those of currents which are flowing just where we are, and which may operate so insidiously that we may not know of their effect until perhaps it is too late to resist their power. These currents in the case of the Hebrews we have already adverted to, and we can see traces of their force in the successes of the Judaizers, to which Paul alludes in his Epistle to the Galatians; but I do not dwell now upon them. I am desirous rather to guard you against those which are running to-day; and, that I may not deal in vague generalities, I will specify three.

I. Take then, first, that which I may call the age-current, or what a recent English essayist, borrowing from the German, has called the "Time-spirit." Every epoch has its own special tendency. Just as there are times when some forms of disease are epidemic, so there are periods when an intelligent observer can discover certain very distinct trends of thought among men. In the days immediately preceding the French Revolution, infidelity of the type of Voltaire was in the ascendant, and its tide swept over many lands. In England, in the wake of the deists who wrote in the early part of the eighteenth century, such unbelief was prevalent that Butler, in 1736, used these words: "It is come, I know not how, to be taken for granted by many persons that Christianity is not so much as a subject of inquiry; but that it is now, at length, discovered to be fictitious. And, accordingly, they treat it as if, in the present age, this were an agreed point among all people of discernment, and nothing remained but to set it up as a principal subject of mirth and ridicule"; and he was himself so much affected by it that all he ventured to say was: "Thus much, at least, will here be found, not taken for granted, but proved, that any reasonable man who will thoroughly consider the matter may be as much assured as he is of his own being that it is not, however, so clear a case that there is nothing in it." The age-current was surely very strong when even a Butler was prevented by it from affirming more than that! But in our own times something of the same sort has made itself felt. It is curious, indeed, that as one looks back over the last three centuries, he sees a kind of family likeness between them in this regard. The years between 1660 and 1688 marked in England the darkest time of that seventeenth cycle. They were the years of persecution, ribaldry, profanity, immorality and scepticism, consequent upon the restoration of the Stuarts to the throne; the years when Jeffries disgraced the English bench, and when the martyrs' blood ran red upon the Scottish moors. Then, a hundred years later—the time between 1760 and the close of the eighteenth century—was that in which England and Scotland both were blighted by a cold moderatism in the pulpits of the State churches, which preached a heathen morality instead of the gospel of the grace of God. And now again, at a similar period in the nineteenth, we find ourselves called upon to contend not for the inspiration of the Scriptures, or for the reality of miracles, or for the divine origin of the Gospel, but for the very existence of God himself. A physical science which has taken up with the doctrine of development, and has insisted that what is at best an ingenious hypothesis shall be accepted as a demonstrated fact, has prepared the way for an agnostic philosophy which refuses to believe that anything can be known save that which can be perceived by the bodily senses, aided by the scalpel and the microscope, and that, in its turn, has given birth to a rank atheism, which has adopted as its creed the terrible negation, *No God*. You meet with this current in our literature. There are first-class reviews every number of which has one or more articles devoted to some one or other of these subjects. Many of our scientific treatises—not all, I am thankful to say—are infected with the same evil spirit. Some of our daily papers give prominence and circulation to the views which it inspires, and the strength of it may be estimated by the fact that it has affected even the ministry of the gospel to some extent, so that we now and then hear of one who has drifted away from everything that the Christian holds dear.

I do not desire to magnify the evil. My own conviction is that the pendulum has had its full swing in the materialistic direction, and that a reaction will speedily take place, if it have not already begun. But I do not believe that any one who has been taking note of passing events will gainsay my statement that a current of the sort which I have described has been flowing for some years and is flowing still. There is a distinct difference between the state of things in this regard to-day and that which existed five and twenty or thirty years ago. And the question I would desire to put to you, and would seek to put to myself, is, How have we been affected by it? It may be very true that we are not disposed to accept either the logic of scientific men or the philosophy of those who would debar all faith in the spiritual, the unseen, and the supernatural. If we were asked whether we joined them in their contemptuous treatment of the word of God, and their rejection of the Saviour, we should answer with an emphatic "No." But are we quite sure that we have not drifted to some extent with the current? After so much has been said on every hand about the "uniformity of Nature's laws," and "prayer-tests," and "the eternal something not ourselves that makes for righteousness," after even a Huxley has spoken of God as "*it*," we might perhaps prudently ask, "Is God the same to us that he was of yore? Do we solace ourselves as much as ever with the assurance that the very hairs of our head are numbered? Is prayer to us the comfort and strength it used to be? Do we prize the Sabbath and the sanctuary as in our earlier life? Do we long for the communion table as we were wont to do? Is the Bible still to us the same old book, and do we find the same joy in its perusal?" We need not flatter ourselves that the age-current can have no effect upon us. If we do, that is the sure precursor of our being ultimately carried with it. We must either resist it or yield to it. And if we have not been consciously and determinedly resisting it, we have been drifting with it, and the drift will show itself in one or other of the ways which I have mentioned. If it be true that the standard of piety and morality is lower among Christians than it was formerly; if it be the case that the Church is less of an aggressive force in our large centers of population than it was a generation ago; if the numbers of those enrolling themselves in its ranks are smaller than they have been in other days; if here, as in England, the census of those who statedly attend the house of God on the first day of the week, is not so great as it was a quarter of a century ago, may it not be owing to the fact that we have not been taking heed to guard against this age-drift which has been flowing beneath us? Brethren, let us get back to Christ, and anchor fast on him. He is the eternal Son of God. His words are truth. His life is our divine ideal. His death is our true and only atonement for sin. His precept is our law. His intercession is our solace. His heaven is our hope. Let us hold the beginning of our confidence in *him* steadfast unto the end, and that will keep us right. There have been many assaults made upon him, but still, as of yore, it is true that "they are dead who sought the young child's life," and he endures. So it will be again; these vagaries in philosophy will pass away, even as the fleecy clouds remove from the summit of Mont Blanc; but he abides like the grand old mountain in its majestic mantle of stainless and eternal purity. Hear him, therefore, and keep fast hold of his sayings: so shall you partake of his stability. But if you allow yourselves to drift away even in the least degree from him, that may be the beginning of a history which will end in outer darkness.

II. The second current to which I would refer is that of the place in which we dwell. Every city has its own peculiar influence. In the Place de la Concorde in Paris, each principal town in France is represented by an emblematic figure; and as I went through that magnificent square, on the day of the great *fête* of the Republic, and saw the statue of Strasbourg draped in mourning, while everything around was dressed in holiday attire, I had a vivid perception of the humiliation and grief which the possession of that city by the Germans has been to the whole French people. But that is a digression. Each city there had its own ideal representative in the statue of a woman. I cannot tell whether the artist intended to delineate the character of the city by the figure which he called by its name; but we all know that there is in each city a spirit which, as it were, inspires it; a current which bears all in it more or less rapidly upon its bosom. Take the capital of New England for example, and you cannot be long in it without knowing that it is especially and distinctively intellectual. A man there is graduated according to his education. The scholar bears the palm, and if in addition to his learning he possess some artistic excellence or some literary ability, he is ranked so much the higher. That current has its own dangers; but that is not the current that is running in New York. It is true indeed that intellect is not despised among us. We have a few names even in this literary Sardis that do honor to the land. Neither do we look with contempt upon scholarship or art. But here commerce is supreme. The "place-current" for us is business. I do not suppose that everybody in the city is fond of money, or desires to possess it, simply and only for its own sake. But everybody loves business. There is an excitement and fascination in that for all, and they cannot tear themselves away from it. They are not all thinking of what they will make, but many of them love it as boys love a game; and if they are in it at all, they must be in it altogether, else they will at length be dishonored and unsuccessful.

Now this current, also, is not without its dangers to the spiritual life. Business, indeed, is not incompatible with piety, and it will not of necessity stir a man up to antagonism against the gospel, but it may so pre-occupy his mind and pre-engage his heart that he ceases to think about religious matters at all; that is, it may drift him away from the things spoken by the Lord. In his earlier days, the young man may have been devout in his closet, and a daily student of the sacred Scriptures. Perhaps, also, he was an earnest teacher in some mission school. You never missed him from the weekly prayer-meeting, and when anything special was to be done for the church, he was always on hand to help. But as his business responsibilities increased, he became less earnest in these respects; and when he went into commerce for himself, he drifted yet farther away. He had to go so early in the morning that he forgot prayer. He came home so tired in the evening that he had no heart to read either the Bible or any other book, and he sought rest in some place of questionable amusement. The prayer-meeting was neglected. Even the Sabbath was less cared for than before, and he was not averse to sandwiching it in between the Saturday and the Monday as a traveling day on some long journey to a Western city; and then, if we spoke to him on the subject, he would be ready with the retort—"Be not righteous overmuch," and go away with a laugh. Now what is all this but drifting on the place-current? and where is it to end? Ah, if there be any of you who feel that I have been holding up a mirror wherein you have seen yourselves, let me urge you to take heed. You are giving too much for your business success, and if you do not return to your old anchorage, you may find yourselves at length among the openly ungodly, who have passed from the neglecting, to the despising and rejecting, of the great salvation. Get back again to Christ. There is no stability save in him. Listen to his exhortations. Lay fast hold upon his principles. Grasp firmly his loving and fraternal hand. If he be the eternal Son, you cannot drift from him without loss, aye, a twofold loss—the loss of him and the loss of yourselves. So, before you are in the rapids where all struggle would be unavailing, before you are carried over the fall to irremediable perdition, let me entreat you to go back to him who alone can make business safe for you, by teaching you to transact it as a part of your worship and service of himself.

But though we may not have gone to such a length as that which I have described, it would not be safe to infer that the "place-current" has had no effect whatever upon us. Even a steamship is affected by the tide. She will make better time coming up the bay with the flow than against the ebb. And it is easier in spiritual things, also, to go with the stream, than it is to row against it. Nay, more, the same effort which we put forth to breast it would, in other circumstances, produce more satisfactory results. I do not hesitate to say that it is a less difficult matter to be an earnest Christian in some cities than it is in others; and in a large metropolitan center like this, the tide is all the time running very strongly against us. We ought, therefore, to allow for that, and be all the more earnest in the maintenance of our spiritual life. Then, so far from being injured by the current, we shall be benefited and strengthened, and rise to a nobler type of Christian excellence than may be found elsewhere. But to do that we must take heed. We must guard against the slightest backsliding; and to succeed in that we must constantly test ourselves by the things which we have heard from Jesus. The navigator is saved from danger from unknown currents by his daily observations. The tides of ocean do not affect the heavenly bodies; and by testing himself by these he knows precisely where he is. So the principles of the gospel are not shifted by the tendencies of any place; and when we measure ourselves by them, we may discover how it is with us. Let us not take it for granted that because we are making some effort in the right direction, therefore we must be going forward. For these efforts may not be enough to resist the force of the current, and we may be drifting backward after all. You remember the case of Sir Edward Parry's crew in the Arctic regions. They set out one day to draw a boat over the ice, expecting thereby to get farther northward and in the open water, but after they had journeyed thus for, if I remember rightly, a day and a half or two days, they took an observation, which revealed to their surprise that they were farther south than they had been when they set out, because while they had been going toward the pole, the ice on which they were had been carried by the drift of an under-current in the opposite direction. I fear, my brethren, that in this great business mart, where we are so exclusively occupied in buying and selling, and getting gain, many Christians among us are like these northern voyagers: they make exertions, and they seem, too, to be making progress; but alas! the drift that carries the whole place has carried them with it, and in reality they are not so far advanced as they were, it may be, years ago. This is a matter which we seldom think about, but it will bear pondering; and I earnestly beseech you to examine well and see whether you are even holding your own against the stream of opposite tendency that is flowing constantly in our city.

III. But I have time now to do little more than name a third current, to the influence of which we are exposed. I would call it the personal drift, the drift in each of us individually. In making astronomical observations, one operator is never precisely the same as another. Some are quick, others are slow; some are exceedingly precise, and others not so perfectly exact; and these differences, of course, affect the results at which they arrive. Therefore, to neutralize, as far as possible, any error which may be thereby occasioned, there is what is known as a "personal equation" for each, and by that his conclusions are rectified before they are sent forth for general acceptance. Now, in a similar way, spiritually, each man has his individual tendencies, which easily carry him in one direction or another. This personal drift, as I have named it, is the same thing as the writer of the Epistle from which my text is taken calls in another place the "sin that doth most easily beset us," and by yielding to that many are carried at last into perdition. How easy it is to acquire an evil habit! Nobody, of mature years at least, ever sets himself deliberately to learn such a habit. On the contrary, every one who has ever known or felt anything like Christian motives working within him, would affirm that he neither desires nor designs to let himself be enslaved by any evil. But yet how many such become drunkards before they will confess it to themselves? How many such become gamblers before they will admit that they are in danger from the facination of the cruel siren? How many such are ensnared and held by the cords of their own lusts, humiliated at their helplessness, and yet hardly able to explain to themselves how they came to such degradation? How many such have become dishonest, who, as they now look back upon the history of the past, are amazed and bewildered, and feel as if they had been in some terrible nightmare? All these have yielded to the personal drift, and if, haply, there should be any such within these walls now, let me beseech them to repent and return unto the Lord. There is no hope, and no help, either for time or for eternity, for you save in him. Rise, then, in the might of the strength which he will give you, and break the bonds of the habit by which you have been enthralled. Rise and he will give you pardon and peace; yes, and purity, too, at length; and oh, do not allow yourself to be allured again to the lap of your seducer, for if you do she will deliver you up to the tormentors, who will set you, Samson-like, to grind for their profit, or to make mirth for their sport.

But prevention is better than cure, and therefore would I urge every one of you to examine well his own heart, that he may discover what his besetment is, and to take special care just there. What a wide difference there is between Lot as he was when he was the companion of Abraham, and when he was hurried by the angel out of the burning Sodom! These two, who came together out of Uz of the Chaldees, are now far apart; and how is it explained? Simply by Lot's personal drift. Abraham was where he had always been, or rather he had gone farther in the direction of excellence which he had been pursuing, and in which for a time he had Lot, as it were, in tow. But when that choice of the well-watered plain was made by the latter, he cut the tow-line and drifted—drifted—into the plain—into Sodom—into fellowship with the Sodomites; and lo! this is the end—nay, not yet the end, for there is a darker, unspeakable history behind which illustrates more terribly the danger I would describe. O friends, let us not be self-confident here, or imagine that there is no fear of us. That imagination is itself the beginning of this personal drift. Distrust yourselves, and trust only, but always, in the Lord. Watch the little things, and let no lust, or appetite, or passion obtain dominion over you. Anchor on to Christ, and that is the sure preventive of all such drifting as I have been seeking to expose. Be not content with coming to him, but follow him; and Oh! beware of following him only " afar off," for it was in that way that Peter came so near apostasy. Follow him fully, and he will bring you at last, in spite of all adverse currents and contrary winds, to the haven of everlasting blessedness and rest.

MARCH 19, 1882

THE INDUCTIVE STUDY OF THE SCRIPTURES.*

MATT. iv. 7. "It is written again."

WHEN Satan tempted Christ to cast himself from the pinnacle of the temple, and sought to enforce his request by a quotation from Scripture, the Lord did not meet him with a denial of the inspiration or authority of the promise which he had repeated; but he brought in the corrective of another passage from the word of God in the light of which the former was to be interpreted and applied. To the "it is written" of his assailant he answered, "It is written again." He did not repudiate the assurance which Satan had so glibly cited, but he intimated that he looked for its verification only in connection with his obedience of the command "Thou shalt not tempt the Lord thy God." The injunction, Thou shalt not put to any unnecessary test, by thy false confidence, or bravado, the Lord thy God, is for all times and circumstances; and only those who are obeying that precept have a right to look for the fulfillment of this promise, "He shall give his angels charge concerning thee, and in their hands they shall bear thee up, lest at any time thou dash thy foot against a stone." What the Saviour did here, therefore, was to fill out and complete the interpretation of the passage which Satan had re-

---

* This discourse was given to the theological students at Yale, Princeton and Rochester Theological Seminaries.

peated, and he did that by showing from another passage the conditions within which alone the former could be rationally and intelligently accepted.

Now the procedure of the Lord in this instance plainly implies that one portion or saying of scripture is to be read in connection with all other portions of it, and is to be understood and interpreted only in that sense which is in harmony with every other utterance of the sacred oracles. "All Scripture is given by inspiration of God," and we accept it all as the only infallible rule of faith and practice in religious things. But then, in so accepting it, we receive its individual statements as they are defined and explained by all the rest. No part of it is to be taken isolated and alone, but it is to be viewed as a whole, and the doctrines of our creed as well as the duties of our life are to be discovered by us through an exhaustive examination, not of separate passages, but of the whole teaching and tenor of the entire collection of treatises which we call the Bible. It is not enough that we be able to quote one text in proof of anything which we mean to advance as an article of faith, or enforce as a duty in daily life; but we must examine how that one passage is related to the place in which it occurs, and to all other portions of the Scriptures which treat of the same subject. That is to say, we must study the Bible inductively, and explore its pages with a purpose and a method similar to those with which the man of science investigates the facts of nature. He gathers his instances, noting everything that is peculiar in the case of each; then, having obtained some general principle which is applicable to them all, he arranges and classifies them; and after that he crystallizes the result into some convenient formula which he calls the law of the phenomena. In this way, out of the facts of vegetable life he has evolved the science of botany; out of the phenomena of the heavens he has distilled the science of astronomy; and out of the strata of the earth he is seeking to complete the science of geology.

Now, what Nature is thus to the physical philosopher, Scripture is to the theologian. It furnishes him with a field of observation. Its statements are to him what the phenomena of nature are to the man of science. They are the things which he has to note, classify and formulate. God has not given us a religious system all arranged and mapped out into its several departments in the Book of Revelation, any more than he has given us a scientific division of phenomena in the book of nature; but there is a divine method alike in both, and it is the duty and the privilege of men to find that out in both by a persevering and exhaustive examination. Thus, whatever it may come to be in man's use of it, a system is, at the beginning, the result of investigation and not a guide to inquiry. Astronomy, for example, is, as a science, the outcome of years of observation, calculation and demonstration on the part of many men of genius from the days of Copernicus down to our own. Yet when we teach our children the great principles which have been deduced by these philosophers and tell them, in apparent contradiction to the testimony of their own senses, that the earth moves round the sun and not the sun round the earth, nobody complains of our interfering with the young people's liberty of investigation, or exclaims that we are binding a yoke of system about their necks. But in precisely the same way systematic theology is, in its origin, a result. It is the formal statement of the conclusions arrived at from the diligent investigation of the Scriptures as a whole, by many men of patient, painstaking, plodding perseverance from the day's of

Augustine to those of Hodge; and there needs be no more outcry against teaching our children the principles at which such men have arrived than there is against initiating them into geology under Lyell or into astronomy under Newcomb. I have said this as a vindication of the much-decried use of the catechism in the religious instruction of the young, and to show you that in the educational employment which is thus made of system, theology does not differ from any other of the sciences.

But while all this is true, we ought, as far as possible, in theology to make, or at least to verify, our system for ourselves, and to do that we must study the Bible inductively; that is to say, we must study it first as a whole; then we must take one subject, and having gathered together into one view all the passages that Scripture contains anywhere concerning it, we must seek some principle of classification among them; reduce them all to some general formula which shall embrace everything which each contributes, and find in that the doctrine which the word of God teaches on the matter. And when any one advances some new dogma, then, even as the man of science seeks to repeat the experiment which is alleged to have demonstrated the new principle, we must repeat his investigation, test his reasonings, examine into the fullness or otherwise of his induction, and decide accordingly. It is not enough that he is able to say "it is written" thus and so; but he must be able to show that his interpretation and application of the words which he cites are in harmony with every other "It is written again" which can be brought before him from the same sacred source.

Now in prosecuting such a systematic and inductive

examination of the Scriptures, there are three things in reference to which we must be always on our guard. In the first place, we must see to it that all the passages, brought together for some such purpose as that which I have described, have a real bearing on the subject in hand. We must not mistake resemblance in sound for similarity in sense and allusion. One cannot examine the references in an ordinary study Bible, without noting how many of the parallels cited have little or nothing to do with the meaning and application of the passage in connection with which they are quoted. When any question arises among geologists, the thing is settled by an appeal to the situation in which the specimen was found. Now in the same way all passages which we bring forth as bearing on a subject must be examined "*in situ*," and only those which are really pertinent ought to be permitted to be heard. As an illustration of my meaning here, let me cite a case which happened in my own experience. The question whether it is right for a sinner to pray—a very foolish question, let me say—being under discussion, one of the disputants quoted from John ix., 31, the words: "We know that God heareth not sinners, but if any man be a worshiper of God, and doeth his will, him he heareth," as if these settled the matter. But a little investigation will show that this passage has nothing whatever to do with prayer. It is the assertion of the man who had been cured of his blindness, and is his own way of alleging that one who could work such a miracle as had been performed upon him, could not be an impostor, and must be more than a mere man. Apart altogether, therefore, from the fact that this poor, unlettered man was not speaking by any divine inspiration, and so cannot be accepted as an infallible authority in the case, his words have nothing to do with the warrant or liberty of a sinner to pray, and have no pertinence to any discussion upon that subject. Thus an examination of the circumstances in connection with which a passage occurs is essential to the discovery of its real teaching; and no saying must be wrested from its connection for the purpose of bolstering up a preconceived theory or opinion.

But, in the second place, we must see to it that we give to each passage its own legitimate weight—no more, no less. Everything that is found recorded in the Bible is not, therefore, to be regarded as of divine and infallible authority. This saying may be startling to some, but a little explanation will make it clear. Thus, the historian, Luke, incorporates in his narrative of the Acts of the Apostles the letter of Claudius Lysias, the commandant of the castle of Jerusalem, to Felix, the governor. Now the inspiration of Luke vouches for the accurate reproduction of that letter, but its appearance in his narrative is not an indorsement of the falsehood which it contains to the effect that Lysias rescued Paul because he understood that he was a Roman citizen; for his own record tells us that it was only after the apprehension of Paul, and just when he was in the act of having him bound in order to be scourged, that he found out that the apostle was a Roman. So, again, there are many records of conversations between different persons in the Bible; and, finding these there, we are entitled to conclude that they are correct reports of what each speaker said; but that does not give infallible authority to the sentiments uttered by each. Thus, take the book of Job, for example, and we have in it an account of a series of discussions between the patriarch and his friends. Now inspiration does not misrepresent the speakers, and we may conclude that each uttered that which is attributed to him. But that is a different thing from saying that Eliphaz, Bildad, Zophar, Elihu and Job were all inspired men, and that, if we find in the speeches of any one of them something favoring a particular opinion of our own, we may conclude that we have Scriptural sanction for its maintenance. The Bible contains the assertion, "Skin for skin, yea, all that a man hath will he give for his life," but that is Satan's word and not God's; and he who should quote that in support of the assertion that a man ought to use all means for saving his life is not giving divine warrant for his doctrine, but rather citing the devil's opinion of human nature—an opinion, moreover, which Satan himself discovered was not universally correct, inasmuch as Job preferred his integrity to his life. Nicodemus was right when he said: "We know that thou art a teacher sent from God, for no man can do these miracles that thou doest except God be with him;" but we may not cite that opinion as if it settled the question as to the evidential value of miracles by divine inspiration. It was simply the view of a candid, honest man, and if we want divine warrant for its correctness we must go to Christ himself, or to one of the apostles. The saying of Benhadad: "Let not him that putteth on his armor boast like him that putteth it off," was a very wise one; but it was a maxim of wordly prudence, and it is not lifted up into divine morality by being reported in the Book of Kings. These and many similar passages which might be cited, may serve to show that when we find a passage bearing on a point in hand, we must take care to give it no more and no less that its legitimate weight.

Thirdly, we must see to it that our induction of passages is complete. In the logical argument which is known as a dilemma, and which proceeds on the assumption that one or other of two things must be true, the conclusion is at once disproved if you can bring forward a third thing which may as easily be true as either of the other two. And, in the same way, the conclusion which one draws from an induction of particulars is fatally vitiated if some other particular of a different sort ought to have been included. Thus, in the case of such a doctrine as the Atonement, if, like Macleod Campbell, one takes his stand merely upon two passages of Scripture, and deals with them as if they were all that had a bearing on the subject, it is enough to upset his conclusion to declare that he has utterly ignored other portions of the word of God having a different aspect and yet clearly referring to the same great theme. One unexplained fact, as Sir Isaac Newton was free to confess, would upset the most plausible and insinuating theory, and in the same way one passage of Scripture fairly bearing on the theme in hand, and yet inconsistent with the doctrine sought to be formulated, demands a reconsideration of the subject and a restatement of the conclusion.

These principles seem to me to be so clear that no further argument is needed in their support. Now let us look at a few subjects in the consideration of which the importance of their application will be seen.

Take, then, in the first place, the doctrine of the Trinity, and it will be found that while there are many passages in both the Old Testament and the New which give the strongest emphasis to the unity of God, "it is written again," and frequently, that the Father is God, and the Son is God, and the Holy Spirit is God; while in such formulæ as that of baptism and that of the apostolic benediction, each is so named as to indicate that there is in each something that is unique and distinctive. Fatherhood is not Sonship; and there is that attributed to the Holy Ghost which is peculiar to him. Now how shall we do in such a case? If we so keep to the divine unity as to repudiate the deity of the Son and that of the Holy Ghost, we fall into the error of the Socinian and are guilty of an imperfect induction. If, again, we begin to describe the distinction between the three in human phraseology, we are in danger of falling into tri-theism, and so repudiating that unity which is everywhere in Scripture predicated of God. We must therefore find some formula in which the deity of each shall be recognized, while yet the unity of the Godhead shall be maintained. If we attempt to explain the "how," we shall immediately land ourselves in difficulty; but if we mean to be faithful to Scripture teaching on the subject, we must find some place for an acknowledgment of both facts. Whether the word "person," which has been settled on as that by which to designate the distinction is the best, may fairly enough be questioned; for if we take that term in its modern sense it is almost suggestive of tri-theism: and if we restrict it to its ancient significance, it may lead us to that Sabellianism which resolved the Trinity simply into modes of the divine manifestation; so, perhaps, it would be better to content ourselves with saying that the Father is God, and the Son is God, and the Spirit is God; and that while each of these terms denotes something distinctive and restricted to him who is called by it, yet the deity of each must not be held in any such sense as violates the incontrovertible truth, that "the Lord our God is one Jehovah." If you ask me to explain how this can be, I acknowledge my helplessness; but if I am to formulate the result of a full Scriptural induction on this subject, I must do it in some such manner as that which I have just expressed. I dare not reject either side of the apparent inconsistency without failing to take note of some of the Bible statements on the subject, and if I do that, I am guilty of setting myself above revelation, and making my reason and not Scripture the infallible standard of my faith. If I do that, I am as unscientific in my treatment of the Bible, as I should be in my treatment of nature if I took note only of such facts as fitted my theory and ignored all others.

Take, again, the doctrine of the Person of Christ, and we have in it an illustration precisely similar to that of the Trinity. The Lord Jesus is really a man. That is everywhere apparent in the gospel history. But then his was a unique manhood, giving constant evidence that there was in him something higher and nobler than common humanity. Moreover he is constantly spoken of by his followers as one possessed of Deity, or rather, to speak more correctly, as one in whom Deity was united to humanity. Thus John describes him in this wise: "The Word was made flesh and dwelt among us;" and in immediate connection with that assertion he affirms: "The Word was God." Again, Paul declares that being originally "in the form of God" he took upon him "the form of a servant," and if any one should shelter himself here under the word "form," as if that meant something different from real godhood, the sufficient answer is found in the fact that the form of a servant describes a very real service; so that the apostle in these expressions virtually claims for him that he is God in human nature. Nor are these isolated passages; multitudes of others might be cited to the same effect, while there are some that speak of his manhood alone, and others which make reference only to his deity. What, then, does a fair induction from all these require? It "is written" that he is a man. But "it is written again" that he is God. Shall I then reject either? No; for that would be unscientific, and would be a repudiation of the Bible as the guide of my faith. I must accept both, however mysterious, and, indeed, incomprehensible the miracle may be; I must declare that in the one person of Christ deity and manhood are united. If I begin to refine into particulars I shall soon find myself lost in uttermost perplexity, for that is always the result of seeking to be wise above what is written, but if I mean to be wise "up to" what is written, and seek to formulate all that the New Testament teaches on the subject, I must declare in the words of the catechism, that "the eternal Son of God became man, and so was, and continueth to be God and man in two distinct natures and one person for ever."

Very instructive in this particular is the record of church history. Almost every conceivable opinion on this subject has been broached by some one; and every new view that is started upon it will be found to be virtually the resurrection of some old heresy, and may be shown to be founded on an imperfect induction of Scripture teaching regarding it; while that which has been settled upon as the orthodox faith upon it may be considered as the final result of a reverent attempt continued for many ages, to give expression to the sum of Scriptural teaching in answer to the question: "Who is this Son of Man?" There is only one way of holding a spirit-level which will keep the vacuum exactly at the center, and if you swerve from that even in the least degree, the vacuum will ultimately move either to one extremity or the other. So in the orthodox statement of the doctrine of the person of Christ you have the only resting-place where you can permanently remain and do justice to all that the Bible says about it; for if you go on the one side, you will land yourself ultimately in the extreme of that humanitarianism which sees in Christ nothing more than a man; while if you move to the other, you will find yourself at length in that error of the ancient Docetæ, who regarded Christ's human body as a phantom or mere appearance, and so believed only in his deity. The true inductive spirit compels us to accept them both, and to hold that he was and is God manifest in the flesh.

We may illustrate this principle, also, by a reference to the doctrine of the atonement. When we examine the New Testament we find that subject spoken of in four different, yet not inconsistent, aspects. It is called a sacrifice, as when Christ is said to have "borne our sins," and is designated as "the Lamb of God that taketh away the sins of the world." It is styled a redemption, as when Paul says, "In Christ we have redemption through his blood, even the forgiveness of sins;" and the Lord himself affirms that "The Son of man is come to give his life a ransom for many." It is characterized as "a declaration of God's righteousness in the forgiveness of sins, that he might be just and yet the justifier of him that believeth;" and the same phase of it is presented to us when the apostle alleges that "it pleased the Father, having made peace by the blood of his cross, by him to reconcile all things unto himself," for the making peace by the blood of the cross is as evidently something prior and in order to the effecting of reconciliation, and must, therefore, be equivalent to the declaration of righteousness whereby he is just and yet the justifier of the believer. And, finally, it is all traced up to the love of God, "who gave his only begotten Son that whosoever believeth in him should not perish but have everlasting life." Thus the death of Christ did not purchase God's love for sinners, but manifested that love and opened for it a righteous channel through which it might flow to guilty men. Under one or other of these four heads I believe that all the Bible references to this great theme may be arranged. But the mere fact that it is presented to us in so many different ways is a proof that no one mode of speech can fully describe its character, and the great source of the discussions which have been waged over it is to be found in this, that each disputant has adopted one of these modes of viewing it, as if that contained the whole truth about it and involved in it the negation of all the rest. But the right induction is that which accepts all the four, and maintains that the doctrine of the atonement fully formulated must be the great whole which accepts them all and holds them all in harmony with each other. It regards Christ's death as a manifestation of God's love in the provision of an all-sufficient sacrifice for human sin, whereby God's righteousness is declared in the forgiveness and salvation of believing men, usually called their redemption. We have heard too much of the 'moral' view, and the 'legal' view, and the 'governmental' view, and so forth, of the atonement. Let us try to get at the Scriptural view, and to find that we must not take one passage and make it interpret all the rest, but we must interrogate them all and receive with reverent faith from each its contribution to the great result.

We may see another field for the application of

the same principles in the investigation of the difficult questions which cluster about the sovereignty of God and the free agency of man. We have some passages which clearly and unequivocally declare that "of God and through God and to God are all things," and there are others which as certainly teach the unfettered moral freedom of man. There are some which affirm that believers are chosen in Christ before the foundation of the world, and others that place salvation unequivocally at the acceptance of the sinner's will; there are some which affirm that saints are kept by the power of God through faith unto salvation, and others which declare that "he that is begotten of God keepeth himself." Now, here again the same questions arise: Shall we choose the one and reject the other; or, shall we accept both, believing both to be in harmony in God, however incomprehensible that harmony may now seem to us? If we take the first alternative, then we are guilty of rationalism—for we accept of Scripture just what pleases us, and reject the rest. If we take the second, then, though intellectual wiseacres may sneer at us as fools, we deal at once reverently and inductively with the sacred oracles. The hyper-Calvinist runs away with the divine sovereignty, as if that were all; and the Arminian walks off with human freedom, as if in that he had found the whole truth. But neither of them accepts the full truth, or has made a complete induction. It is the old story of the knights and the shield over again. Both are correct in what they affirm and wrong in what they deny; and, curiously enough, in the union of the affirmations of both the full truth is obtained. "It is written," the one may truly say; but "it is written again," the other may as truly reply; and if we are to have a

Scriptural theory, we must hold by both, looking to God as if all depended upon him, and at the same time exerting ourselves as if all depended upon us.

But to mention only one illustration more—let me take the practical subject of prayer, all the more that, just for the neglect of the principles on which I have been insisting, many hold the most erroneous views regarding it. It is written: "Every one that asketh receiveth, and he that seeketh findeth, and to him that knocketh it shall be opened." And again: "Whatsoever ye shall ask in my name that will I do, that the Father may be glorified in the Son; if ye shall ask anything in my name I will do it." Now from these and many similar passages multitudes have inferred that by prayer they will obtain anything which they choose to seek from God, and some of the wildest statements have been made by them in this matter, savoring, as I cannot but think, both of superstition and delusion. For it is written again: "If ye abide in me and my words abide in you, ye shall ask what ye will, and it shall be done unto you." And again: "Delight thyself also in the Lord, and he shall give thee the desires of thine heart." Moreover, it cannot be forgotten that when David fasted and wept and prayed for the life of his child, he did not obtain that which he desired; and when Paul besought the Lord that the thorn in his flesh might depart from him, he did not get the thing which he requested. From all this, therefore, it is evident that the universal promise is to be understood as qualified by some indispensable conditions which connect themselves with the character of the suppliant, with the nature of the thing requested, and with the purpose and prerogative of God himself. If the petitioner be not abiding in Christ, or if the thing which he seeks be something that will do him real harm, or if by refusing his prayer God can train him into something better and nobler than he would become if his request were granted, then his desire will not be given to him. It would be easy to dwell on each of these three conditions and show you how much is involved in each; but what I now insist upon is that they *are* conditions as constant and as invariable, as in the case of my text, the obedience of the command, "Thou shalt not tempt the Lord thy God," is alleged to be the condition of the fulfillment of the promise, "He shall give his angels charge concerning thee." But how seldom all this is taken note of by many modern Christians? They seem to think that the Lord exists simply and only to answer prayer. They forget that he is the Father of his people, and that as such he is disciplining his children for heaven. They know, indeed, that they train their own children by the manner in which they deal with their requests, but they think God as a Father is to be so indulgent as to grant them everything, without regard either to his own honor or to their good; and so they are troubled about their "unanswered prayers." But in reality there are only two prayers for which we have an unconditional assurance that we shall have a full answer. These are: Father, glorify thy name," and, "The will of the Lord be done"; and as the true believer who abides in Jesus has these two petitions as the under-tone of every request, he always carries away a blessing. So let us not be ignorant, unreasonable and unscriptural in our expectations when we pray, but accepting the full teaching of the Word of God upon the subject, let us make our plea and leave ourselves with joyful trust in our Father's hand, full sure that even the denial of a request may be itself the means of answering some of the deepest yearnings of our hearts.

Many other illustrations of the application of the inductive principle to the investigation of the sacred Scriptures might be given, but these, must suffice for the present. Let me conclude by little more than mentioning three important inferences which may be drawn from the course of thought which we have prosecuted and the remembrance of which may be of great service to those who are looking forward to the ministry of the Gospel.

In the first place every heresy has in it a certain modicum of truth. The poet has said that "There is a soul of goodness in things evil, could we observingly distill it out;" and no one can read thoughtfully the history of doctrine in the Christian Church without discovering that even in those systems of error which have from time to time made their appearance there has been a side of truth. Not only so: the error has been formidable not because of the error, but because of the truth that was mixed up with it. One can much more easily deal with that which is wholly wrong than with that which is partly right; and the great misfortune in controversy has been that the defenders of the faith have not always had the discrimination to distinguish the fraction of truth from the error to which it has given vitality, and both have been assailed together. Thus, whether the issue were victory or defeat, there was sure to be some injury done to truth. Whenever, therefore, some system of doctrine becomes prevalent, and you see it to be dangerous in its tendency yet attractive in its presentation, accustom yourselves to ask first of all concerning it what is the portion of truth in it that gives it feasibility, and that will at once indicate how it is to be met.

For, in the second place, the truth thus mixed up with error is very generally something that has been too largely overlooked. That which has been neglected revenges itself at length by claiming more than its due share of importance. The continual presentation by old divines of the federal theology with its clean-cut legal formulæ, provoked the assertion that the whole virtue of the atonement was of a moral sort, and that there was no reference to God's justice or satisfaction of law whatever in it. So, again, the constant prominence given to the deity of Christ and the almost universal ignoring of his humanity, swung men off into that early Unitarianism which made such exquisite use of the brotherhood of the Lord Jesus. And the insistence by multitudes on the mechanical verbal-dictation theory of inspiration, struck out of Coleridge those "Letters of an Inquiring Spirit" which have been the germ of almost everything that has been written by the Broad School on the subject since his day.

Now if these two general principles be true, you will see at once, as a third inference from our subject, how error is to be most effectually met. Recognize the portion of truth which it contains. Bring that back to its proper importance. Then supplement it by putting it along with those other sides of the truth which are needed to give it full-balanced completeness. Let it be acknowledged fully and frankly "it is written," but then let it be added it is written "again." Admit freely the reality of the Redeemer's manhood, but put with that the genuineness of his deity. Concede willingly the moral theory of the atonement as far as it goes; but make it clear that there is more than that in the Scripture statements on the subject, and show that the moral view can have no place unless the other be held along with it: grant all that is required concerning the individuality of the inspired writers; but yet insist upon it that through that individuality God sent his message to mankind. Thus you will kill error without injuring truth. Thus, too, you will keep yourselves from becoming narrow-minded and intolerant, and will cultivate that spirit not more truly philosophic than Christian which is open-eyed toward all truth, and welcomes it even when it comes, apparently, in no good company.

January 30, 1881.

AN OPEN DOOR FOR LITTLE STRENGTH.

Rev. iii. 8.—Behold I have set before thee an open door, and no man can shut it; for thou hast a little strength and hast kept my word and hast not denied my name.

"Thou hast a little strength." The words were addressed to the angel of the church at Philadelphia by the Lord Jesus after its members had passed, with honor, through some fiery ordeal, which had been designed by their enemies to make them deny his name. They do not mean, as some might be inclined to suppose, that the persecution had been so oppressive as wellnigh to exhaust the church, so that though it had come off with unstained loyalty, it had only a little strength remaining. Rather they describe the condition of the church before the terrible trial came upon it. From the very beginning its ability had been but small. It had never been what outsiders would have called a strong church. In numbers, in wealth, in rank, in influence, in every other constituent which is popularly regarded as contributing to power in the world, it had been always poor. Yet small as its strength was, its members had stood firm in the the face alike of cruel threatenings and alluring promises. And lo! as the reward of their steadfastness, the Lord declares that he has set before them "an open door" which no man could shut. That is to say, through the gateway of their fidelity, feeble as they were, they went under the leadership of Christ to a sphere of usefulness, which was peculiarly and pre-eminently their own, and which no mortal could prevent them from filling. Thus interpreted, this text has been to me full of comfort and inspiration, and I desire to-day to make you sharers with me in the blessing it has brought to me.

"Thou hast but little strength." How many in all our congregations may be truly thus addressed! They are painfully conscious of their feebleness, not only when they contrast themselves with those who are more favorably circumstanced, but also when they look abroad on the work which is yet to be done for Christ in the world. Sometimes the weakness is physical, and the frailness of the body prevents the man from undertaking that which, in vigorous health, he would have entered upon with joy. Sometimes it is intellectual, and as he thinks of the undeniable eminence in science and philosophy of some of those who are arrayed against God's truth, he is almost tempted to wish that he had the ability to cope with them in argument and show the fallaciousness of their reasonings. Sometimes it is social; he has little wealth, and no great standing in the world; it may be that he is even in a subordinate place as the servant of another, and as he desires to do something for Christ, and has, perhaps, the claims of different causes urged upon him from the pulpit or elsewhere, he is apt to become despondent when he discovers that he is literally unable, from the necessity of his situation, to do anything for any one of them. I believe that cases of this kind are commoner than multitudes imagine; and that there is much secret sorrow in the hearts of many humble followers of Christ, because in one or other of these ways they are being continually made to feel that they have only "a little strength."

Now, I know few passages of Scripture more admirably fitted to give encouragement and direction to those who are distressed in this way than that which is now before us. For one thing it suggests to us that the having of but little strength is not a matter of which we need to be ashamed. The Lord here does not blame the Philadelphians for their feebleness. There is not a single syllable of reproof in this whole letter; and we must not suppose that weakness is always and of necessity wickedness. If one has brought it upon himself by his own iniquity, then it may be a matter of disgrace; but if it come in the allotment of God's providence, there is no moral reproach to be associated with it. No doubt the tendency among men is to despise feebleness. The law of "the survival of the fittest," whether there be much or little in it in natural science, is certainly not unknown in human life, for almost invariably by selfishness the weakest is driven to the wall. If a boy has some constitutional defect, whether lameness of foot, or obliquity of vision, or impediment of speech, it will too often be turned into ridicule by his companions; and in this matter I am afraid that many men may truly be described as children of a larger growth. So, because in common society weakness is too often counted a reproach by men, the feeble Christian is apt to think that God will despise him because he has only a little strength. But that is not the case. Look again at this epistle. Christ did not overlook the church of Philadelphia, weak though it was; and neither does he now forget his feeble children. Is it not written, "A bruised reed shall he not break, and the smoking flax shall he not quench"? Nay, do we not see in the description of the children's angels as beholding the face of God, that the care of the least is the special charge of the highest? Lack of strength, therefore, so far from making us the objects of the Divine contempt, only gives us a new claim upon his assistance. Whoever may upbraid us with our weakness, we may be sure that Jesus never will; and if he do not condemn us for it, why should we be ashamed of it in the sight of men? He giveth power to the faint and to them that have no might he increaseth strength.

But more than this, when we take this letter and read it in connection with the others which have been framed and hung up here for our perusal in the porch of the book of Revelation, there is suggested to us the truth that the having of but a little strength may even come to be, in some respects, an advantage. For it is not a little remarkable that the two churches which received unqualified commendation are those of Smyrna and Philadelphia, neither of which was strong in the ordinary sense of the term; while on the other hand the severest reproof is addressed to the church of Laodicea, which any outsider would have spoken of as at once prosperous and influential. Thus we are reminded that where there is much strength there is also a disposition to trust in that; while, on the other hand, where there is conscious feebleness there is felt also the necessity of making application for the might of the Most High. That was the secret of Paul's paradox, "When I am weak, then am I strong;" and there are many among us who feel that if it had not been for the blessing of God imparted to them through physical affliction, or pecuniary straits, they might, and in all probability would, have grown proud and defiant, and thus might have cut themselves off from the grace of God. So let the weak be reconciled to his weakness, and accept it as being the will of God in Christ Jesus concerning him.

But pursuing this line of thought a little farther we may see from my text that the having of only a little strength does not utterly disqualify us from serving the Lord. Feeble as they were, the Philadelphians had kept Christ's word and had not denied his name. They glorified him where they were, and in the manner appropriate to their circumstances. They kept their loyalty to him even in their weakness. And it is possible for every one of us to do the same. If God has given us only one talent, he does not hold us responsible for five. If my strength is small he does not require of me that which only a larger measure of power could enable me to perform. Wherever I am, it is enough if there I keep his word; and however limited be my resources, he asks no more than that I use all these resources in advancing the honor of his name. He is no hard master, reaping where he has not sown, and gathering where he has not strewn. If he has not given me wealth, he asks only that I consecrate my poverty to him. If he has not bestowed upon me commanding intellectual abilities, he seeks only that I use those which I possess in serving him; and if "obstacles and trials seem like prison walls to be," he requires only that I do the little that I can, and leave the rest to him. Nay, if there is nothing active that I can undertake, it will be sufficient if I resist all temptations to let go his word and to deny his name. From this none of us can excuse himself, and every one who earnestly sets himself to act after this fashion may rely upon the assurance, "My grace is sufficient for thee; my strength is made perfect in weakness."

Still further, if we proceed upon this principle, my

text affirms that a wider sphere will be ultimately opened up to us. Look at it again: "I have set before thee an open door, for thou hast but little strength and hast kept my word, and hast not denied my name." Fidelity is rewarded by greater opportunity. "He that is faithful in that which is least" is promoted to that which is greater, and has given to him a loftier position and a wider range. The man who is always murmuring over the limits of his lot will never do anything in the world. He whose pride is wounded because he has received only one talent will be sure to bury that one in the earth. But if he will only use his little all to purpose, laying it out to usury with faithfulness, earnestness, and prayer, he will find at length his opportunities doubled. Thus it is always that men have risen, alike in the church and in the world, to the thrones of their individual power. From those who have not, even that which they have is sure to be taken away; but they who have begun by doing their little faithfully have risen through that into something nobler, and through that again to something higher, until at length they have reached a position which at first seemed quite beyond the possibility of their attainment. They have had set before them an open door, which none has been able to shut. Fidelity always rises. It is, in fact, irrepressible; for when Christ says to it, "Come up higher," no one can hold it down.

Such, as it seems to me, are the main teachings of this suggestive verse, and if I have been right in thus interpreting it, one or two inferences of a wholesome sort will follow.

I. In the first place we may learn that usefulness is not the primary object of the Christian's attention. I would not be understood, indeed, as seeking in any way to discourage those whose desire it is to benefit their fellow men by leading them to the Lord Jesus. It is right to aim after the welfare of those who are still ignorant and out of the way. But I am persuaded that many among us fail in securing that because we do not seek it in the right manner. We are apt to make it a primary and immediate end in and of itself, and to forget that the first thing Christ sets us to do is to be faithful where we are, by keeping his word and confessing his name. Usefulness is the result of character, and therefore character ought to have our earliest care. Not what we can do for others, but rather what we are in ourselves, demands our first attention, for to do good to others we must first be good ourselves. Usefulness is to character what fragrance is to the flower. But the gardener does not make the fragrance his first or greatest aim. Nay, rather his grand design is to produce a perfect flower, for he knows if he succeed in that the fragrance will come of itself. In the same way the Christian's first concern should be with his own character. His prime ambition ought to be, where he is, to keep Christ's word and to confess his name; and when he has succeeded in that, the door to legitimate and lasting usefulness will open to him of itself, or, rather, Christ will open it for him and no man will be able to shut it.

The first results of our Christianity are to be looked for not in the effects of our work upon others, but in the development of holiness in ourselves; and when our characters are thus Christianized we shall find through them a short and easy way to usefulness, for indeed the effluence of them will be the finest means of telling upon others. Hence I cannot but regard it as unfortunate and indeed unnatural when young converts who have only just found their way to Christ, are encouraged forthwith to begin to labor among others. They may be instrumental in doing something, but in that way they will never attain to anything like the highest usefulness. Their first duty is in the sphere in which Christ found them, to keep his word and to confess his name. Their first care ought to be for the manifestation of the Christian character in the lowly and limited place to which they originally belonged, and through their faithfulness in that the Lord will open up for them a door to something higher. To be holy is our primary duty, and through that we pass to usefulness. If, therefore, there be those before me who are eager for the crown that is to be won by turning many to righteousness, let me urge them not to go after that in the wrong way. The shortest path to it is not that which seeks it directly, but that which lies through faithful holiness in the discharge of duty or the endurance of trial where you are. Nor let any one be discouraged if by reason of the pressure of immediate obligations, or the circumscribing influence of weakness or of suffering, he may seem to be shut out from doing anything for others. That which he has to look to for the moment is the cultivation of holiness within the limits of his providential surroundings, and it is only through the keeping of Christ's word by himself there, that he is to expect the opening of a door into wider work among others. Everything in its own order, and here the order is, first, cultivation of personal holiness, and then the attainment of a sphere of usefulness.

II. But if these things are so, we have as, another inference suggested from this text, an easy explanation of the great usefulness of many who are in no wise noteworthy for strength. Few things are more commonly spoken of among men than the fact that the most successful soul-winners in the ministry are not always those who are most conspicuous for intellectual ability or argumentative power. If you take up the sermons, for example, of John Wesley or of George Whitefield, you will find it hard to believe that such effects as we read of in the records of the period were produced by them. In point of mental power and suggestiveness they are not for a moment to be put into comparison with those of many other men who had apparently scarcely any success; and if we look at the sermons alone, there is no explanation of their results to be found in them. But no printing-press can reproduce the preacher; and the secret of the power in all such cases was in the men. Their greatness was their goodness. Their holy characters, formed and molded by the Spirit of God, exhaled through their discourses, and these gave them their usefulness. In the same way you will sometimes find a church whose members are poor in this world's goods, and not remarkable for that culture which modern circles have so largely deified, yet famous for its good works among the masses, and foremost in the successes which it has achieved in evangelistic work; and when you look into the matter you find the explanation in the consecrated characters and lives of those who are associated in its fellowship. They have sought their usefulness through their holiness, and not their holiness through their usefulness; and therefore it is they have had such signal triumphs. On the other hand, when we see churches great in numbers, wealthy in resources, and fully equipped with all the machinery required for home missionary work, yet mourning over their lack of success in its prosecution, my text suggests a possible explanation of the anomaly. Their communion rolls, perhaps, are burdened with those who are not distinguished for holiness, and who have a name that they live while they are dead. Their members, it may be, are lacking in consecration; they are not thorough-going in the maintenance of the principles of the gospel in their daily lives, they are unfaithful to their profession in their conduct, and so Christ has shut the door in the face of their church, and no man can open it. When we are unsuccessful in work for others, let us see whether it be not because we are somewhere unfaithful in our motives. Israel could not take Ai when Achan with his hidden wickedness was in the camp; and who can tell how sorely our churches are crippled in their work, and how largely their exertions are neutralized by the inconsistencies of those who are nominally connected with them. When doors are closed against us it is time to inquire whether it be not true that we have not been keeping the Lord's word, and have been denying his name. Unfaithfulness shuts us out of opportunity. A man is useless because he has been heedless of the Word; a church is useless because it has denied Christ's name. The thought is full of solemnity alike for minister and people, and if it should be that we are mourning over our comparative failure in telling on the outlying world, let us search and see lest the cause of our lack of success be not in our denial somewhere of the Lord that bought us. Nor let us forget that the noblest contribution we can give to the work of the church is our own personal holiness, for without that no money offering can be fully blessed, and yet, even if we be poor in this world's goods, that is a gift which we may always lay upon Christ's altar if we will.

III. Finally, if the principles which I have tried to deduce from this text are true, we see at once how such apparently opposite things as Christian contentment and Christian ambition are to be perfectly harmonized. The full discharge of duty on the lower level opens the passage up into the higher. We see that illustrated in secular departments, if I may call them so, every day. If the school-boy wishes to gain a high and honorable position as a man, he must be content, so long as he is at school, to go through its daily round, and perform in the best possible manner its common duties. The better he is as a scholar, the more surely will the door into eminence open for him as a man. But if he trifle away his time, if he neglect his work, if he despise what he calls the "drudgery" of education, and so leave school without having learned those things which he was sent thither to to acquire, then there will be nothing for him in after days but humiliation and failure. Doors enow may open to him, but he will never be ready to enter one of them, and will be to the last, unless he go back and make up for what he has lost, a useless hanger-on to the skirts of society. In the same way if a servant would seek to be a master, the shortest way to that end is for him to accept his present lot and be in it the very best of servants. He who is always scheming for a sudden elevation, as if he would vault at one leap into the chair of his ambition, never reaches it in that way; or if he do, he cannot keep in it. But the wise plan is to be content for the time with the place we have, and show the highest excellence in filling that; for in the long run the door always opens before character. The "candidating minister" who is forever gadding about among vacant churches seeking a suitable sphere, until at length he becomes known as the "solicitor-general," never gets one to his mind. But the man who is conspicuously diligent where he is, and is doing there his utmost for the honor of the Lord, will be sought for by others without any agency of his own, and will receive the recognition of the Master in a nobler opportunity.

Now it is not otherwise in every other department. The first thing we have to do, if we would pass from a lower to a higher post of usefulness, is to adapt ourselves thoroughly to our present sphere, and set ourselves diligently to perform its duties. If we are conscious of its limitations then let us not rebel against them, but accept them and make the best possible work within them. Then when we have turned our little strength to good account, we shall find the door opened to us by the Master's hand. Contentment with the present thus, paradoxical as it may seem, is the surest means of securing in the future that on which, as Christians, we are taught to set our desires. Fretting over our weakness will not make things better, but it will prevent us from bringing anything out of the little strength we have. He who is constantly complaining that he has no more, makes little or no use of that which he has; whereas the man who is reconciled for the moment to his position and deliberately seeks to serve God in the best way there, is already in the sure and safe way to promotion. This is a most important consideration, for it brings all the hopes of the future and focuses them on the duties of the present, making the commendation of the Judge at last depend upon even so small a thing as the giving of a cup of cold water to a disciple in his name, or the visiting for his sake of one of his imprisoned brethren.

Here, then, is comfort as well as direction for the weak. Present fidelity is the door through which we pass to future eminence. The disciple of the Lord is content with the sphere in which he is placed; but he seeks to fill that thoroughly, in order that he may rise the sooner to something better. Nor does he seek in vain, for the Lord does not overlook the faithfulness of the feeble, but opens for them a door of opportunity which all the sticklers for ecclesiastical propriety, and all the votaries of intellectul culture, and all the influences of fashionable society will not be able to shut. And then when the best use has been made of earth's opportunities, when he has employed to the utmost in the Master's service and the service of his generation that strength which even at its best in this life is but small, the Lord will open for him the door of heaven, saying, "Well done, good and faithful servant; thou hast been faithful over a few things; I will make thee ruler over many things; enter thou into the joy of thy Lord."

October 31, 1880.

THE SORROWFUL "IF."

John xi. 21 and 32. Lord, if thou hadst been here, my brother had not died.

Every reader of the Gospels is perfectly familiar even with the minutest details of this most interesting chapter. For that reason, therefore, and also because the most important points in it will come incidentally up as we follow the line of thought which I have marked out for this discourse, I shall not attempt to give you any summary of the narrative by way of introduction, but proceed at once to indicate and illustrate the practical and experimental truths which it suggests.

I. Notice, then, in the first place, that the friends of Jesus are not exempted from affliction in the world. If such immunity might have been expected in any case, it surely would have been in that of the members of the Bethany family who so often received and entertained the Lord. The household consisted of three members—a brother and two sisters—to each of whom Christ was bound by ties of human friendship, as well as of spiritual fellowship. He was, in fact, almost like another brother in the family, one to whom they were all most tenderly attached, and who loved them very specially in return. Their house was one of the few places—perhaps the only place—on earth in which he was perfectly at home. Thither he often went after a weary day of labor and debate with the Jews in the streets of Jerusalem or in the courts of the temple, and there he always found congenial companionship unshadowed by the presence of enemies who were watching to entangle him in his talk. No painful association connects itself with Bethany. We cannot think of Bethlehem without remembering the massacre of the infants; of Nazareth without recalling the rejection of the Saviour by the men of the city in which "he had been brought up;" of Capernaum, without recollecting the woe which its inhabitants drew down upon their heads; of Jerusalem, without having brought to mind the sad scene of the crucifixion; but Bethany is linked only to memories of blessedness, and the home of Lazarus stands out from among the scenes of the gospel history with a sacredness that is peculiar to itself; for there the Lord Jesus was honored and beloved. Yet, dear as Christ was to its inmates, and tenderly as they were regarded by him, they were not on that account exempt from affliction; for here we have these statements in the closest proximity. "Now Jesus loved Martha and her sister and Lazarus;" and again: "A certain man was sick, named Lazarus, of Bethany, the town of Mary, and her sister Martha."

This suggests the question, why affliction is sent upon those who are the friends of God? It is the old problem which Job and his three visitors debated, and which, taken in connection with the frequent prosperity of the wicked, perplexed the souls of the authors of the 37th and 73d psalms; and though the full materials for its solution are not furnished to us anywhere, we may yet find some light cast upon it by this and other portions of the word of God. For we may conclude that such trial is not necessarily the result of any special sin. Even in regard to those who had no such tender relationship to himself, the Saviour warned his disciples against drawing the inference that particular suffering is always the consequence of some particular wickedness, and in a case like that of Lazarus and his sisters, it is clear that all such reasoning would be unwarranted. Nay, more, in affirming, as he did in answer to the application of the sisters, that "This sickness is for the glory of God, that the Son of God might be glorified thereby," he laid down a general principle which may guide us in all similar instances. The great design of God in the affliction of his people is to show the exceeding riches of his grace, and thus to commend himself to them as the strength of their hearts and their portion forever. And if it be asked in what respects his glory is thus advanced through the trial of his own, different answers must be given to the question. It may be so in the development of the character of the afflicted one himself; for there can be no doubt that spiritual growth is often promoted by such discipline. Hezekiah is not the only one who has felt and said that "By these things men live." Luther numbered trials as among his best instructors; and the Psalmist records the experience of multitudes when he says: "It is good for me that I have been afflicted." Again the afflictions of God's people may redound to his glory in their effect upon others, either as silencing the gainsayer, or as converting the careless, or as educating the weak believer into stronger faith. The calamities of Job came on him to prove the utter falseness of the assertion made by Satan, that the truly godly man is moved only by utilitarian considerations, and serves the Lord simply for what he can make thereby; and I have no doubt that even in our own days many Christians have been sorely afflicted, just to show to the scoffing crew by whom they were surrounded how sure and abiding their confidence was, and how lovingly God could sustain them in the deepest distress. Sometimes, again, through the sufferings of a believing friend the indifferent have been awakened and led to the Lord. The affliction of a parent has been, as we express it, "sanctified" to a son or a daughter; and the illness of a companion, borne with Christian submission, has led many a man to Christ; while, again, a weak believer has often been strengthened by the sight of the calm bearing and simple trustfulness of a dear one on whom God's hand has been laid. Christ said to his followers in this very case: "I am glad, for your sakes, that I was not there, to the intent ye may believe." We have all known such instances, and when we think it through we come to see that vicarious suffering is not confined to Christ. In the highest sacrificial sense of the words, indeed, we must say that no one ever suffered for others as He did; but in a lower sense it is true that believers often do suffer for others; and when their benefit is secured thereby, the afflicted ones discover that their sickness has really been for the glory of God, so that they enter in a very real way into "the fellowship of the Saviour's sufferings." I think if this view were more frequently taken, affliction would not so often lead the sufferer to morbid introspection, as if God was somehow offended with him and it was essential that he should search in himself for some reason for his trial; while, again, it would sustain him under his visitation with the hope that others might be benefited through his tribulation. If Lazarus or his sisters could have foreseen all that was to result from the trial to which they were subjected, they would have been thoroughly upheld thereby; and their history is written here from first to last, just to give us a revelation of the possibilities that may spring out of our sorrows. These considerations may not, perhaps, quite solve the problem why the friends of Jesus are afflicted, but they do most undoubtedly lessen the mystery, and they may serve to put a staff into our hands when God shall cause us to walk through the valley of shadow. In any case the narrative on which now I am commenting, ought to keep us from rashly concluding that because we are afflicted we cannot be the objects of the love of God. When the teacher desires to demonstrate his own excellence as an instructor he takes his ripest scholar and subjects him to the sorest examination, not because he is suspicious of his attainments, but just because he knows that they are so thorough: so sometimes I think the Lord exposes his dearest people to fiery trials, not because he would expose their weakness, but because he knows their strength, and would thereby commend that grace by which they stand to the acceptance of their fellow men. If he had not been so sure of Mary and Martha they might have been spared, at this time, the affliction which befell them; but it came on them that, through them, untold multitudes might be blessed. This may be a view of the matter that is strange to some of you, but I am sure it is a right view, and I have dwelt upon it now because of the consolation which it yields.

II. But notice now, in the second place, that the friends of Jesus in their affliction turn directly and immediately to him. So soon as Martha and Mary awoke to the seriousness of their brother's illness, they sent unto Christ a messenger to say: "Lord, he whom thou lovest is sick." They believed that he was "the Christ, the Son of God, that should come into the world," and they made instant application unto him in that capacity. They know his power; they cherished fondly the remembrance of their happy fellowship with him, and they trusted implicitly in his grace—so implicitly, indeed, that they made no definite request, but contented themselves with the simple announcement of their brother's distress, believing that no more was needed to bring the Lord Jesus to their side. Yet even in making this intimation, their confidence was not in anything about themselves or Lazarus, but simply in himself. They did not say, "He who loves thee," but rather, "He whom thou lovest." It was an appeal to his own heart, all the more eloquent because it left the manner of the response entirely to himself, and made no suggestion as to how he should relieve them. It was enough for them to make sure that he simply knew their need. Just as the disciples of John the Baptist, when they had lost their master by the cruel deed of Herod, "went and told Jesus," so these sisters in their hour of extremity sent straight to the Lord. Now here is an example for us, for, though Jesus is no longer upon the earth, we may repair to him in all our time of trouble; nay, just because he is no longer on the earth, we may get to him more easily than these sorrowing sisters did; for their messenger had to go away across the Jordan to Bethabara before they could reach him, but now we can breathe a prayer into his ear at any time and in any place, with the full assurance that he hears our request.

Nor have we here only an example, for we may make of the conduct of the Bethany sisters a test wherewith to try ourselves. To whom do we go *first* in the time of our extremity? What is our resource in the day of trouble? To what refuge do we run when calamity is overtaking us? Can we say with David, "From the end of the earth will I cry unto thee when my heart is overwhelmed?" or do we betake ourselves to some other helper? The answer to these questions will determine whether we are the friends of Jesus or not. To take an illustration which I have used elsewhere: "Traveling once upon a railroad car, I had among my fellow passengers a little laughing child who romped about and was at home with everybody, and while she was frolicking around it might have been difficult to tell to whom she belonged, she seemed so much the property of every one; but when the engine gave a loud, long shriek, and we went rattling into a dark tunnel, the little one made one bound and ran to nestle in a lady's lap. I knew then who was her mother!"* So in the day of prosperity it may be occasionally difficult to say whether a man is a Christian or not; but when, in time of trouble, he makes straight for Christ, we know then most surely whose he is and whom he serves. Take a note of it, then, and when affliction comes, observe to whom you flee for succor—for that will tell you whether you are or are not a friend of Jesus.

III. Notice, now, in the third place, that the response of the Lord comes often in such a way as seems to aggravate the evil. Instead of hastening at once to Bethany, the Saviour sent for answer these words: "This sickness is not unto death, but for the glory of God, that the Son of God might be glorified thereby;" and deliberately remained where he was for two days, so that when the messenger returned, Lazarus was dead. How strange it all seems, and how bewildered the sisters must have been! First of all,

---

* David, King of Israel, p. 145.

the Master did not come, and therefore it looked as if he did not heed their distress. Then their brother died, though they might perhaps have expected that, as in the case of the servant of the centurion, Jesus would have spoken the word where he was, and their brother would have been healed. Then, after Lazarus had died, their courier came back with the assurance from the lips of Jesus, "This sickness is not unto death." What could they make of all this? We now, looking at the history as a whole, can see the meaning of the mystery. But to them, as they were passing through the suspense, the ordeal must have been severe, and the conduct of the Lord incomprehensible. When, however, we read this history in the light of other narratives, we see here only a parallel case to the treatment of Jacob by the Lord at Peniel, and that of the Syrophenician woman by Jesus on the coasts of Tyre, and that of the disciples while they "toiled in rowing" all through the night upon the tempestuous lake. He delayed only that he might bring a larger blessing when he did come, and might thereby discipline a weak faith into strength, as well as furnish a support to his afflicted people in every after age. And when we get to the perception of that truth, we understand the striking language of the Evangelist as he records the fact (verses 5 and 6): "Now Jesus loved Martha, and her sister, and Lazarus," "when he had heard, therefore, that he was sick, he abode two days still in the same place where he was." He loved them, *therefore* he did not come immediately at their call. That looks like a *non sequitur*, but it is the sober truth. He had in store for them a greater kindness than they could have dreamed of; and therefore he delayed until he could confer that upon them. It seemed that their prayer was unanswered; but the answer was deferred only that it should be surpassingly benignant. The faith of the Roman centurion was rewarded by the cure of his servant; but the faith of beloved friends like Martha and Mary was to be surprised by the yet grander gift of the restoration of Lazarus from the grave. They did not know it at the time; if they had known it, what a burden would have been taken from their hearts; but we know it, and that should keep us from ever being burdened with anxiety about the treatment of our prayers. When, therefore, the Lord seems to stay away from us though we cry to him; when that which we request from him appears to be denied to us; when the gathering storm grows darker, and at length, in spite of our application unto him, breaks over our heads, let us remember the peculiar "*therefore*" of this narrative, and "be still." There is nothing for us at such a time but to wait in patient, trustful expectation; but when we get to the end we shall see that there was love in the discipline, and shall give our glad indorsement to the good Toplady's lines:

> "Blest is the man, O God,
>   That stays himself on thee;
> Who wait for thy salvation, Lord,
>   Shall thy salvation see."

IV. But advancing another step, observe, in the fourth place, that the friends of Jesus have different individualities, but a common danger in their sorrow. The peculiarities of these two sisters are very marked, and it is a striking proof of the truthfulness of the Evangelists Luke and John, that, though they wrote independently of each other, and describe Martha and Mary in quite different circumstances, we clearly recognize the similarity of the portraits which they draw. Luke describes them as entertaining Jesus as their guest; and in his picture we see in Martha the kind-hearted hostess, stirring about in earnest activity to have on her table everything of the best for her Lord. Indeed such was her eagerness in that regard that she was "cumbered with much serving," and could give attention to little else for the time. She has been harshly blamed by many commentators for that, because they have forgotten that it was Christ whom she was seeking to serve, and that in these attentions she was showing her love to him in her own way, just as Mary showed hers, in her way, by breaking the alabaster box of precious ointments over his feet, and by sitting reverently to hear his word. She did not understand the Lord so thoroughly as Mary did, but she loved him just as earnestly, and believed in him just as implicitly. Mary's nature was deeper than Martha's, and she would at any time have chosen rather to hear the Lord utter his suggestive sentences on the profoundest themes, than to partake of the richest banquet that could be set before her. So in the account of the feast, in Luke, she shows to most advantage. But such a brooding spirit is always more affected by grief than is an active soul; and hence, in the narrative of John here, Martha shows to the greater advantage, as being the first to welcome Jesus, and as having composure to converse with him upon their trial. Mary was utterly prostrated. She took no notice of the announcement of the Saviour's arrival; and so completely overwhelmed was she, that when at length she rose to accompany her sister, those who were beside her said, "She goeth to the grave to weep there;" while when she came to the Saviour she fell at his feet in a paroxysm of grief, and could only articulate through her sobs a few words of broken agony. Thus while at the feast the composure was Mary's, at the grave the composure was Martha's; and that just because of the deeper nature of the one and the more active disposition of the other. A superficial reader might be apt to say that the two pictures are utterly inconsistent; but a profounder study will only make it plain that the sorrow of each is stamped with the same individuality that was so conspicuous at the feast. Thus, as Dr. Candlish* says, "In different circumstances, the same natural temper may be either an advantage or a snare. Martha was never so much occupied in the emotion of one scene or subject as not to be on the alert and ready for the call to another. This was a disadvantage to her when she was so hurried that she could not withdraw herself from household cares to wait upon the Word of Life. It is an advantage to her now, that she can, with comparative ease, shake off her depression and hasten of her own accord to meet her Lord. The same profound feeling, again, which made Mary the more attentive listener before, makes her the most helpless sufferer now, and disposes her almost to nurse her grief until Jesus, her best comforter, sends specially and emphatically to rouse her." I am particular to note all this, because from one-sided expositors Martha has received anything but just appreciation, and because the prostration of Mary in the time of affliction has been almost entirely overlooked.

But though thus there was individuality in their sorrow, they had both fallen before the same temptation, for both alike said to Jesus: "Lord, if thou hadst been here my brother had not died."

---

* "Scripture Characters," by R. S. Candlish, D.D., p. 235.

This was not a reproach of him, but it was a conviction deeply entertained by them, and because it was the first utterance of both to Jesus we may infer that it had been often said between themselves during his mysterious absence. And yet, deep as the conviction in their hearts was, we can see that it was wrong. For as we know the Lord Jesus was there. He could say to his disciples, even at Bethabara, "Lazarus is dead." He was at Bethany, therefore, in his omniscience, and being so, he was there also in his omnipresence and omnipotence. They did not know it, but it was none the less true: *he was there and yet their brother died.*

Again, they had no warrant for their belief that if he had been visibly with them their brother's life would have been saved. That was merely their own supposition. For anything they knew, he might have permitted Lazarus to languish and die, even if he had been their guest at the time, in order that some larger and more lasting blessing than his recovery would have been might be conferred upon them. So their feeling, however natural, was simply wrong; and wrong as it was, it added a bitter element to their grief, for it led them to say that their affliction might have been prevented, and so it opened the way to murmuring and made resignation harder.

But it is much easier to point out the error of the sisters here than it is to keep from falling into it ourselves. For unhappily, in all our trials, we are prone to lose sight of the universality of God's providence, and to torment ourselves with this unbelieving "if." Have we lost a dear friend by death?—then we are apt to exclaim: "If we had only taken it in time;" "if we had only been able to get our own physician;" "if we had only called in the help of that eminent medical man;" or "if we had gone with him in time to some milder climate, then he might not have died," and so forth. Have we become involved in business perplexities?—then the burden of our complaint is: "If our debtors had not disappointed us, or if we could only have received temporary help from our friends, we might have tided over the embarrassment and need not have suspended." Have we lost some object on which our hearts were set?—still the refrain is: "*If, if, if,* then we might have retained it." But all this is utterly unbelieving, for it proceeds on the principle that the providence of God is not concerned in everything, and it gives to secondary causes a supremacy that does not belong to them. The Christian utterance is that of Paul: "We know that all things work together for good to them who love God": *All things,* not simply those which are apparently prosperous, but those also that are seemingly adverse; all things, not merely those which depend on the operations of external nature, but those also which are the results of the actions of voluntary agents. Until we get to this belief we can have no solid comfort in the hour of trial. Look away, therefore, all ye who are afflicted, from mere secondary causes, and have faith in the providence of him without whom a sparrow cannot fall to the ground. When calamity comes upon you, be sure that it is not because this or that accident prevented relief, nor because the Saviour was not with you, but because it was his will, and his will only, to bring about that which shall be better for you and others than your deliverance would have been. Be still and confide in him, and soon your mourning will be ended by the discovery that he hath done all things well. "All these things are against me," said the sorrowful Jacob when he was asked to let Benjamin go with his brothers into Egypt, but he lived to see that they were all for him, for God was in them all, and Joseph could say to his brethren: "Ye thought evil against me; but God meant it unto good, to bring to pass, as it is this day, to save much people alive." God meant it unto good. Yes, that is a more wholesome way of looking at things than it is to deal in "*if's*," and when we get to that conviction it will not be so hard to wait in patience for the issue.

V. But now, finally, let me ask you to observe that the friends of Jesus have a blessed end to all their sorrows. You know the sequel of this touching history. At the command of Jesus, Lazarus was recalled to life, and in the joy of receiving him back to their fellowship and affection all the mystery of the dark dispensation was made clear to the gladdened sisters, while by the whole discipline, as well as by the words which the Master himself had spoken to them, their faith was quickened, their characters were strengthened, and they were the better prepared for the deeper, darker, and more tremendous mystery of his own crucifixion and burial. Now, of course, we cannot expect just such an issue to our afflictions as that; but without any straining of interpretation, I think we may say that in all this we have a prophecy and prelude of the ultimate result of all our earthly trials, when in the higher resurrection life we shall be reunited to the loved ones who before us have fallen asleep in Jesus, and shall look back from the vantage ground of heaven upon all God's providential dealings with us here below. Then broken fellowships shall be resumed, and those chapters in our histories which seemed here the most incomprehensible shall there be all resolved, so that we shall clearly see how it came about that the very love of Jesus to us held him back from coming immediately to our relief: or rather we shall perceive that even when we thought him absent he was most truly present with us, arranging and overruling everything for our highest good and the glory of his name. He does not come to interpose against the death of our beloved; neither does he recall our dead to our embrace, but in our case, as in that of the Bethany mourners, we shall discover that there was love in the delay, and we shall be glad that he acted as he did when we behold the grand result. Nor only in the case of such an affliction as bereavement will that be the issue. We shall find that the same thing is true of all our tribulations, for "the trial of your faith, being much more precious than of gold that perisheth, though it be tried with fire, shall be found unto praise and honor and glory at the appearing of Jesus Christ." "Rest in the Lord, therefore, and wait patiently for him," for the day is coming when you shall be constrained to say: "Because the Lord was with us our trials came upon us, and he brought us safely through them into his wealthy place."

And now, dear friends, I have completed the course of thought which I had marked out for this discourse, and I leave it to make its own impression on your hearts. Some of you have lately been called to pass through deep affliction. Each winter, as it goes, takes with it some of those whose forms and faces were familiar in our place of assembly, so that now as I look across my audience, I miss the countenances of many who, years ago, were wont to worship with us here, and during the last few months the homes of not a few among us have been saddened with a desolation akin to that which fell upon the cottage of Bethany. To them especially I have spoken to-day. Take to yourselves the consolations in which this history is so rich, and be careful lest you fall before the temptation to which the sisters yielded. Be done with all unbelieving "ifs;" do not deify secondary causes; but say with Job, "*The Lord* hath taken away," and then it will be easy to add, "Blessed be the name of the Lord," for he is perfect wisdom and perfect love, and ordereth all things well. And, remembering that those who have lived for Christ depart only to be with him, lift your thoughts to the place into which they have entered—so shall your hearts be comforted, and your memories of the past be transformed into hopes for the future. For you shall see them again in that glorious home into which neither sin, nor sorrow, nor pain, nor death shall enter. Here is a beautiful adaptation of my text, that brings out both the danger of murmuring and the joy of faith; let me commend it to your attention, that you may be at once warned and cheered:

    We sadly watch'd the close of all,
      Life balanced on a breath;
    We saw upon his features fall
      The awful shade of death.
    All dark and desolate we were;
      And murmuring nature cried:
    "Oh! surely, Lord! hadst thou been here
      Our brother had not died."

    But when its glance the memory cast
      On all that grace had done,
    And thought of life's long warfare pass'd
      And endless victory won,
    Then faith prevailing wiped the tear,
      And looking upward, cried:
    "Oh! Lord, thou surely hast been here;
      Our brother has *not* died."

And you who heretofore have been largely exempt from sorrow, think not that it will be always so with you. Trials will come. Tribulations will come. Bereavements will come on you as on others. Therefore, let the thoughts which I have this morning uttered sink into your hearts, that so you may be kept from misjudging your Saviour in the hour of your calamity, and may be upborne through all by the consciousness that he is with you, and the assurance that by and by you shall be with him. May God add his blessing. Amen.

May 6, 1883.

THE HIDDEN SUPPORT OF LIFE.

John iv. 32. But he said unto them, I have meat to eat that ye know not of.

WEARY, hungry and athirst, Jesus sat beneath the glare of an Oriental noon on the ledge of Jacob's well. His disciples had left him all alone for a season while they went into the neighboring city to buy food, and on their return they were surprised to find that he was speaking with a woman who had come to draw water, and who, almost as soon as they appeared, left her pitcher behind her and hastened, like one who was on a special errand, into the town from which they had just come. And she was on a special errand, for after a conversation which had probed her heart to its depths and brought to light the secrets of her life, she had found the Messiah in the mysterious stranger and was off in eager joy to say to all her people, "Come and see a man that told me all things that ever I did: is not this the Christ?" But all that was at the moment unknown to the disciples, and so when they urged their Master to partake of the food which they had provided and he declined, saying: "I have meat to eat that ye know not of," they were puzzled and asked among themselves: "Hath any man brought him aught to eat?" Their perplexity was natural in the circumstances, for they imagined that he had referred to ordinary material food, but when he added, "My meat is to do the will of him that sent me and to finish his work," they began to understand that during their absence he had been engaged in his "Father's business," and that he was describing the inner satisfaction which he had enjoyed in its discharge. But when he went on to speak of their entering into his labors, they recognized also, that in the unfolding of his own experience he was testifying to a fact which might be verified in theirs. It is indeed true that no one else can affirm as unqualifiedly as he did, that the doing of the Father's will and the finishing of the Father's work is his meat; but still all who have believed in him and have received his spirit, can so far forth at least adopt his words, and therefore I do not misuse them when I regard them as suggesting for our consideration *the hidden support of life.*

Before entering on the exposition of that topic however, it may be well to set clearly before you the general principles which underlie the expression which the Lord has here employed. It is an affirmative way of enunciating the same truth which, in its negative form, he uttered when, in reply to Satan's suggestion that he should command stones to be made bread for the removal of his hunger, he said: "It is written, man shall not live by bread alone, but by every word that proceedeth out of the mouth of God." Now putting these two sayings together, and having regard both to their undoubted significance and to the circumstances in which they were spoken, we get some valuable results.

I. For one thing, they teach that, in the case of human creatures at least, life is a higher thing than existence. Man is a complex being, having a soul as well as a body. His soul allies him with God and the unseen, while his body links him to the animal and the material. The meat by which the soul is supported is spiritual; that by which the body is maintained is material. The soul, from the very nature of the case, is superior to the body—is indeed the tenant of the body; and so the body is for the soul and not the soul for the body. The gratification of the body in its material support is simply animal existence; but life for a man is the culture and development of his soul through the doing of the will of God. True, the body has its wants which must be cared for; but the supply of these is only means to the attainment of a higher end, that end being the doing of the will of God by the soul. When, however, the means are elevated into the end, and a man seeks the pampering of the body only, he has thereby abdicated his manhood and sunk into a mere animal. The first question, therefore, which faces the youth when he awakes to moral consciousness and recognizes that he has a soul within him is this: "Am I content merely to exist? or do I mean to live indeed?" Or, to put it in other words: "Am I to be my body's? or is my body to be mine? and mine for God? What shall be my aim henceforth? Shall I exist simply to eat and drink; or shall I eat and drink in order to live by glorifying and enjoying God?" That is the great hinge on which the quality of a man's career turns; and according as he swings it to this side or to that, he will become a slave of appetite or a servant of God. Ah! how often is the young man tempted into sensuality by the invitation of his companions: "Come, let us see life!" But sensuality is not life *for a man*. Life for a man is something higher, nobler, more glorious by far, even "to do the will of him that sent us, and to finish his work." It is not, as the gourmand fancies, to enjoy the pleasures of the table; not, as the drunkard madly sings, to drown care in the flowing bowl; not as the sensualist declares, to give loose rein to the lowest passions of our nature. All these are but forms of animal enjoyment, and the man who makes these the ends he seeks is simply existing, and has sunk beneath the dignity of a rational and immortal being. He only can be said to live a man's proper life who, by faith in God and obedience to his word, is striving constantly to serve the Lord.

II. But these words suggest to us, in the second place, that in the prosecution of life, as thus understood, we must lay our account with manifold privations, difficulties and conflicts. For we have not now a perfectly harmonious environment. We do not begin, as Adam did, in a paradise of innocence. But we come into a world where sin is abounding, and we bring with us natures all too prone to listen to the tempter's blandishments; so that the very first motions of real life within us often take the form of conflict, either with ourselves or with those influences by which we are surrounded. Sometimes we have the longings of the flesh so strong upon us that when we "would do good evil is present with us;" and the will, to use the words of another, may be "struck down by the lightning of passion, or may move creaking with the friction of temper, or may sink in the collapse of depression."* And even if all should be at peace within, we may have much to try us from without. The strain of labor may be severe, or the course which we feel impelled to take may estrange our friends from us and leave us in utter solitude, or the claims of interest may be so strong for the moment as almost

---

* James Martineau, D.D. "Hours of Thought," 1st series, p. 141.

to outweigh in our regard those of duty, or at least to make the sacrifice seem something terrible—or the sight of the apparent prosperity of those who are not burdened with conscience may tempt us to exclaim with the Psalmist: "Verily, I have cleansed my heart in vain," so that our feet may almost slip. Ah! who is there among us that has begun to live indeed, and knows not experiences like these? But let us not be discouraged. These are the evidences that we do live; for if we had been content with simple existence we should have had no such conflicts. It is not *the having of them* that should distress us, but rather *the being worsted by them*, for the promise is not to him who has had no battle, but "to him that overcometh."

III. But these words suggest to us, in the third place, that under such experiences the strength of the man comes from hidden support. He has meat to eat of which others know not. He could not sustain himself if he had not. If he deny himself present gratification he feeds upon the future food for which he has given up the fleeting joy. If he brave the condemnation of the ungodly, he delights in the consciousness that he has the approval of his God. If he have to go without many of the worldly advantages which others possess, he has the satisfaction of having accomplished much which they have never attempted. If he be left apparently "in the blank and solitude of things" to endure affliction or suffer persecution, he has a constant solace in the assurance that he is still on the side of God, and that ere long "He will bring forth his righteousness as the light and his judgment as the noonday." These are things which the world cannot give him and which the world cannot take away; and by these things, and such as these, all those whose lives have benefited and blessed humanity have been sustained. This hidden meat is the food of heroes, and has always been the nourishment of those who have "resisted unto blood striving against sin."

IV. But these words suggest to us, fourthly, that when a man has no such secret support his life loses all spiritual importance and becomes a mere groveling thing of animal enjoyment. The soul in such circumstances is starved, and all true nobleness disappears from the character. The wretched one has put out his faith eyes, and his own passions have set him, Samson-like, to grind in ceaseless drudgery for their gratification. It is a terrible thing to think of, and yet, alas! how many there are in this great city of ours who, beginning on Delilah's lap, have ended in a slavery and degradation more horrible by far than that of the old Hebrew giant! When the hidden food that God in Christ supplies is despised, be sure that the noblest life is thenceforward unattainable; the man is descending to the animal; the life is degenerating into mere existence, and the soul is being sacrificed for the body. These principles are of immense importance. They are absolutely fundamental, and they cannot be neglected without disastrous consequences resulting from our imprudence. For these reasons I have felt constrained to put them thus in prominent and distinct relief before you, not without the hope that through their instrumentality the Divine Spirit may quicken some among you into life indeed.

But now, leaving mere generalities, let me endeavor to particularize some of the forms under which the Christian receives this hidden support of life—some of the ways in which he has meat to eat which others know not of.

And first, I remark that he has often such food in a "good conscience." I enter not now into any metaphysical analysis of the faculty of conscience. Let it suffice to say that it is that within us which gives us the distinction between right and wrong, along with the feeling of obligation to do the one and to refrain from doing the other. It deals in the words "ought" and "ought not." It lays down the law to the soul, and cannot be better described than it has been by Bishop Butler, as "that superior principle in every man which distinguishes between the internal principles of his heart as well as his external actions, which passes judgment upon himself and them; pronounces determinately some actions to be in themselves just, right, good; others to be in themselves evil, wrong, unjust; which, without being consulted, without being advised with, magisterially exerts itself and approves or condemns him the doer of them accordingly; and which, if not forcibly stopped, naturally and always, of course, goes on to anticipate a higher and more effectual sentence, which shall hereafter second and affirm its own." This is the law written in the heart, of which Paul makes mention; and though depravity has in some degree corrupted it, yet when it is purified and rectified by the operation on it of the Holy Spirit, through the belief of the truth as it is in Jesus, it may be regarded as being, in a very true sense, God's representative in the soul. Its approbation, therefore, being the reflex and echo of the approval of God, is a great source of support to a struggling and tried believer, even as its condemnation must be always a cause of weakness and of pain. When one is accused he is not so much to be pitied if he be accused falsely, as he would be if the accusation were true. In the one case, he knows that whatever men may say or do, God will vindicate him in the end. In the other, he is already condemned by himself, and that is only the sure foretaste of his condemnation by God. Thus conscience makes of a man either a hero or a coward—a hero if he has its unqualified indorsement, but a coward if he feels already its sharp upbraidings. See how this was proved by the contrast between Paul and Felix. By all ordinary laws the Apostle ought to have been daunted before the governor. He had little of power or pomp about him, but Felix had all the style and authority of a Roman magnate; and besides, Paul was a prisoner at the bar, and Felix the judge upon the bench. Yet what do we see?—the prisoner giving a charge on righteousness, temperance, and judgment, and the judge trembling as he listens. Why? Because the one could say: "Herein do I exercise myself to have a conscience void of offense toward God and toward man;" and because the other was haunted by the remembrance of his unjust decisions, his robberies, his cruelties, and his impurities. Thus Paul had meat to eat of which Felix knew nothing, and in the strength of that food he grew into a greatness which we have never seen equaled since his day. In the same way we explain, to a very large extent at least, the robustness of each member of that "noble army of martyrs," to whom the world has owed so much, who "met the tyrant's brandished steel, the lion's gory mane," and gave up the existence of the body that they might maintain the life of the soul in the preservation of their allegiance to their Lord. A good conscience is a continual feast, and they who have that within themselves can do without the banquets of the world. I know, indeed, that in these days it has become fashionable to sneer at all this, and there are many who will say that they "cannot afford to keep a conscience." But be not ye among the number. Cannot afford to keep a conscience! What is gold compared with the assurance that you have done that which God would have you do? and what will whole mines of wealth or whole burnt-offerings of human applause avail if, after all, you are despised by yourself, and have that within you which constantly upbraids you with meanness and corruption? O, it gives a manly erectness to you when you can hold up your head and say with Paul: "With me it is a small matter to be judged of by you or of man's judgment; yea, I judge not mine own self; there is one that judgeth me, even God." A crust with the consciousness of unswerving loyalty to God is better far than affluence with remorse gnawing at the heart; and he may well defy all human antagonism who is only sure of these three things—a good God, a good conscience, and a good cause—for then he has "meat to eat of which the world knows nothing."

But a second form in which the Christian often enjoys this hidden support is that of a worthy ambition. If we are intent upon the attainment of some fixed purpose, then our steady contemplation of that will sustain us amid distractions and difficulties and trials which otherwise would have overmastered us. We see that exemplified even on the lower level of ordinary temporal pursuits. Every reader of Macaulay's Essays must remember how that fascinating writer describes the boy Warren Hastings lying, when just seven years old, on the banks of the rivulet that flows through his parental domain, and resolving that he would recover the estate which had belonged to his father, and then adds: "This purpose, formed in infancy and poverty, grew stronger as his intellect expanded and as his fortune rose. * * * When under a tropical sun he ruled fifty millions of Asiatics, his hopes, amidst all the cares of war, finance and legislation, still pointed to Daylesford." Yes, that was the secret meat by which he was sustained. And to take a more recent instance. As I was wandering with a friend, some summers ago, through a Highland glen in the island of Arran, he pointed out a rock to me, and said: "There's where Louis Napoleon used to sit when, during his exile, he was here as the guest of the Duke of Hamilton, and the story is told that, one day after he had been resting there in solitude for hours, another of the visitors at the castle came and said to him: 'What are you thinking about so long and all alone?' and received for answer: 'I was planning a system of sewerage which I mean to carry out in Paris when I become the ruler of France.'" That was his secret food, by the eating of which he kept up his heart in those days of darkness; and though I am no great admirer of the man, I see through such an incident some glimmerings of greatness in him. Now a similar effect is produced by a worthy ambition in the heart of the Christian. Let him be but thoroughly resolved to make the world the better for his being in it; let him set his soul upon the attainment of some good, not for himself, but for his fellow men; or, let him live for the bringing of multitudes to Christ, and then that purpose will enable him "to bear up and steer right onward," keeping a steady course in spite of the darkest night or wildest weather. It is written of the Lord himself, that "for the joy set before him"—and that was the joy of saving men—"he endured the cross, despising the shame." And we find precisely the same thing in the history before us, when the joy of saving this Samaritan woman, and the eager expectation of benefiting those who were coming to him at her invitation, made him forget for the time his hunger and his weariness. So it will be with us also in the measure in which we follow him. This is the secret of the strength of those who have given their lives to the missionary cause. They have discounted the future for the benefit of the present, and in their anticipation of the results which shall spring from their work in generations to come, they have that which sustains them in their labors now. They see the harvest already in the handful of seed which they are preparing to scatter, and seeing that, they have new strength to sow. At the unveiling of the Livingstone statue, in the city of Edinburgh, the venerable Dr. Moffat, Livingstone's father-in-law, as reported in the newspapers of the day, spoke to this effect: "When Livingstone was led into the unknown regions of Africa, they all knew the dangers to which he was exposed, but nothing could influence him to desist. He had an Africa in view over which they had talked many times together, and in which he could see vessels sailing on the lakes, and spires rising and churches built. He never lost sight of that." And that was a part of his hidden food. If, therefore, you would have something within you that will uphold you amid difficulty and discouragement, get a benevolent ambition, resolve to do some Christian service for your generation, set your heart on the righting of some wrong, or the removing of some ignorance, or the undoing of some burden for others, by the propagation of the gospel of Christ, and you will have therein meat to eat of which others know not.

But akin to that which I have just described is the

third form in which the Christian enjoys this hidden support, that, namely, of a strong faith in the unseen and in the future. This enables him to distinguish between things as they appear to men, and as they really are before the eye of God, and gives him an inward ideal toward which he is always striving, and the attainment of which by him will be heaven itself. Now where can we find a better illustration of this than that furnished by Moses, of whom it is said that "he endured as seeing him who is invisible," and again, that "he chose rather to suffer affliction with the people of God than to enjoy the pleasures of sin for a season, esteeming the reproach of Christ greater riches than all the treasures of Egypt, because he had respect unto the recompense of the reward?" Through the veil which conceals the spirit realm from mortal sight his faith-eye saw the living throne of the eternal God; and that for him neutralized all the influences of earth, so that the compass of his conscience trembled sensitively yet steadily to Jehovah. In his light he saw clearly the relative position of earthly and heavenly things, the infinite difference between the temporal and the eternal, and he reckoned that the light afflictions which were but for a moment were not worthy to be compared with that "far more exceeding and eternal weight of glory." Beyond the boundary of earth and time he saw a glory and a greatness which dazzled into dimness the glittering pomp even of an Egyptian royalty, and the contemplation of the one gave him strength to sacrifice the other. Here again we see that the conduct of the believer is only an application to the relation between this life and that which is to come of the principles on which men act in seeking the honors and rewards of earth. The ideal with both dominates over the real; the only difference is that with him the ideal is higher than with them. They labor for a corruptible crown, "but he for an incorruptible." What the student is doing for his scholarship, and the merchant for his wealth, and the statesman for his office, and the author for his fame, he is doing for his recompense of eternal reward. Each has his own secret food. Each is giving up a present advantage for a future good. Both alike are walking and working by faith; but the Christian's faith takes in eternity. He hears a voice they cannot hear; he sees a hand they cannot see. So he follows after in the sure confidence that in the end there shall be for him a crown of righteousness that fadeth not away. This assurance is the hidden food by which his soul is supported amid all the privations and afflictions of his earthly lot.

But to mention only one other thought. I remark that the Christian enjoys this hidden support in the form of divine companionship. When Jesus was passing into Gethsemane he said to his followers: "Ye shall be scattered every man to his own, and shall leave me alone; and yet I am not alone, because the Father is with me." And when Paul at his first answer was forsaken by all his friends he affirmed that "the Lord stood by him and strengthened him." So also when he and Silas were in prison at Philippi, with their backs smarting from the scourging to which they had been subjected, and their feet fast in the stocks, "they prayed and sang praises unto God." They had meat to eat of which their adversaries knew not, and by that they were supported when others would have fainted. Nor are these exceptional instances. The believer "walks with God;" and in that fellowship has his sure support. He can say, in the words of the hymn:

> "I find him lifting up my head,
>   He brings salvation near;
>   His presence makes me free indeed,
>   And he will soon appear."

God is to him "a very present help in trouble;" and by the words of his promises, by the suggestions of his Spirit, haply also by the ministrations of his angelic servants—unrecognized at the moment, yet full of encouragement—he gives cheer to his people in their despondency, and strength to them in their weakness. "The best of all," said the dying Wesley, "is that God is with us." "Come," said Luther in his days of trial, "and let us sing the 46th Psalm—'God is our refuge and our strength.'" There is no solace or support to be compared with that. To know that we are on God's side and that God is on our side, that is meat indeed, and there are experiences in which nothing else will avail to hold us up. As one has well said: "On the bed of pain, when thought and will swim feebly away and we are condensed into the poignant moments, when we long for the night, but when it comes the stars glide too slowly and the silence will not let us moan; and we watch for the morning, but when it dawns the soft light mocks us with its sweetness and the birds with the blitheness of their song: in the vigils of anxiety when some life which is our all trembles in the scale, and we extort a thousand contradictory oracles from the flush upon the features or the cloud upon the eye; under the sting of calumny when things we most abhor are told of us, and averted faces and sarcastic words show that the lie has proved too strong and the love of friends too weak; in the countless vicissitudes of broken fortunes and shattered health and disappointed hopes; all must look like ruin if we have no stay beyond the impression of the hour."* But if then there break in upon our perplexity a voice saying unto us: "Fear not, for I am with thee; be not dismayed, for I am thy God; I will help thee, yea I will strengthen thee, yea I will uphold thee with the right hand of my righteousness." "Lo I am with you always even unto the end of the world. I will never leave thee, no, no, I will never forsake thee;" immediately there is a calm. "In loneliness we have still an ever-living communion. Deserted by the voices of affection, we are with him who attuned their sweetness and will console their loss; and dying we but pass to the very source and home of life."

Nor only for such great emergencies is this companionship a secret fountain of support. It is as valuable for the common weariness of a common day, and under the dull monotony of that constant routine whose

> "Sameness doubles cares,
> While one unbroken chain of work
> The flagging temper wears."

For if, exhausted by such labors, we can get "the unexpanded thought of the eternal God" to lie closer to our hearts, we shall find that by itself "that thought is bliss," and the assurance "I will not fail thee nor forsake thee" will send us on our way rejoicing so that we shall ply

> "Our daily task with busier feet
> Because our secret souls a holy strain repeat."

Happy, O thrice happy! they who thus have meat to eat of which the world knows not.

And now, in conclusion, tell me what the hidden

---

* James Martineau, D.D. "Hours of Thought," first series, as before, pp. 151, 152.

support of your life is, and I will tell you whether you are a Christian indeed. To what or to whom do you resort in times of weakness, depression and spiritual exhaustion? When your heart is overwhelmed, to what or to whom do you go for strength? To the stimulants of the world, whether in the shape of its beverages, or its amusements, or its pleasures, or its business? or to God in Christ? To the rock that is higher than you? or to some of those that are beneath you? to Christ or to the world? The answer will infallibly reveal whether you are or are not the followers of him who here did say, "I have meat to eat that ye know not of." Shrink not, I beseech you, from applying the test, and if you find that you are none of his, may the truths which have now been set before you lead you to repair at once to him who alone can say with truth to a human soul, "My grace is sufficient for thee, my strength is made perfect in weakness."

Feb. 11, 1883.

THE RECTIFYING INFLUENCE OF THE SANCTUARY.

PSALM lxxiii. 16, 17. When I thought to know this, it was too painful for me, until I went into the sanctuary of God; then understood I their end.

THERE has been some little difference of opinion among expositors as to the precise reference of the word here translated "sanctuary." Literally, it means "the holies" of God; and so it may be taken either as the holy things or the holy places of God. A few would understand it in the first sense as designating "the righteous plans of God's government," or "the secret grounds of his dealings with men;" while others would take it, in the second sense, as denoting "the eternity where God dwells as in a holy place." But to me it seems self-evident that by "going into the sanctuary of God," in this seventeenth verse, the writer describes the same exercise which in the twenty-eighth verse he has called "a drawing near to God;" and so, in the mouth of one belonging to the old dispensation, the primary reference of the term must be to the temple, which was the earthly residence of God and the place where he communed with his people. Thus understood, the main drift and teaching of the psalm, as a whole, is that in approaching God through the recognized channels of access unto him, and in appropriating him to himself, Asaph found the antidote which neutralized the poison of the insidious temptation by which he had been almost destroyed.

What that temptation was has been most graphically described by himself. He had been greatly disturbed by the anomalies which were continually occurring in the world around him. He had seen the wicked so often prosperous and the righteous so often in distress that he was almost ready to conclude that God was unrighteous, and that it made no matter how a man lived; or rather, perhaps, that it would be better for him to become unscrupulous too. But when he entered into the sanctuary and took in all the revelation made there through sacrifice and symbol, he was enabled so to grasp anew the truth that God is righteous, and so to appropriate the God of the mercy seat as his own God as to find there the compensation for all his privations and the solvent for all his perplexities. For thus he sings: "Nevertheless I am continually with thee. Whom have I in heaven but thee? and there is none upon earth that I desire besides thee." As if he had said: "Whatever else I may be without, yet I have thee for the strength of my heart and my portion forever; and having that, I have infinitely more than wicked men possess, even in their highest prosperity, so that I am delivered from all envy of them and lifted out of all distrust of thee."

Under the New Testament dispensation, the true antitype of the temple is the Lord Jesus Christ, in whom the real Shekinah dwells, for he is God manifest in the flesh; so that the right gospel use of such a text as this would be to show that when by faith we enter into the Lord Jesus Christ, we have the true corrective influence, by which we are enabled to rectify the false judgments of the world and to preserve our faith in God, amid all the perplexities that suggest themselves when we look at the course of things upon the earth. But as, in the sanctuary commonly so-called among us, the sincere worshiper seeks thus believingly to enter in to Christ, we may, without any hesitation, apply the words of the psalmist here to that; and in a day when so many criticisms are made upon public worship, it may be useful to set distinctly before you what I may call the rectifying influence of the sanctuary on those who regularly and devoutly enter it on the first day of the week. Of course I must take for granted that the worship of the sanctuary is such as to bring us near to God. I do not enter now on the discussion of those things which are best adapted to secure that end. I must postulate that the hymns of praise which are sung are such as carry up the tribute of our hearts to God; that the prayers which are offered are such as lead us into the very secret place of the Almighty, and that the discourses delivered are such as clearly explain and cogently enforce the word of God—in short, that the services are such as to bring us from first to last face to face with God, as he has revealed himself to us through the written word and through the living Christ. Now, my assertion is that in the sanctuary, thus understood, there is a rectifying influence which corrects the errors into which, from his close and constant intercourse with worldly men, the Christian is apt to fall. That this is true will appear if you look at the matter from one or two different points of view:

I. Take it, first, as it bears upon the standards of judgment commonly in use among men. Nothing is clearer than that the maxims of the Lord Jesus are in almost all respects opposed to those that are most popular in the world. Now, when a man accepts him as his Redeemer, Lawgiver, and King, he declares that he is determined to be ruled in all respects by the principles of Christ. No doubt, too, when he makes that declaration he is sincere. But in his daily business he is thrown continually among those who consider that the laws of his Lord are fanatical, or impracticable, or ridiculous, and who tell him that if he is determined to act upon them, he may as well make up his mind to be defeated in the race of competition. More than that, his observation convinces him that as things now are their assertion is largely true; and so, as the days go on, he is in danger of being lowered to their level. But the Sabbath comes, and he enters into the sanctuary, where he is confronted with God, and then and thereby all the webs of sophistry that his fellow men have spun are swept away as easily as one brushes from his path the gossamer of the morning. Did you ever see a vessel swung for the purpose of having her compass adjusted? The process, as carried on in the river Thames in England, is something like this. The ship is moved in the bight at Greenhithe, and by means of warps attached to certain buoys she is turned with her head toward various points one after another. The bearing of the compass on board, influenced as that is by the attraction of the iron of which she is composed, or which she carries, is accurately noted by some one appointed for the purpose, and the true bearing is signaled to him by another observer on shore, who has a compass out of reach of all local disturbance. The error in each position is ascertained, and the necessary corrections are made. Now, it is just similar with Christ and the devout worshiper in the sanctuary. During the week the consciences even of the best among us have been more or less affected by things immediately around us, so that we are in danger of making serious mistakes in our life voyage. But here Christ comes to us and gives us our "true bearings," as they are in the standard of his word, undisturbed by any earthly or metallic influences, and so the needful rectifications may be made by us and we may start out afresh.

But, to take one or two particular illustrations, let us look at the judgment which Christ gives of wealth, and see how much there is in that to rectify the current opinion. With many—may I not say with most—wealth is the supreme good. They estimate everything by the money scale. They subordinate everything to the acquisition of a fortune. They live and move and have their being mainly to get riches, and even when that is not the case, yet there is in the air around them such a deference to money, altogether irrespective of the means by which it has been acquired, that, almost insensibly to themselves, they become infected with the same spirit. Now see what Christ's standard says on this subject. He does not allege that wealth is a thing to be despised, but he dethrones it from its position of supremacy to one of inferior importance. He shows that it is not the great end to be sought, but at the best only a means which may be made conducive to the furtherance of that end. He declares most emphatically that "a man's life consisteth not in the abundance of the things which he possesseth," but in those inner treasures which the world can neither give nor take away. Hear these words: "The ground of a certain rich man brought forth plentifully, and he thought within himself, saying, 'What shall I do because I have no room where to bestow my fruits?' and he said, 'This will I do: I will pull down my barns and build greater, and there will I bestow my fruits and my goods, and I will say to my soul, Soul, thou hast much goods laid up for many years; take thine ease, eat, drink and be merry.'" Now mark what was wrong in all that. The evil was not that he had so much, but that he had nothing else. His error was, not that he had well considered what he should do with his goods, but that he had never considered what he should do with himself. In the filling of his barns he had starved his spiritual nature, and when death deprived him of his earthly fruits he discovered that he had nothing left. Hence God said to him: "Thou fool! this night thy soul shall be required of thee, then whose shall those things be which thou hast provided? So," adds the Saviour, "is he that layeth up treasure for himself, and is not rich toward God." There it is—to be rich toward God—that is the true aim of life. To have a heart at peace with God, a soul renewed by the Spirit of God, a life devoted to the service of God; that is to be rich indeed. With that a man will take care how he seeks earthly wealth, and will know how best to spend it for the glory of God and the service of his generation; without that, no matter how much of this world's goods he may possess, he has missed the great purpose of his being. My hearer, what does your conscience say to that? Look in and see, and if it has been deflected by the metallic influences round you during the week, be sure that you correct it now, lest, like the fool in the parable, you should make shipwreck at the last.

But, as another illustration, look at the Saviour's standard of greatness. Men generally connect that with power. That which raises one above his fellows and gives him some advantage over them for his own honor or aggrandizement, is, in the estimation of the world, greatness. It is a thing of personal pre-eminence, making others minister to its comfort or state; and so it comes to be sought by the individual for his own sake, and not for that of others. But when we get near to Christ in the sanctuary, we discover that his estimate is entirely different. You remember what he said to James and John when, through their mother, they presented the request that they might sit, one on his right hand and the other on his left hand, in his glory. He did not affirm that it was wrong to seek after greatness. He knew the nature which God had given to men too well to do anything like that. But, as in the case of wealth, we have just seen that he gave a new definition to riches, and said, "Seek to acquire such treasure as will make you rich toward God," so here he gave a new direction to ambition by making greatness consist in service. "Ye know," said he, "that they which are accounted to rule over the Gentiles exercise lordship over them, and their great ones exercise authority upon them, but so shall it not be among you; but whosoever will be great among you shall be your minister, and whosoever of you will be the chiefest shall be servant of all. For even the Son of Man came not to be ministered unto, but to minister and to give his life a ransom for many." Thus to those who are filled with the love of greatness, the Lord preaches the greatness of love, and to those who are enamored of the service which authority commands he reveals the influence which service ultimately secures; while, with a sublime egotism only to be explained by his consciousness of deity, he holds himself up as the brightest exemplification of his own principle. Now, here again, what does our conscience say? Each of us is striving after some greatness; so much is natural; but is the greatness after which we are striving of this self-sacrificing sort? or is it selfish and self-seeking? Search and see, and if you have lowered your standard before the world's opinion, see that you rectify the mistake here and now. It is one great purpose of the sanctuary service to secure such a result. Here is the standard. The highest of all is the servant of the lowest of all, and the test of greatness in a man, according to the estimate of Christ, is not, how much does he know? or how much does he possess? or what office does he hold? or what power does he wield? but what service has he rendered to his generation by the will of God? Ah, if human competition were to be as eager for the prize in that as it is for pre-eminence in other matters, how much better would it be for the world at large, and for the prize-takers themselves!

But, to mention only one thing more under this head: take the matter of success, and see how Christ, in the sanctuary, rectifies the views of men regarding that. When we speak of success we are prone to think of it as a merely outward thing. The successful merchant is one who has built up a large business and acquired a fortune. The successful author is one who has obtained the ear of the public so that his works are circulated in thousands, and he becomes honored and wealthy as the result. The successful statesman is one who comes to be the recognized leader of his party and is everywhere acknowledged as its ablest man. And so on in every other department. To such an extent is this true that we have books on "Self Help" and "How to Succeed," and the like, detailing the steps by which some have risen from the very lowest round of the ladder to the very highest. And I do not wish to depreciate such works; they have a value of their own in their own place; but the success which they depict is not the true success in life, as Christ has defined success. For tried by such a standard his own life must be pronounced a failure, and we all know that it was anything but that. Success, in his view is in character, in the drinking of the cup which he drank of, and in the being baptized with the baptism wherewith he was baptized; and one may attain that while yet, in a worldly point of view, he may be so poor as to have nowhere to lay his head. Show me the man, therefore, who, as he has tried to mount the ladder of which I have been speaking, has been evermore beat back and beat down—the man whose life has been apparently one long struggle with difficulties, but who, in spite of all, has become only the sweeter and the purer in the process—who has kept all his tenderness in disposition toward his fellows, because he has retained his faith in God—who has learned in and through and by means of all his struggles to hold more freely by God's hand and cling more closely to Christ's cross, and walk more in accordance with Christ's example—and I tell you that man's life has been a success, even though there has been no external accumulation of property. There is the success of the unsuccessful; and I would we could have nowadays a little more of that; for character is nobler than any outward thing—yea, is the only thing that will remain when we shall stand naked and open before the eyes of Him with whom we have to do. Here again, then, let us look in and ask ourselves what that is which we account success; and if we have been adopting the worldly ideal, let us unlearn our mistake and accept the corrective which the sanctuary supplies in Christ. It was well said by Dr. Mark Hopkins, at the funeral of one of our noblest philanthropists some weeks ago, that what we most of all need in these days is " the rectification of our standards." Let us therefore to-day receive the spirit of Christ into our hearts, that we may judge according to his estimates; for if the standards be wrong, everything must be wrong, according to that saying of his own, "The light of the body is the eye; if, therefore, thine eye be single, thy whole body shall be full of light; but if thine eye be evil, thy whole body shall be full of darkness. If, therefore, the light that is in thee be darkness, how great is that darkness?" Divine Illuminator, open our eyes, that "in thy light we may see light clearly!"

II. But proceeding now to another department of the subject, let us look at the rectifying influence of the sanctuary on what I may call the perspective of life. Standing close up to our work, the thing which we are doing at the moment is apt to grow into undue importance in our minds, to the inevitable neglect of other and greater matters. The painter needs to retire now and then from his easel in order that he may not exaggerate some objects and diminish others, but may put each in its proper proportion; and so in the sanctuary, as we draw near to God in Christ we learn to give its relative value to each province of our lives and to keep each in its own place. The Sabbath is a weekly day of review; and as we meet Christ in the sanctuary, everything in our conduct is contemplated in its relation to him. We thus discover whether or not we have been allowing things material to exclude from our thoughts things spiritual, or have been letting the means take the place which belongs only to the end. Perhaps the devotional has unduly preponderated over the active; or, what is much more likely, the pressure of active duties has crushed contemplation and devotion into a corner, and while we have been busy here and there about concerns which might have been postponed without detriment, the opportunity for fellowship with Christ in the closet has irrevocably gone. The ephemeral pamphlet has, it may be, overlaid for us the enduring word of God, or we have given to society and amusement hours which ought to have been sacred to duty or filled with service. But now as we sit here in the presence of Christ, and feel how little we have to bring to him out of the bygone week, we are ashamed. We see how much we ought to have done and might have done, which yet has been entirely neglected; and the experience of the past thus becomes a warning for the future, for the failures of last week are set up as the beacons wherewith we mark the channel of the next, and we set out from the church porch anew with the determination to keep closer to our ideal than ever before. Has it not been so with us very frequently in the past? Do we not feel that it is so with us now? Even with the Sabbath and the sanctuary our lives are poor trailing things enough, but how much more so would they be if we had not weekly the rectifying influence of which I speak! We shall fail again, no doubt, this week as we did the last, but we shall not fall quite so low as before, and the next Lord's day will lift us up anew; and so, week by week, we shall go on rising by slow degrees into the measure of the stature of the perfect man in Christ Jesus. Mark well, therefore, the things on which you cannot look with complacency here in the sanctuary, that you may avoid them in the future; and if you have been giving undue predominance to any matter, let the revelation of that fact administer its own corrective to your heart.

III. But, narrowing in to a conclusion now, let me

note finally the rectifying influence of the sanctuary on the estimate which we form of the relative importance of things present and things to come. When we draw near to Christ here, we recognize him as the risen and ascended Lord who has brought life and immortality to light, and who has gone into another mansion of the Father's house to prepare a place for his people. In this way we bring the motives of eternity to bear upon the duties of time, and call in the glories of heaven to sustain and support us under the afflictions of earth. In the toil and trouble of daily life we are too apt to forget the issues which hang upon our existence here. I do not think that we Christians dwell as much on heaven in our meditations as we ought to do. It is not that, like Bunyan's man with the muck-rake, we are so much occupied in gathering together the refuse of earth that we do not see the glorious crown that is above us; but that we are so engrossed with the present duty, or the present conflict, or the present suffering, that we forget to look before us into the better land. We desire to be true to Christ, and yet so occupied are we with the effort that we neglect to think of the reward that is in store for us, and thus deprive ourselves of much comfort and inspiration which we might otherwise have enjoyed. But in the sanctuary, when we get near to Christ, we have heaven also brought nigh to us, and as we catch a glimpse of its glories, our afflictions dwindle into insignificance, while we are fired by the joy that is set before us to make more strenuous efforts to overcome the evil that is in us, and to endure the hardships that may come upon us. Thus Paul says, "If so be that we suffer with him that we may be also glorified together, for I reckon that the sufferings of this present time not are worthy to be compared with the glory which shall be revealed in us;" and again: "Our light affliction, which is but for a moment, worketh for us a far more exceeding and eternal weight of glory; while we look not at the things which are seen, but at the things which are not seen; for the things which are seen are temporal, but the things which are not seen are eternal." It was said by a great British statesman on one occasion that "he brought in the new world to restore the balance of the old," and in the same way in the sanctuary the Lord Jesus reconciles us to the present by the revelation of the future. Are we weary and heavy laden, suffering under long continued trials, or pressed by grievous burdens, then he bids us look forward and upward to the inheritance "that is incorruptible, undefiled, and that fadeth not away," where "there shall be no more death, neither sorrow nor crying, neither shall there be any more pain;" and he assures us that in a little while we shall be there. Are we wounded in the constant conflict with self, and with the world? and do we cry out for relief? Is the language of our hearts that of the aged believer who exclaimed, "Am I never to be done with this warfare? Is there to be no victory—no rest?" Then he lets us see the vision by which he sustained the spirit of the early Christians amid their sorest persecutions, even that of "the white-robed throng before the throne," and as we gaze with rapture on the sight he says: "These are they which came out of great tribulation, and have washed their robes and made them white in the blood of the lamb. They shall hunger no more, neither thirst any more; neither shall the sun light on them, nor any heat. For the lamb which is in the midst of the throne shall feed them and shall lead them unto living fountains of waters; and God shall wipe away all tears from their eyes." So he encourages us to be faithful even unto the death, and gives us assurance of ultimate and unending triumph, and we go back again to renew the battle of life with eagerness and enthusiasm, feeling that "it has been good for us to draw near to God."

Thus have I sought to set before you as briefly and suggestively as possible the rectifying influence of the sanctuary when we seek sincerely to approach Jesus in it. And if all that I have said be true, then two things are thereby most easily accounted for. First, we understand at once how it comes that the true Christian "loves the habitation of God's house." It meets his need. It rests him when he is weary; it comforts him when he is sorrowful; it cheers him when he is desponding; it reinvigorates him when he is faint, and in the hour of his gladness it sanctifies and elevates his joy. His week to him is robbed of its brightest portion when he has not been able to begin it in the house of God. Something has been lacking to him all through when he has missed the sanctuary. He has been conscious of less spring and elasticity in his walk because he has been deprived of what one called "the weekly tonic" of the public services on the Lord's day. It is not the ritual, it is not the accessories of music and fellowship with earthly friends, that so invigorates him, but it is the drawing near to God, the having of his spirit reminted by the Holy Ghost, and the having of his conscience rectified by him who is its only Lord. This lifts him up and sends him on with new fervor and enthusiasm; and he leaves the porch of the sanctuary after such a time of reinvigoration, saying, "If this be not heaven it is the way to it. Blessed are they that dwell in thy house; they will be still praising thee." My brethren, do I exaggerate here? or is it not rather the case that you are ready to corroborate and confirm my words?

But if this be all true, then we come to understand in the second place how it is that so many dislike the sanctuary. Much attention has been recently directed to the subject of church attendance, and only a week or two ago I was asked to write a contribution to a symposium in a popular review on the question why the people do not go to church. I made answer at once that the pressing duties of my daily life would not allow me to give any time to the preparation of such an article; and when, on reading the paper which I was expected to criticise, I found that it was an indictment of ministers for grievous mistakes in their manner of preaching, and was signed by one who called himself vauntingly a "non-church-goer," I was confirmed in the wisdom of my resolution; for if a man does not go to church, what does he know of that which goes on in church, and of how much worth is his criticism on it? But, indeed, there is no mystery in the case. The church, in so far as it is the ordinance of Christ, exists for the rectification of the world's standards, and, naturally, the men of the world do not like it. They must come to Christ first, and then there will be no difficulty about the sanctuary; but until they submit themselves to him they cannot but be dissatisfied with it. Suppose a man whose great object in life is to amass a fortune should come into the house of God. He is there confronted with the principle laid down by the Saviour, that "a man's life doth not consist in the abundance of the things which he possesseth," and therefore one or other of two things must follow; either he accepts the maxim of the Lord, and consents to reconstruct his life in accordance with it; or he rejects it, and goes away railing at the gospel and its ministers. In like manner, if one who is bent on acquiring such greatness as shall enable him to command the services of others is confronted with the doctrine that to be the greatest of all one must be the servant of all, we cannot wonder that he rebels, and counts the sanctuary a weariness. Unless he is prepared to accept Christ as his redeemer and guide, he can do no otherwise. "The natural man receiveth not the things of the Spirit of God, neither can he know them, because they are spiritually discerned." The critic may exclaim against that as he pleases. He may call it fanaticism or mysticism, and may characterize it as ridiculous, but it is none the less true, and it contains in itself the explanation of the whole matter. Unless, therefore, we consent to alter the fundamental principles of the gospel to suit the world's fancy we must be content to hear such fault-finding to the end. But we dare not think of any such treason to the Lord, whose messengers we are; and so, whether we speak to admiring crowds or not, we must continue to expose the falseness of the world's standard, and to show how that can be corrected in Christ alone. Whether men hear, therefore, or whether they will forbear, this is our determination; and though the self-styled "leaders" of the present generation may sneer at us for our lack of appreciation of their culture, and for our failure to comply with their demands, we know that a day is coming when our vindication shall be complete.

April 15, 1883.

THE RESPONSIBILITIES OF LIFE.

ROMANS xiv. 7. For none of us liveth to himself.

THESE words may be regarded by us in three different lights, each of which will be found to bring out vividly before us some important practical truth; and as the illustration and enforcement of these will require all the time at my disposal, I shall proceed at once, without any formal introduction, to the work which I have taken in hand.

I. Let us look at the text then, in the first place, as it is interpreted for us by the section of the Epistle to the Romans in which it is found. That section is devoted to the elucidation of the principles by which the early Christians were to be guided as to their observance or non-observance of particular festival days, and as to their abstinence or non-abstinence from certain kinds of meats and drinks. To understand the matter fully we must have a clear perception of the difficulty with which the Apostle was seeking to deal. In those times, living as they were in the midst of paganism, the Gentile Christians were frequently invited to feasts at which meat was served which had been offered to an idol. Some partook of it without any hesitation, believing as Paul himself did, that "an idol was nothing in the world," and that nothing was "unclean of itself." Others having less enlightened and more scrupulous consciences refused to touch it, believing that if they did eat it they would be guilty of countenancing idolatry. The Jewish converts, again, were divided on the question of the observance of their national feasts. Some of them maintained their old habits in the matter of these Mosaic appointments, and others contented themselves with the simple keeping of the Lord's day. All of them relied upon the sacrifice of Christ for justification, and therefore are to be carefully distinguished from those against whom the Epistle to the Galatians was written, and who insisted on circumcision as essential to salvation. No vital principle in this instance was at stake. The error of the scrupulous was that of asceticism and not that of legalism; and so the Apostle here counsels mutual forbearance. He condemns everything like intolerance and recrimination. Those who had attained to such breadth of view that they felt no difficulty about eating anything that was set before them, were not to arrogate to themselves superiority over those who felt no such liberty; and on the other hand, those whose consciences would not allow them to partake of every sort of food were not to condemn such as had no scruples on the matter. The Jewish believer who kept all the festivals of his nation was not to look upon himself as better than he who observed only the Christian festival of the first day of the week; and neither were they whose strength of mind had raised them above such things to despise those who still considered that they were important. There was to be an agreement between them to differ in love; and if in any case the exercise of his undoubted liberty by one should seriously imperil the spiritual welfare of another by leading him to commit sin, then that liberty was to be cheerfully sacrificed in order that a brother should not be destroyed, for "the kingdom of God" was not a thing of "meats and drinks," but of "righteousness and peace and joy in the Holy Ghost."

Now the ground on which these injunctions were based was, that each believer—if he were a believer at all—was living, not unto himself, but unto Christ. "None of *us*," says the Apostle, "liveth unto himself." However it may be with others, none of us Christians liveth unto himself. Each of us has accepted Christ as his Redeemer and Lord and is seeking in all things to serve him; so if one eateth, he eateth unto the Lord; and if another eateth not, he eateth not unto the Lord. Each of us follows Christ as his Master; therefore, in all such things we must not judge each other, but rather judge that "no man put a stumbling block or an occasion to fall in his brother's way." One man is not to be condemned by another for that which he does in the exercise of conscientious Christian liberty; and yet, liberty to be Christian must be conditioned by love, so that we ought to forego even that which we feel free to engage in, if our indulgence in it should be the means of a brother's falling into sin. Thus the principle here enforced is precisely the same as that laid down by the Apostle in his Epistle to the Corinthians when he says: "All things are lawful for me; but all things are not expedient." Because we are seeking to live to Christ, there is, in reference to all matters indifferent, perfect liberty to the individual conscience, and no one has a right to judge or set at naught another for doing that of which he is "fully persuaded in his own mind," and which he is seeking to do "as unto the Lord." Each is responsible not to his fellows but unto the Lord; and while we may try to enlighten the conscience of another and bring him to see precisely as we do, we must not subject him to ridicule, or insult, or reproach, or hold him up in any measure to contempt, for doing that which he believes to be right. "To his own master he standeth or falleth." Conscience is the inner sanctuary of the human temple, and into that may enter only the Great High Priest who has made atonement for the world's guilt, and who alone "can purge it from dead works to serve the living God." It behooves us, therefore, to keep every unhallowed intruder out of that sacred domain, to stand up for our liberty in things indifferent, and so long as we maintain loyalty to Christ in his revealed word, to insist that no man shall judge us in respect to those matters of custom or conformity which are not in themselves sinful, and in regard to which we take that course which seems to us to be most honoring to the Lord we love. Only let us see to it that we are taking it for the Lord's sake and not simply and solely for our own gratification. That is the one side of the subject.

But there is another which is equally important; for the liberty being maintained, the question of love then comes into operation. If I live to Christ and not to self, then I live also to Christians, for they are one with him. I cannot be true to him if I am inconsiderate of them. Therefore, though I may, nay, must *assert* my liberty, yet, if my *exercise* of that liberty should seriously wound my brother's heart, I shall be acting uncharitably if I insist on carrying it out. "I know and am persuaded by the Lord Jesus," says Paul, "that there is nothing unclean of itself, but if thy brother be grieved with thy meat, now walkest thou not charitably. Destroy not him with thy meat for whom Christ died." Nay, even more strongly, if thy brother is led into sin through the exercise of thy liberty, if he thereby stumbleth, or is made weak, or is offended—not in the sense of being displeased, but in that of being made to stumble—then the Christian course is for thee to sacrifice thy liberty for love of him, even as Christ pleased not himself that he might redeem us from all iniquity; or as Paul has put it in the Epistle to the Corinthians (I quote from the Revised Version), "Give no occasion of stumbling, either to Jews, or Greeks, or to the church of God; even as I also please all men in all things, not seeking mine own profit, but the profit of the many that they may be saved; be ye imitators of me, even as I also am of Christ." Here then are the two principles; first, that things non-essential or indifferent are to be determined by each for himself in the exercise of individual liberty and as unto Christ, and that no one is to judge another for his determination, since none of us liveth unto himself, but unto Christ, and each is responsible to him alone; and second, that while the right to this liberty is inalienable and may not be yielded on any ground, the acting on it is conditioned by the effect of our conduct on the brotherhood of believers, so that if it should provoke evil and not good, or give occasion to the falling of others into sin, we should abstain from carrying it into exercise, since "None of us liveth unto himself," but the actions of each affect the welfare of the brotherhood to which all alike belong.

Now the application of these principles to modern things is too obvious to need remark. In regard to all matters not in themselves sinful, the conscience of each believer is at liberty to judge what his conduct may be; and to his own master he standeth or falleth. "All" such "things are lawful." But while it would be quite expedient to do certain things under one set of circumstances, it would be just as inexpedient to countenance them in another. What is above all to be regarded is that "the work of God" shall not be "overthrown" either by the uncharitable judgments of the more scrupulous, or the inconsiderate and inexpedient exercise of their liberty by the more enlightened. Not our own pleasure, but rather the glory of Christ, and the edification, and peace, and progress of the brotherhood, is to be made the rule of our lives. There are no specific prohibitions in the New Testament, except of such things as are positive sins; and in regard to all others these principles must be our guides. It would be convenient no doubt, if the book or the preacher should decide for us whether we should go to particular places, or take part in particular amusements, or engage in particular practices concerning which we are perplexed; but all these things are left to each conscience—not to do as it pleases, but to take the course which in the light of loyalty to Christ and love to the brethren, seems to be the best; and it is in the decision of such questions for ourselves, that we grow into strength and develop into true Christian manliness. Insist upon liberty therefore in all such matters, but let the exercise of that liberty in every case be conditioned by love, for "it is good neither to eat flesh, nor to drink wine, nor to do any thing whereby thy brother stumbleth. All things are lawful, but all things are not expedient; all things are lawful, but all things edify not. Let no man seek his own, but each his neighbor's good," for "none of us liveth unto himself."

II. But leaving now the consideration of the text as it is interpreted for us by the section of the epistle in which it is found, let us proceed to regard it more generally, in the second place, as an inevitable condition of human existence. No man's life terminates on himself alone, but each of us exerts an influence through his character and conduct upon all with whom he comes into contact. We are so constituted, and have been placed in such circumstances, that, whether we are conscious of it or not, others are affected by our actions and example. Those nearest us are in a greater or a smaller measure molded by what we are, and these again have a like influence on those by whom they are surrounded, so that what emanated originally from us is at once perpetuated in its existence and amplified increasingly in its range. To use the trite illustration, just as the stone cast into the pool makes undulations which continually widen until they reach the edge, so the moral force generated by our character constantly widens through those on whom it operates. It would be easy to illustrate this by typical instances drawn from the pages both of sacred and secular history. Who does not remember how, long after the first king of Israel had gone to his account, the sad results of his idolatry remained active in the land, so that his name never occurs without the appended description, "the son of Nebat, who made Israel to sin?" The papacy to this day bears the impress of the mind of Hildebrand, and almost every country on the globe has felt the effect of the life of Ignatius Loyola, whose successors in the so-called Society of Jesus have gone to the ends of the earth. The same is true of the great reformers of the sixteenth century, as well as of the pioneers of freedom and the founders of our nation. But these are not exceptional cases. True, they are the cases of men who had great abilities and exalted opportunities, and therein they were exceptional. But these abilities and opportunities have only put, as it were, in their case, into larger type, a truth which holds of every man. Influence is as inseparable from character as the fragrance is from the flower or the shadow from the substance. Every one that lives, therefore, lives not merely unto himself, but has a subtle effluence always radiating from him that produces some effect on others. On the rocks beneath us you will find the impress of the tiniest insect as well as that of the largest megatherium; and so in the strata of society each man has his own place to fill, and will leave his own mark behind him for blessing or for the reverse. A little Hebrew maid in the house of Naaman was a most important factor in bringing about the cure of that great captain's leprosy; and often yet a child's tiny hand may fire the mine that shall shake down even granite rocks.

But, to come nearer ourselves, think how true it is in our homes that "none of us liveth unto himself." The influence of parents upon their children is positively incalculable; for the young are given to imitation, and are all the time taking on a living likeness of their elders. The words they hear and the actions they see day by day have all a power, and though they may pass away from the memories of both, they will live permanently in their results, so that parents will meet their children at the bar of God wearing the characters which by their daily lives they did so much to fashion. And the children, too, produce very marked and indelible effects upon their parents, while brothers and sisters twine around each other like runners up the wall, so that for every bend in the one there is a corresponding inclination in the other, and there is in each a difference from what might have been if the other had not been there. In like manner it is true of friends that there is ever going on between them an assimilating process, as the result of which they become like each other in tastes, opinions and habits. Nathaniel's friendship with Philip was the means of introducing him to Jesus, and Jehoshaphat's companionship with Ahab placed his life in jeopardy that day in the field of Ramoth Gilead. So still the intimate associates of a man have a molding influence on each other and on him, while he in turn is helping to form them. This influence on others is what I have called an inevitable condition of human existence. We cannot rid ourselves of it. It is the attendant shadow of each life, and takes its shape from the life. What a solemn thing it is, in this view of it, to live! It is to be continually receiving from others, and as continually giving to others. How careful, therefore, we ought to be lest we should be contaminated by others, or should contribute to the undoing of others! And if you would secure yourselves against both of these dangers, let me urge you to seek deliberately and prayerfully to live to Christ. Receive him into your hearts, and he will keep all evil out of them. Retain him in your hearts, and he will make them centers out of which nothing but good will issue. Watch the flower and the fragrance will take care of itself. Form your character after the pattern of Christ and your influence will be always Christian. To have the unconscious effluence of the best, you must have the conscious purpose always of the purest. To resist the evil you must retain the good. The moistened hand may hold with impunity the bar of white-hot iron, and he who is bedewed with the influences of the Holy Spirit will take no harm from those of the ungodly men by whom he is surrounded. Nor will he do harm to any by his example, but, contrariwise, that may be like the shadow of Peter, which healed the sick ones over which it passed. Ah! how momentous the thought that each of us, by our very existence, is either blessing or blighting some one else, according as our influence is good or evil! Which is it? Make haste and see, for you may start a train which you shall never be able either to overtake or to arrest, and though you may repent and return to God yourself, that other whom you introduced into the broad way may go on his downward course and end in destruction! Make haste, then, and see whether the effect of your life on others is good or evil; and if it be evil, seek forgiveness and renewal at the hands of Christ.

III. But now, finally, let me view this text as it expresses the deliberate purpose of every genuine Christian. The true believer forswears self. Other men, in one form or other, live for self. They seek their own pleasure, or their own interest, or their own honor. They make themselves the centers of all their ambitions, and care neither for other men nor for God when their personal predilections are in the case. But with the Christian it is different. And it is different not because some authority outside of him has said, Thou shalt not worship self, but because he has of his own motive, and out of love to Christ, renounced self and accepted Christ as the God of his heart and the sovereign of his life. Look here, for illustration, to the case of the Apostle Paul himself. In writing to the Philippians, he said, "To me to live is Christ;" and in his second letter to the Corinthians he uses these words: "The love of Christ constraineth us, because we thus judge, that if one died for all, then were all dead, and that he died for all that they which live should not henceforth live unto themselves, but unto him which died for them and rose again." So also to the Galatians he says: "I live, yet not I but Christ liveth in me," while in the very next verse to that in which the text for this morning is found, he affirms that, "whether we live, we live unto the Lord; whether we die, we die unto the Lord; whether we live, therefore, or die, we are the Lord's." Now all these expressions imply that Christ had taken in Paul the place which was formerly occupied by self. Where before he wrought for his own interest or glory or position, he now sought Christ's honor and labored for the advancement of his cause; or, as he puts it in another phrase, "what things before were gain to him, those he counted loss for Christ." He felt himself so identified with Christ that his own interest and the Redeemer's glory seemed to be one and the same. He had become, as it were, merged in Christ. John the Baptist said, on a memorable occasion, concerning Jesus: "He must increase, but I must decrease." Now that which was true externally of John was true internally and spiritually of Paul—the self in the apostle had decreased, and the Christ in him had increased, until it was all Christ and no self, so that in everything he did his dominating motive and main purpose were to honor Christ. In judging of any alternative put before him, the determining element always was, "Lord, what wilt thou have me to do?" When fashion was on one side and Christ on the other, he never hesitated, for now the approval of others was nothing to him in comparison with the commendation of Christ; and no sinful pleasure—even in the days before his conversion—had for him a tithe of the enjoyment which he now derived from the consciousness that he was serving Christ and was beloved by Christ. Now it is the same with every real Christian. From the moment of his conversion his whole being runs Christward. The volume of the river may be small at first, but, small as it is, its direction is decided, and it gathers magnitude as it flows, for it drains the valley of his life. He keeps himself for Christ, because he owes everything to Christ. He realizes that he has been bought with a price, and therefore he seeks to glorify Christ in his body and his spirit, which are his. Duty and delight now coalesce in his experience. That which he ought to do, and that which he finds happiness in doing, are now to him identical, and his life illustrates the beautiful epigram of Philip Doddridge, whose family motto, "Dum vivimus, vivamus," was thus rendered by him into English verse:

> "Live while you live, the epicure would say,
> And seize the pleasures of the passing day.
> Live while you live, the sacred preacher cries,
> And give to God each moment as it flies.
> Lord, in my view let both united be:
> I live in pleasure while I live to thee."

Now, this determination to live to Christ I have called the deliberate purpose of every genuine Christian, for so soon as a man believes that Jesus Christ loved him—gave himself for him—he is moved by the Holy Ghost to give himself up to Christ, and then discovers that

> "A life of self-renouncing love
> Is a life of liberty."

But living thus *to* Christ, the believer lives also *for* his fellow-men, for the two are inseparable, inasmuch as the great principle at the root of the cross is the sacrifice of self for the benefit of others; and Jesus himself has indicated that our gratitude to him should take the form of ministering to the necessities of others for his sake. He bids us recognize himself in every ignorant one whom we can instruct, in every naked one whom we can clothe, in every hungry one whom we can feed, in every suffering one whom we can relieve, and what we do for them he regards as done for him. Thus, while we live to him, we live also in the very highest sense for others, and find the purest and the sweetest happiness for ourselves, for we are enjoying a pleasure even when we are doing a duty. The "must" of benevolence in us is not that of outward constraint, but of inner impulse. It is the irrepressible "cannot but," and not the shuddering "I dare not but." We find our joy in seeking to make others joyful. The selfish man makes happiness the *end* he seeks, and so he never gains it, for when pursued in that way it flees from before him as the rainbow recedes from the deluded child who runs to find the pot of gold that is fabled to be at the place on which the ethereal arch doth seem to rest. But when, renouncing self, we seek to make others better, holier, and nobler for Jesus' sake, then true happiness comes unsought, and comes to stay. When in the midnight hour you lie awake and wish for sleep, the more you try expedients to bring it to your pillow, the more it seems to flee from your pursuit. But when you turn your mind away from all such things and think on something quite apart from self, then, with muffled footstep, the angel of the night steals into your chamber and steeps your senses in forgetfulness. And so, the more eager you are for happiness as an object in itself, the more hopeless is your effort to attain it; but when, renouncing self and seeking to live to Christ, you labor for the benefit of others; then happiness will come of itself and fill your heart with a foretaste of heaven's own blessedness. Thus, by living to Christ, the Christian secures these three things—the glory of Christ, the benefit of his fellow men, and his own highest happiness.

And now, my unbelieving friends, what have you to

say to all these things? Are you still determined to live to yourselves? What profit have you had therein in the past? You may have added to your wealth, but have you increased your happiness? You may have multiplied your possessions, but what have you done that has served your generation, or honored your God, or glorified your Saviour? And what of all that you have lived to accumulate or to enjoy can you take with you into that state where character shall be your only property? Live, I beseech you, for something that you can keep when death shall overtake you. Live to glorify God here, in the obedience of Christ and the love of your fellow-men, and you will find that in that way you will make friends of the mammon of unrighteousness, who, when you fail, shall receive you into the everlasting habitations which Christ has prepared for them that love him.

And, my fellow Christians, shall not we renew our dedication to the Lord to-day, and seek henceforth more than ever to bless and benefit our fellow men for his sake? What joy, what usefulness, what honor, have come to us as we have attempted to act on these principles in the past? Let us, therefore, carry them out only more thoroughly than ever in the future. Few men in his generation sought to live so much for Christ and for his people as did Thomas Guthrie, the Scottish pulpit orator and philanthropist, and the secret of all was that he had learned at the foot of the cross to sacrifice self and to love all for whom the Master died. I have heard him often, and always with delight, but never, I think, with such quivering emotion tingling through my frame, as when, at the close of a glowing appeal for his ragged children, he repeated, with the deepest fervor, these lines, which were peculiarly appropriate on lips like his:

> "I live for those who love me,
>   For those who know me true;
> For the heaven that smiles above me,
>   And awaits my spirit, too;
> For the cause that lacks assistance,
> For the wrongs that need resistance,
> For the future in the distance,
>   For the good that I can do."

That was his motto, because he had learned the meaning of the love of Christ to his own soul. Shall we not adopt it as our own from this time forth? Let us live for the good that we can do as the disciples of Christ, and then we may very well leave all other things to take care of themselves, or rather, we may be sure that the Master whom we serve will take care of them for us. "Not unto ourselves, but unto Christ, and unto our fellow men for Christ's sake;" so let us live here, and death when it comes will only promote us to a higher sphere, where we shall live to nobler purpose and to yet grander fruitage.

MARCH 18, 1883.

THESE THINGS DONE AND OTHERS NOT LEFT UNDONE.

MATTHEW xxiii, 23. *Woe unto you, scribes and Pharisees, hypocrites! for ye pay tithe of mint and anise and cummin, and have omitted the weightier matters of the law, judgment, mercy and faith: these ought ye to have done, and not to leave the other undone.*

The denunciations of the Pharisees, in connection with which these words occur, are the sternest utterances which came from the lips of Jesus. Indeed, they are in this respect so exceptional that they have occasioned much perplexity to many sincere Christians, and have been held up to scorn and execration by many antagonists of the gospel. But a clear conception of the real nature of Phariseeism is all that is needed for their complete vindication, and as that will materially help us to a right understanding of the text, especially in its primary application, it may be well to set it distinctly before you in the outset of my discourse.

The error of the Pharisees was not superficial, but fundamental. Their religion was not simply defective, but positively false. They were not insincerely striving after that which was right; but they were sincerely striving after that which was wrong; or to take the Saviour's own illustration, they were building their house on a foundation of sand and not upon the firm and unyielding rock. I know, indeed, that to many among us the Pharisees stand as the representatives of those who are deliberately seeking to impose upon others by professing to have that which they are conscious that they do not possess. That this was true of some who were called by that name is certain, for the Saviour speaks of them as "for a pretense making long prayers;" but such a view cannot be entertained, for example, of Paul before his conversion. Neither his conduct in reference to the early disciples nor his subsequent allusions to his experience as a Pharisee will allow us to rest in the conviction that he was at that time willfully and deliberately seeking to deceive others. He was just as truly in earnest then as he was in his later life as a Christian Apostle; but he was in earnest after the wrong thing. And so, judging of the others as a class by him, we may say that they had a radically false idea of what religion was; and thus their very sincerity in its practice was fraught with the deepest danger to themselves, and the greatest mischief to others. Bishop Butler, in a somewhat neglected portion of his writings, has put the case in a way which reveals his accustomed insight, when he says: "They were not men without any belief at all in religion, who put on the appearance of it only in order to deceive the world; on the contrary, they believed their religion and were zealous in it. But their religion which they believed and were zealous in was in its own nature hypocritical, for it was the form, not the reality." * This witness is true. They resolved religion into a bundle of separate acts of ritual and prescription instead of regarding it as the character of the man himself; or what in Scripture language is called the relation of the heart to God. They lost sight of that "moral unity" in the individual which makes him "a

---

* Butler's Sermon before the House of Lords on the day appointed to be observed for the martyrdom of Charles I.

good being as distinguished from a bad being," and which in the words of a great thinker* is "that general virtue which covers the motives" and which, "like some essence which we can hardly get at," is not itself so much as it is the goodness of everything else in him; "not a virtue so much as the substratum of all virtues; the virtue of virtue; the goodness of goodness." Thus their religion was a super-position from without; not a manifestation of that which was within; a garment by which the body was covered, and not the life of the body itself; a something separable from themselves, instead of their very innermost self; a fraction cut off from their lives and devoted to a special object; instead of the very life of their lives, of which everything they did was but a part.

Now to one who came, as the Lord Jesus did, to give prominence to the truth that "the Kingdom of God cometh not with observation," but is in very deed within men's hearts, the Pharisees stood forth as the representatives of the most pestiferous error. They occupied, so to say, the very center of the position which it was his mission to storm, and very naturally, therefore, against them his heaviest bombardment was directed. So as Mozley says,† the sternness of these denunciations "is part of the judicial language of the first advent," and "laid the foundations of the final judgment." The doctrine of the Pharisees was the fundamental heresy in human life it; baptized into the name of religion that which had no right to such an appellation; it robbed God of the whole, while ostentatiously seeming to give him much more than he asked; and therefore it called forth from the Lord

---

* See Mozley's University Sermons, p. 29.
† Ibid, p. 29.

Jesus the most scathing and indignant words which he was ever known to utter.

But this is not all. Such radically erroneous notions concerning religion lulled the Pharisees into absolute self-security. The very essence of their hypocrisy was that it imposed upon themselves. Believing religion to consist in a certain round of ritual observances and seeking zealously to perform that, they conceived that all was well with them; thus it came that appeals which reached the hearts of others never affected them. It was awfully true that "the publicans and harlots" went into the kingdom before them. Calls to repentance did not effect them, for why should they repent of their goodness? It was a false goodness indeed, as we have seen, but then its falseness was the very thing of which they were not conscious, and so extraordinary measures had to be taken in order to rouse them, if possible, to a sense of their danger. Hence in portions of the Sermon on the Mount, their exclusion from the kingdom at the last is represented as coming upon them as an awful and humiliating surprise; and hence in the chapter before us the most terrible woes are pronounced over them, if haply the reverberations of the thunder might awake them to a true perception of the nature of the case. Thus the indignation in these verses sprang from the root of love, as you may easily see by reading on to the end of the chapter, for after "the whirlwind, the earthquake and the fire," comes this still small voice of plaintive yet baffled tenderness, "O, Jerusalem, Jerusalem, thou that killest the prophets and stonest them which are sent unto you, how often would I have gathered thy children together, even as a hen gathered her chickens under her wings, and ye would not! Behold, your house is left unto you desolate."

But still further, we may account for the severity of these denunciations, from the fact that the Saviour foresaw that Phariseeism would, in after ages, become the greatest hindrance to the progress of his cause in the world. As one has pithily said,* "there are no extinct species in the world of evil;" and most certainly this is true of the evil of which now we speak. For it is the shadow that invariably attends on spiritual life and follows after it. What was the Genesis of the Phariseeism of the Saviour's day? Something like this. There was a great religious revival among the Jews after their return from the captivity, which continued for a considerable time; and which, after they had rebuilt the Temple, sent them back to the law with a sincere desire to honor God by keeping its commands. So long as the life remained, the obedience was the real outcome of an inward principle; but when the life died out, then the obedience became only a fossil, and was soon covered over with corruption, until it became what we see it to have been, in the days of the Saviour upon the earth. But the same danger attends on every great spiritual movement, and we have many illustrations of it in the Christian Church. Thus a real devotion to Christ stimulates to reverent attention to the forms of worship, and so long as that is simply an expression of loyalty to Him, all is well; but by and by all thought of him drops out, and then only the ritual remains, becoming the idol of the heart and so the life departs. Who does not recognize in this the natural history of Ritualism, whether in the Church of Rome or elsewhere? So again the founders of the great monastic orders were all sincere and ardent reformers, and in

---

* See Mozley's University Sermons, p. 32.

them and their immediate followers we see great self-sacrifice and devotion from the holiest motives; but as years rolled on the life evaporated, and only the Pharisaic fossils of their orders remained. Thus we see how it comes that "the real virtues of one age are the spurious ones of the next,"* and that what was a voice full of sincerity in one generation is often only an empty echo in that which follows. So Phariseeism has to be guarded against in every age of the Church's history, and more especially after times of special activity and life. The constant tendency is to retain the form after the life has departed, and to keep on doing as our fathers did, when we no longer feel as our fathers felt; and any one who thinks deeply on the subject will be compelled to admit, that in the strength of that tendency, we have one of the greatest sources of the Church's weakness at the present day. Hence the words of the Lord in this chapter were prophetic as well as judicial; and the very terror of them was intended to direct the attention of his people in every age to a danger that would be always imminent. We for example, have come in for the legacy of the church forms and customs of those who have gone before us, and so we must take heed that we do not continue these for their own sakes, but rather that we have the life of which they were the expression, and that we adapt the expression of that life to the circumstances and requirements of our own times.

These considerations will be enough, I hope, to vindicate the severity of the Saviour's words in the chapter before us, while, at the same time, they will show the importance of this subject to ourselves, and

---

* Mozley, as before.

prepare us to understand what I have called the primary application of the text, to the special consideration of which I now proceed.

It charges that the Pharisees were strictly attentive to the minutest matters of tithe, but omitted the weightier concerns of the law, judgment, mercy, and faith; and then lays down the general maxim, "these," that is the weightier matters, "ye ought to have done, and not to have left the others undone." Now here two or three very important principles are implied.

We learn, for example, that the commands of God are of different degrees of importance. There are matters of more weight than others, among the divine precepts. That God has commanded a thing, always invests it with a certain importance, but all his commandments are not of equal gravity. The heart that reverences him, indeed, will seek for his sake to render obedience to them all, but each in its own order. There are higher and lower obligations; and the higher will be first attended to, nay if need be, will absorb into them the lower. This is a distinction in morals kindred to that between things essential and non-essential in matters of faith, and it will be recognized by all. In any case it lies here upon the very surface of the text so plainly that I need not stay either to prove its existence or to point out its importance; the rather as these will both be brought out in the second thing which the text teaches, namely: That the weightiest of all God's commands have respect to judgment, mercy, and faith. That is a truth which is emphasized over and over again both by the prophets of the Old Testament, and the Apostles of the New. Thus Samuel said to Saul, "To obey is better than sacrifice, and to hearken than the fat of lambs." The same thought quivers through the solemn music of the fiftieth psalm; while Isaiah represents the Lord as saying to the rulers of his day whose hands were full of blood, "Your new moons and your appointed feasts my soul hateth; they are a trouble unto me; I am weary to bear them." So also Paul exclaims in the most solemn manner, "Though I bestow all my goods to feed the poor, and though I give my body to be burned, and have not love, it profiteth me nothing." He does not mean that it is not a duty to feed the poor, or that it is not right to "resist unto blood striving against sin;" but as both of these things may be done from sinful motives, the one from love of ostentatious display, and the other from a disposition not essentially different from that which animates the combatants in earthly war, neither of them may, in itself considered, be put into comparison with that love to God and love to men which is the result of the reception of Christ into the heart; and which, wherever it exists, will always prompt to the performance of those things which are for the glory of Jehovah and the welfare of mankind. The inner is more important than the outer; the spirit than the letter; the principle than the action; the character than the isolated deed. The heart is the great thing, "for out of it are the issues of life," and therefore it should have the first and the greatest attention. If that be wrong nothing can be right; but if that be right, everything will partake of its quality. Therefore, in regard to "judgment, mercy, and faith," the Lord says positively, "these ought ye to have done;" while in matters of tithe and prescription, he contents himself with the negative expression "and not to have left the others undone." Do the great things, and the smaller will follow in their train. Attend to the principle, and the exemplifications of it will come of themselves. Look well to the character, and the conduct will correspond thereto. Keep the heart, and everything flowing from it will testify to that vigilance. This is of prime importance, and clearly indicates why so many who are awakened to a sense of the value of religion do yet fall short of its attainment. They try to reform their conduct in certain particulars. They resolve and re-resolve, but only to break their vows; and all this because they are proceeding on a wrong plan. They are working from a point in the circumference instead of from the center. They are trying to reform the heart from the conduct instead of the conduct from the heart; and so they have to lay afresh the whole foundation; and they have to do that by building upon Christ, and coming to him for the renewal which only his Spirit can effect. This looks very simple, yet simple as it looks, there are many among us who have never truly apprehended it, and therefore I have tried with all plainness of speech to make it clear.

But another thing taught us in this verse is, that attention to the matters of less importance will not compensate for the neglect of those which are of essential moment. Punctilious tithe-paying will not condone oppression, or injustice, or the lack of humble faith in God. It was no answer to the charge of "devouring widow's houses" for the Pharisee to say "I fast twice in the week and give tithes of all that I possess." Ritual is not religion; it is only, even at the best, the outer garment which she wears on certain occasions; but religion herself is character; and that is a moral unit, giving its quality both to the worship and to the ordinary conduct of the man. It is no vindication for my not doing a most important duty, to say that I have done something else that is on a far lower plain. If a man has dishonestly appropriated the money which was intrusted to his care, he is not to be excused because he can say, "I was a regular attendant upon church, I was a Sunday-school teacher, or I was a liberal giver to benevolent objects." That does not alter the character of his dishonesty; it only reveals the radical wrongness of his religion, and shows that he is a modern Pharisee, who regards religion as a thing of rubrics and ritual, and times and seasons, and temporary engagements, instead of a matter of heart and life. Oh! my hearers, how many such cases there have been in recent years! and how necessary, therefore, it becomes for us to examine into the foundation on which we are building; whether the rock, with its moral unity of character solidified by the regeneration that comes from the Holy Spirit through faith in Jesus Christ; or the sand, with its particles of separate and isolated actions held together by no principle of regard to God, and fused into no firm coherence by love to Christ.

And to mention only one other point this text suggests, that where the heart is right with God through faith in Jesus Christ, both the weightier matters and those of less importance will be properly attended to. Not in so many words, indeed, are we taught this truth here. But we must put this passage alongside of many similar utterances of the Lord Jesus. Take the following as a specimen: "Either make the tree good and his fruit good, or else make the tree corrupt and his fruit corrupt, for the tree is known by his fruit. A good man out of the good treasure of the heart bringeth forth good things; and an evil man out of the evil treasure bringeth forth evil things." "The light of the body is the eye; if therefore thine eye be single thy whole body shall be full of light. But if thine eye be evil thy whole body shall be full of darkness; if therefore the light that is in thee be darkness, how great is that darkness!" "Marvel not that I say unto thee, ye must be born again." These and kindred sayings which might be quoted in abundance all go to show that a new nature is the fundamental need of the sinner. With that he must begin; and for that he must go in humble faith to him of whom it is said, "as many as received him, to them gave he power to become the sons of God, even to them that believe on his name—which were born, not of blood, nor of the will of the flesh, nor of the will of man, but of God." This is the beginning of the whole matter. True holiness, which is that character that performs every duty in its own place, and gives to each its own importance, is not the result of human effort alone, but the work of God's Spirit promised to those and only to those who cordially receive Jesus Christ as their Redeemer and Lord; and so if we wish to have it we must commence not with working, but with believing; or, if you choose to express it differently, our first work must be believing in Christ, for "this is the work of God, that ye believe in him whom he hath sent." Begin there, my hearers, and that will save you from the insidious danger of the Phariseeism, which I have been trying this morning to analyze and to expose.

But while thus in its contexual application the text is full of instruction and warning to those who have been hitherto simply and only Pharisees, it has in it also a principle of great value for the guidance of Christ's own disciples, for it clearly teaches that the performance of one duty must not be pleaded as an excuse for the neglect of another. In all such matters what is put before us is not an alternative, as whether we shall do this *or* that, but an aggregate, for we are to do this *and* that. Now thus understood, the lesson of the text is susceptible of manifold applications.

It speaks to the minister in the pulpit, and tells him that in his discourses his question ought never to be, whether shall I preach for the conversion of sinners, or for the edification of believers; but rather how shall I prepare my sermons so as to secure both the *up*-building of God's people, and the *in*-building of those who are yet out of Christ? He is to do the one but he is not to leave the other undone. Of the two in some circumstances the preaching to sinners may be the more pressingly important; and in others, the training of those who are already disciples may demand the larger attention; but always he ought to have both in his aim; for both alike are duties required at his hands. If the Acts of the Apostles be in the New Testament to show him how to "do the work of an Evangelist," the Apostolic Epistles are also there to let him see how to "feed the flock over which the Holy Ghost has made him overseer;" and if he will study these well and faithfully he may perhaps find in the example of Paul something that will help him to edify believers even when he is preaching to sinners; or to probe the consciences of sinners even when he is seeking the promotion of holiness in those who are already Christ's. But if he neglect either, he is, so far forth, unfaithful, and for the passing over of the one, the doing of the other will be no excuse. Nay the effect in either case will be disastrous. If he continually preach for the awakening of sinners, then in proportion as his hearers are converted, they will pass away from him and seek a teacher who shall lead them forward; while if he confine himself to the training of believers, his church will ere long become depleted by death and removals, and no others will come to take the vacant places. In this way, undue preponderance of either will work injuriously to the permanent usefulness of the church, and he is the wise and well instructed scribe who, while doing the one, will contrive also not to leave the other undone.

But there is in this principle, thus understood, a lesson also for the church. It exists, as our own manual has well put it, "for mutual edification and encouragement in Christian life; and for the advancement of the Redeemer's Kingdom." Therefore it must not neglect aggressive work on the outlying world, for the fostering of the growth and comfort of its members; and neither must it neglect the growth and comfort of its members for the prosecution of evangelistic effort among those who are "ignorant and out of the way." Here again it may be said "this ought ye to have done, and not to leave the other undone." There have been times when the aggressive has somewhat eclipsed the educational; and then extravagance and emotion have set in like a flood. But again there have been times when the educational has overshadowed the aggressive, and then intellect has run to seed into doctrinal error, and often also into absolute unbelief. Thus there are dangers on either hand. The Salvation Army, with its irreverent modes of speech and somewhat shocking methods, will illustrate the peril of becoming simply and only aggressive; the Unitarian defection, with its ultimate developments into such disintegration as Boston saw in the breaking up of Theodore Parker's company of followers, and we in New York have witnessed in the dissolution of Mr. Frothingham's congregation, will illustrate the danger of devoting ourselves entirely to self-culture.

The wise church will steer clear of both extremes by carrying on the work of mutual edification abreast of that of evangelistic aggressiveness. I know not in which direction our danger lies. Perhaps in that of giving undue preponderance to the simple maintenance of our own church life, and yet after the announcement which I have made this morning in reference to our Bethany enterprise,* I may not indulge in any such suspicions. Let me content myself rather with uttering a warning against the one-sidedness that would give the preference to either, and then, by the guidance of God's Spirit, we may be able to keep each in its normal proportion in our thoughts and prayers and efforts.

But speaking still of the Church, the same principle holds in regard to the home and foreign missionary enterprises. Concerning these also we must say, "This ought ye to have done, and not to have left the other undone." Both alike are duties; and as far as possible, both should be carried on abreast. Sometimes the Home effort may claim the larger share of attention, as I think it does, in a country like our own into which we are receiving foreign population at the rate of hundreds of thousands every year. But then, work prosecuted among these is, in a very true sense, foreign work as well as home. Sometimes, again, as in a country like Scotland, which, if anything, is rather overchurched than underchurched, the main effort should be put forth in the foreign field. But always there should be an

---

* The New Bethany Church on Tenth Avenue was dedicated on the Sunday after this discourse was preached.

outlook upon both, and work put forth on both. If we content ourselves with home work, we shall become selfish, self-conceited, and disagreeable—the Pharisee among the nations saying with contempt, "Thank God we are not as they!" and that will issue in national humiliation. If, again, we restrict ourselves to foreign, we may find our own cities, like the garden of the sluggard, overrun with "thorns" and "nettles," and "the stone wall thereof broken down." They who have true leal-hearted love to Christ will take a warm and living interest in both, as is evident in the fact that we find the same individuals on the platforms of both, and the church that labors earnestly in both will make sure and steady progress, and be marked with holy peace. If you seek to propel a boat with one oar, you will simply turn it round and round; but if you use both you "go forward;" and so true church prosperity depends on the carrying forward of both home and foreign missions.

But turning now to the household, we may see how there also the same principle holds good. Public religious services must not be made the substitute for home duties; and again home duties must not be pleaded as an apology for the neglect of public ordinances. Arrangements ought to be made for rightly engaging in both. The instructing of other people's children must not be allowed to keep us from giving needed attention to the godly upbringing of our own. And again the training of our own families should not be made a plea for exemption from all effort for the spiritual welfare of those of others. It is sometimes seen that the children of those who have been prominent in Sunday-school work grow up in utter carelessness; but then occasionally we also see that the sons of those who kept themselves rigidly at home for their training have become absolute reprobates. So that both extremes are bad, simply because they are extremes. Home is the weightier, and of its duties we may say unhesitatingly, "these ought ye to have done;" but then other forms of effort claim assistance, and of these we must say, "and not to leave the other undone." A workman meeting a friend on the street in Edinburgh, one Monday morning, said to him, "Why were you not at church last night? our minister preached an excellent sermon on home religion. Why were you not there to hear it?" "Because," was the answer, "I was at home doing it." That was a good answer, for the service was an extra one, and the man had been at church twice before. So he was right, with the third, to give his home duties the preference. But then, on the other hand, the "at home doing it" is not all, and it should be so provided for as not to take away from proper attendance on regular ordinances, otherwise the result will be that after awhile religion will not be much cared for either in the church or in the home. A tardy student coming late into the class was asked by his professor to account for his want of punctuality, and replied that he had delayed for purposes of private devotion. But his teacher very properly reproved him by saying, "you had no right to be at your prayers, when you ought to have been here; it is your duty to make such arrangements that the one shall not interfere with the other." So I say in regard to the conflicting claims of the household and the church upon you. Make arrangements for giving due attention to both, and do not sacrifice the one on the shrine of the other.

Finally, take it in its individual bearing, and you will see at once to how many things this principle may be applied. Does business say one thing, and the closet another? then do not give up the one for the other, but see to it that you secure both. Are you interested in evangelistic operations? well, that is excellent; but do not so neglect your business for them that it shall get into confusion and bring you and your Christian profession alike into reproch. Not many years ago, Mr. Spurgeon publicly reproved some in his church for so neglecting their business for the work of preaching that they found themselves at length in the bankruptcy court. That was bad. But then it is equally bad for merchants to become so absorbed in business on all days and at all hours, that they have neither time nor strength to give to efforts for the welfare of others, and allow our missionary Sunday-schools and churches to languish for lack of their assistance. It is all a matter of proportion, and it ought to be solemnly pondered by every one of us. Let us, therefore, in the light of the principle on which I have been insisting, look at our lives and see if there be not many things in them out of proportion; the weightier being sacrificed for those which are less important. When the painter is at work, you will see him stepping back every little while from his canvas that he may be sure his perspective is right. So let us go apart a little by ourselves to-day and test the perspective of our lives. Let us examine whether we are not neglecting some things of great moment for the sake of others of mere transitory interest and may God enable us to act out the principle which we have found this morning in the Saviour's words. Amen.

MARCH 4, 1883.

CHOICE STANDARD WORKS.

NEW AND REVISED EDITION
OF
HALLAM'S COMPLETE WORKS,
With New Table of Contents and Indexes.

IN SIX VOLS., CROWN, 8VO, CLOTH.

PRICE, $7.50 PER SET. (Reduced from $17.50.)
(Bound in Half Calf extra, $3 per vol.)

THIS UNABRIDGED EDITION OF HALLAM'S WORKS COMPRISES

The Constitutional History of England, 2 Vols.
The Middle Ages, The State of Europe During the Middle Ages, 2 Vols.
Introduction to the Literature of Europe, 2 Vols.

REPRINTED FROM THE LAST LONDON EDITION, REVISED AND CORRECTED BY THE AUTHOR.

MACAULAY, in his famous estimate of Hallam, says: "Mr. Hallam is, on the whole, far better qualified than any other writer of our time for the office which he has undertaken. He has great industry and great acuteness. His knowledge is extensive, various, and profound. His mind is equally distinguished by the amplitude of its grasp, and by the delicacy of its tact. His speculations have none of that vagueness which is the common fault of political philosophy. On the contrary, they are strikingly practical, and teach us not only the general rule, but the mode of applying it to solve particular cases. . . . Mr. Hallam's work is eminently judicial. Its whole spirit is that of the Bench, not that of the Bar. He sums up with a calm, steady impartiality, turning neither to the right nor to the left, glossing over nothing, exaggerating nothing, while the advocates on both sides are alternately biting their lips to hear their conflicting misstatements and sophism exposed."

This "STANDARD EDITION" of HALLAM'S WORKS, in 6 Vols., AVERAGES NEARLY 800 PAGES IN EACH VOL., and is sold at $7.50 PER SET (formerly published in 10 Vols. at $17.50.)

Sent on receipt of price, charges prepaid.

CHOICE STANDARD WORKS.

THE MOST ELEGANT EDITION PUBLISHED
OF
CHARLES LAMB'S COMPLETE WORKS,

Including ELIA and ELIANA (the last containing the hitherto uncollected writings of Charles Lamb), corrected and revised, with a sketch of his life by Sir Thomas Noon Talfourd, and a fine Portrait on Steel.

3 VOLS., CR. 8VO, CLO. PRICE, $3.75 PER SET. (REDUCED FROM $7.50.)
(Bound in Half Calf extra, $3 per vol.)

With a volume of Letters and Essays collected for this edition by the industry of, and arranged with much taste and skill by, J. E. BABSON, *Esq., of Boston, " who literally knows Lamb by heart."*

In Mr. Babson's preface to this additional volume, he says:

"Other writers may have more readers, but none have so many true, hearty, enthusiastic admirers as he. * * * With all lovers and appreciators of true wit, genuine humor, fine fancy, beautiful imagination and exquisite pathos, he is a prodigious favorite. Indeed, there is something—a nameless, indescribable charm—about this author's productions which captivates and enravishes his readers, and though Lamb found many admiring readers in his lifetime, since his death his fame and popularity have increased greatly. Then he was generally looked upon as a mere eccentric—a person of more quaintness than humor, of more oddity than genius. Now he is acknowledged to be a most beautiful and original genius—one of the 'fixed stars of the literary system'—whose light will never pale or grow dim, and whose peculiar brightness and beauty will long be the wonder and delight of many. * * * For years I have been hopefully and patiently waiting for somebody to collect these scattered and all but forgotten articles of Lamb's. * * * Without doubt, all genuine admirers, all true lovers of the gentle, genial, delightful 'Elia,' to whom almost every word of their favorite author's inditing is '*farsed with pleasaunce*,' will be mightily pleased with these productions of his inimitable pen, NOW FIRST COLLECTED TOGETHER."

As this "SUPERB EDITION" of LAMB'S WORKS, in 3 Vols., AVERAGING NEARLY 800 PAGES IN EACH VOLUME, is sold at the EXCEEDINGLY LOW PRICE OF $3.75 PER SET (formerly published in 5 Vols. at $7.50), the Publishers confidently believe IT WILL COMMEND ITSELF TO ALL FOR PERSONAL USE AND FOR LIBRARIES.

Sent on receipt of price, charges prepaid, by
A. C. ARMSTRONG & SON, 714 Broadway, New York.

CHOICE STANDARD WORKS.

A NEW AND HANDSOME LIBRARY EDITION
OF
MILMAN'S COMPLETE WORKS,

With Table of Contents and Full Indexes.

IN 8 VOLS., CROWN 8VO, CLOTH.

PRICE, $12.00 PER SET. (Reduced from $24.50.

Bound in Half Calf extra, $25.00 per set.)

THIS EDITION OF MILMAN'S WORKS, THOROUGHLY REVISED AND CORRECTED, COMPRISES

The History of the Jews, 2 Vols.
The History of Christianity, 2 Vols.
History of Latin Christianity, 4 Vols.

DR. MILMAN has won lasting popularity as a historian by his three great works, HISTORY OF THE JEWS, HISTORY OF CHRISTIANITY, and HISTORY OF LATIN CHRISTIANITY. These works link on to each other, and bring the narrative down from the beginning of all history to the middle period of the modern era. They are the work of the scholar, a conscientious student, and a Christian philosopher. DR. MILMAN prepared this new edition so as to give it the benefit of the results of more recent research. In the notes, and in detached appendices to the chapters, a variety of very important questions are critically discussed.

The author is noted for his calm and rigid impartiality, his fearless exposure of the bad and appreciation of the good, both in institutions and men, and his aim throughout, to utter the truth always in charity. The best authorities on all events narrated have been studiously sifted and their results given in a style remarkable for its clearness, force and animation.

MILMAN'S WORKS HAVE TAKEN THEIR PLACE AMONG THE APPROVED CLASSICS OF THE ENGLISH LANGUAGE. The general accuracy of his statements, the candor of his criticisms and the breadth of his charity are everywhere apparent in his writings. His search at all times seems to have been for truth, and that which he finds he states with simple clearness and with fearless honesty. HIS WORKS ARE IN THEIR DEPARTMENT OF HISTORY AS VALUABLE AS THE VOLUMES OF GIBBON ARE IN SECULAR HISTORY. THEY DESERVE A PLACE IN EVERY LIBRARY IN THE LAND. THIS NEW EDITION, in 8 vols., contains AN AVERAGE OF OVER 900 PAGES per volume. PRICE, $12.00 PER SET. (Formerly published in 14 vols. at $24.50.)

Sent on receipt of price, charges prepaid.

CHOICE STANDARD WORKS.

A NEW EDITION OF
THE HISTORY OF THE CRUSADES.
A. D. 300–1270.

IN EIGHT PARTS, WITH AN INDEX OF 47 PAGES.

By **JOSEPH FRANCOIS MICHAUD.**

And a Preface and Supplementary Chapter by Hamilton W. Mabie. 3 vols., crown 8vo, Cloth. $3.75.

(Bound in Half Calf extra, $3 per vol.)

"The ability, diligence and faithfulness with which MICHAUD has executed his great task are undisputed, and it is to his well-filled volumes that all must resort for copious and authentic facts and luminous views respecting this most romantic and wonderful period in the annals of the world."

This work has long been out of print, and its republication is opportune. It narrates very fully and in a picturesque and interesting manner, the most striking episode in European history, and will add an invaluable work to the historical literature which has recently been put into the hands of the reading public in editions combining sound scholarship and reasonable prices. Of the first excellence as an authority, full of romantic incident, graphic in style, this new edition of that which is by universal consent

THE STANDARD HISTORY OF THE CRUSADES,
will have equal value for the student and general reader.

RIVERSIDE EDITION OF
MACAULAY'S ESSAYS,
Critical, Historical and Miscellaneous. With a Biographical and Critical Introduction from the well-known pen of Mr. E. P. Whipple. 3 vols., crown 8vo, Cloth, 3,000 pages. With a fine Portrait on Steel. Price, $3.75.

(Bound in Half Calf extra, $3 per vol.)

In this edition the essays have been arranged in chronological order, so that their perusal affords, so to speak, a complete biographical portraiture of the brilliant author's mind. It contains the pure text of the author and the exact punctuation, orthography, etc., of the English editions.

A very full index (55 pages) has been specially prepared for this edition. In this respect it is superior to the English editions, and wholly unlike any other American edition.

Sent on receipt of price, charges prepaid.

CHOICE STANDARD WORKS.

A NEW EDITION
OF
D'ISRAELI'S COMPLETE WORKS.
Edited by his Son, LORD BEACONSFIELD,
With a fine Portrait on Steel. 6 Vols., Crown 8vo, Cloth.

PRICE, $7.50 PER SET. (Reduced from $15.00.)
(Bound in Half Calf extra, $3 per vol.)

THIS NEW EDITION OF D'ISRAELI'S WORKS COMPRISES

THE CURIOSITIES OF LITERATURE,	3 Vols.
CALAMITIES AND QUARRELS OF AUTHORS AND MEMOIRS,	1 Vol.
AMENITIES OF LITERATURE, SKETCHES AND CHARACTERS,	1 Vol.
LITERARY CHARACTER, HISTORY OF MEN OF GENIUS,	1 Vol.

A collection of literature which no judiciously selected library will fail to have, and no person of literary taste and culture willingly do without.

They are, in truth, a history of literature and of literary men, gathered from the writings of centuries and from living authors, philosophic and learned, yet easy and fascinating.

The Curiosities of Literature treat of everything curious in the literary kingdom. The formation of libraries, past and present, bibliomania, the oddities of authors, their labors, anecdotes, successes, failures, etc., containing a valuable mass of rare information.

The Amenities of Literature " is in a different strain, and treats of Language, the origin and growth of our own, the discovery and progress of the art of printing, the growth of literature, its patrons, followers and builders, and of other matters which have a broad and general bearing upon the subject in hand."

The Calamities and Quarrels of Authors " contains an account of authors' struggles, difficulties and poverty as a class * * * teaching them their failings and holding up the mirror for those who may be benefited by a view of the difficulties which beset authors."

Literary Character " is probably the most searching and distinctive treatise of its kind extant, made up, as it is, from the feelings and confessions of men of genius."

This NEW IMPRESSION of the famous works of the elder D'ISRAELI, IN 6 VOLS., PRICE $7.50 PER SET (formerly published in 9 Vols. at $15.00), has been aptly said to comprise the cream of English Literature of Europe from the times of Dr. Johnson to our own, and to constitute a whole library in themselves.

Sent on receipt of price, charges prepaid, by
A. C. ARMSTRONG & SON, 714 Broadway, New York.

NEW AND IMPORTANT BOOKS.

I.
Chas. Loring Brace's New Work,
GESTA CHRISTI;
Or, A History of Humane Progress Under Christianity.
1 vol., octavo, 500 pages, $2.50.

This work is designed to show the practical effect of Christianity on the laws, customs, and morals—1st, of the Roman period; 2d, of the Middle Ages; 3d, of the Modern Period. The position of Woman, Slavery, Serfdom, Parental Rights, and similar subjects in each period are treated of: in the Middle Ages, such as Feud, the Peace of God, Judicial, Duel, Ordeal, Torture, Private War, and Arbitration are discussed. In the Modern Period, the Influence of Christianity on International Law, Arbitration, the Limitation of War, and Modern Reforms are examined, as well as on Education and Liberal Government, the Distribution of Property, Temperance and Chastity. A brief comparison is made with the influence of the Hindoo, Buddhist, Chinese, Mohammedan religions on the position of women and humane progress. The closing chapter considers objections and examines the relation of Christianity to Evolution and future progress of mankind. The book is an effort to make plain the great Christian ideas of the age, and to show both what the Christian religion has done for progress in humane practices, and what it is adapted to do.

"THIS WORK CONTAINS A VAST AMOUNT OF USEFUL AND HELPFUL KNOWLEDGE OF THESE GREAT SUBJECTS. IT IS LIKELY TO BE ONE OF THE MOST EFFECTIVE CHRISTIAN APOLOGETICS OF THE AGE."—N. Y. Christian Union.

II.
REVIVALS: HOW AND WHEN?
By Rev. W. W. NEWELL, D. D. With steel portrait.
1 vol., 12mo. $1.25.

This is no ordinary book on the subject of Revivals of Religion. It does not commend great excitement followed by depressing apathy. It favors a religious quickening and an ingathering of souls every passing year. It does not commend a theory. It is eminently practical. It gives the exact experience of persons who, in the greatest variety of seemingly hopeless conditions, have been taught of the Lord just how to secure a spiritual blessing. It shows how the Revival has been secured and conducted in the Church, the Household, the Bible-class, the Sabbath-school, the Missionary and the Temperance circle.

Copies sent by mail, post-paid, on receipt of price, by

www.ingramcontent.com/pod-product-compliance
Lightning Source LLC
Chambersburg PA
CBHW030404230426
43664CB00007BB/741